D1595655

ESSAYS ON ETHICS, SOCIAL BEHAVIOR,
AND SCIENTIFIC EXPLANATION

THEORY AND DECISION LIBRARY

AN INTERNATIONAL SERIES

IN THE PHILOSOPHY AND METHODOLOGY OF THE

SOCIAL AND BEHAVIORAL SCIENCES

Editors:

GERALD EBERLEIN, *University of Saarland*

WERNER LEINFELLNER, *University of Nebraska*

Editorial Advisory Board:

VOLUME 12

JOHN C. HARSANYI

Professor of Business Administration and of Economics, University of California, Berkeley

ESSAYS ON ETHICS, SOCIAL BEHAVIOR, AND SCIENTIFIC EXPLANATION

D. REIDEL PUBLISHING COMPANY

DORDRECHT-HOLLAND / BOSTON-U.S.A.

170
H25e

77-0552

Library of Congress Cataloging in Publication Data

Harsanyi, John C
    Essays on ethics, social behavior, and scientific explanation.

    (Theory and decision library; v. 12)
    Includes bibliographical references and indexes.   1.
    Ethics—Addresses, essays, lectures.   2.   Social ethics—
Addresses, essays, lectures.   3.   Social status—Addresses, essays,
lectures.   I.   Title.
BJ1012.H33   170   76-21093
ISBN 90-277-0677-8

Published by D. Reidel Publishing Company,
P.O. Box 17, Dordrecht, Holland

Sold and distributed in the U.S.A., Canada, and Mexico
by D. Reidel Publishing Company, Inc.
Lincoln Building, 160 Old Derby Street, Hingham,
Mass. 02043, U.S.A.

TABLE OF CONTENTS

FOREWORD BY K. J. ARROW   VII

INTRODUCTION   IX

ACKNOWLEDGEMENTS   XV

PART A / ETHICS AND WELFARE ECONOMICS

I. Cardinal Utility in Welfare Economics and in the Theory of
Risk-Taking   3

II. Cardinal Welfare, Individualistic Ethics, and Interpersonal
Comparisons of Utility   6

III. Ethics in Terms of Hypothetical Imperatives   24

IV. Can the Maximin Principle Serve as a Basis for Morality?
A Critique of John Rawls's Theory   37

V. Nonlinear Social Welfare Functions: Do Welfare
Economists Have a Special Exemption from Bayesian
Rationality?   64

PART B / RATIONAL-CHOICE AND GAME THEORETICAL
MODELS OF SOCIAL BEHAVIOR

VI. Advances in Understanding Rational Behavior   89

VII. Rational-Choice Models of Political Behavior vs.
Functionalist and Conformist Theories   118

VIII. Game Theory and the Analysis of International Conflicts   145

IX. Measurement of Social Power, Opportunity Costs, and the
Theory of Two-Person Bargaining Games   162

X. Measurement of Social Power in n-Person Reciprocal
Power Situations   185

XI. A Bargaining Model for Social Status in Informal Groups and Formal Organizations 204

PART C / SCIENTIFIC EXPLANATION

XII. Explanation and Comparative Dynamics in Social Science 227

XIII. Popper's Improbability Criterion for the Choice of Scientific Hypotheses 243

INDEX 255

FOREWORD

When John Harsanyi came to Stanford University as a candidate for the Ph.D., I asked him why he was bothering, since it was most unlikely that he had anything to learn from us. He was already a known scholar; in addition to some papers in economics, the first two papers in this volume had already been published and had dazzled me by their originality and their combination of philosophical insight and technical competence. However, I am very glad I did not discourage him; whether he learned anything worthwhile I don't know, but we all learned much from him on the foundations of the theory of games and specifically on the outcome of bargaining.

The central focus of Harsanyi's work has continued to be in the theory of games, but especially on the foundations and conceptual problems. The theory of games, properly understood, is a very broad approach to social interaction based on individually rational behavior, and it connects closely with fundamental methodological and substantive issues in social science and in ethics. An indication of the range of Harsanyi's interest in game theory can be found in the first paper of Part B – though in fact his own contributions are much broader – and in the second paper the applications to the methodology of social science. The remaining papers in that section show more specifically the richness of game theory in specific applications.

Harsanyi has maintained consistently the importance of founding ethics as well as descriptive social science on the basis of the rational behavior of society and of individuals. The result has been a vigorous defense, rehabilitation, and reinterpretation of classical utilitarianism. In particular, Harsanyi introduced the ideal of considering the choice of an ethical criterion in a hypothetical situation where individuals do not know who they are or what their interests will be (this approach was used independently and somewhat later by John Rawls, under the now widely-used term, 'original position'; it has also been introduced independently and somewhat earlier by William Vickrey). Hence, the social rule amounts to maximizing under uncertainty. The clarity of analysis implied by this perspective is well represented in the papers here.

The foundations of ethics have been a source of dispute among human beings since conscious reflection upon them began. After all, man is one of the most social of all animals; the nature of social interactions and the conflict between social bonds and individual assertiveness are issues very close indeed to the deepest of human motives. It is not surprising that this depth of feeling remains manifest in ethical controversies even in the most rarefied reformulations in abstract terms. Even apart from naïve egotism, human beings, even scholars, come to ethical problems with differing life experiences and hence differences in perception which can be lessened only to the extent permitted by communication.

Ethical discourse is precisely the attempt at communication which may serve to reduce differences by clarifying the issues. The construction of a descriptive social science has similar obstacles and similar aims, for scholars bring with them perceptions of society depending on their experiences and their learning. In such endeavors, clarity of thought and empathetic understanding of the human roots of social processes are both needed, and both are found in the work of John Harsanyi.

Harvard University   KENNETH J. ARROW

INTRODUCTION

I

This book contains thirteen papers, written over the period 1953-1975. *Part I* consists of five papers, which try to provide a modern decision-theoretical foundation for a *utilitarian* ethical theory. It is argued that a moral value judgement is a judgement of preference based on impersonal and impartial criteria. Thus, each individual has two sets of preferences. One consists of his *personal* preferences, defined as his *actual* preferences, which will be typically based mainly on his own personal interests and on the interests of his closest associates. The other consists of his *moral* preferences, defined as his *hypothetical* preferences that he *would* entertain if he forced himself to judge the world from a moral, i.e., from an impersonal and impartial, point of view. Mathematically, and individual's personal preferences are represented by his *utility function,* whereas his moral preferences are represented by his *social welfare function.*

More specifically, an individual's moral preferences can be defined as those preferences that he would entertain if he assumed to have the same probability $1/n$ to be put in place of any one of the n individual members of society. According to modern decision theory, in such a situation a rational individual would try to maximize his expected utility, which, under this model, would amount to mazimizing the *average utility level* of the individual members of society. This means that a rational individual will always use the average utility level in society as his social welfare function.

Of course, this definition of social welfare functions presupposes that we can meaningfully add up different people's utilities, i.e., it presupposes the possibility of *interpersonal comparisons* of utility. Contrary to what probably still is the majority view among economists, other social scientists, and philosophers, I am trying to show that the possibility of interpersonal utility comparisons is a very natural assumption. Suppose I am trying to compare the utility that *you* would derive from reading a good novel, with the utility that *I* can derive from it. Then, I am essentially trying to compare the

X INTRODUCTION

utility that I myself would derive from reading this book if I had *your* social situation, *your* personality, *your* education, *your* past experience, etc., with the utility I do derive from it, with *my* own actual social situation, personality, education, and past experience. It is essentially the same kind of mental operation as trying to compare the utility I myself would derive from the book under two different sets of conditions, such as when I was in one mood or in another mood, etc. In other words, *inter*personal utility comparisons are essentially the same kind of mental operation as *intra*personal utility comparisons are.

Apart from the equi-probability model for moral value judgments, two other arguments, both of them based on *axiomatic* approaches, are proposed in order to show that the social welfare function W_j of a rational individual j will be a *linear* function (such as the arithmetic mean) of the utility functions U_i of all individuals i. In particular, it is shown that if (1) All individuals i follow the standard Bayesian rationality postulates with respect to their *personal* preferences, and if (2) Individual j follows these rationality postulates with respect to his *moral* preferences, and finally if (3) Individual j is always *morally* indifferent between any two alternatives X and Y whenever all individuals i are *personally* indifferent between X and Y – then the social welfare function W_j of j *must* be a linear function of the individual utility functions U_i. In short, Bayesian rationality *plus* an individualistic interpretation of social welfare mathematically *entail* a linear social welfare function.

The last two of the five papers on ethics try to defend this utilitarian ethical theory against recent objections by Rawls, Diamond, and Sen. Against Rawls's theory of justice, based on the maximin principle, it is shown that the maximin principle is a thoroughly irrational principle as a decision rule and, therefore, cannot serve as a basis for a rational ethics. Against Diamond's objections it is shown that, if his objections were accepted, highly counterintuitive implications would follow. Finally, against Sen's objections it is argued that his theory is based on what may be called the *utility-dispersion* argument for *social welfare,* which has no more validity than the well-known utility-dispersion argument for *lotteries,* commonly rejected by decision theorists, has. It is also argued that, in addition to these logical difficulties, both Rawls's and Sen's anti-utilitarian theories are also *morally* unacceptable because they involve morally highly objectionable discrimination against those individuals who happen to enjoy high utility levels

(even if they have achieved these high utility levels by morally perfectly legitimate behavior).

My views on ethics and welfare economics, described in Part A, are based
on the concepts of cardinal utility and of interpersonal utility comparisons. This means that they are in obvious conflict with the ordinalist
and anti-comparisonist positions entertained by probably still the
majority of the economics profession. They were, of course, even more
unorthodox views in 1953 and 1955, when they were first stated in print.
   Yet, since that time, there have been slow but significant changes in
the climate of opinion. Several eminent economists, including some who
used to be strong advocates of an ordinalist position, have expressed
views very close to my own. Paul A. Samuelson recently came out in favor
of cardinal utility and interpersonal utility comparisons; and even went
as far as calling my theory "one of the few quantum jumps" in welfare
economics. (Samuelson, 1974, pp. 1266-67. See also Theil, 1968, p. 336)
In any case, I hope the reader will examine my views and my arguments with
an open mind, even if he happens to come from an ordinalist intellectual
tradition.

II

Part II of the book contains six papers, dealing with rational-choice models
and, in some cases, with game-theoretical models, of social behavior. The
first of these papers starts with a discussion of the relationship among the
three main branches of the general theory of rational behavior, viz. *utility
theory* (which includes individual decision theory), *ethics,* and *game theory.* The second part of the paper provides a nontechnical summary of
some recent work in game theory on games with incomplete information
and on noncooperative games. It is argued that the theory of noncooperative games is now in a position to supply common foundations for game
theory as a whole, since any *cooperative* game can always be represented by
a *noncooperative* bargaining game.
   The second paper in Part II of the book discusses the advantages of rational-choice models of social behavior, over functionalist and conformist
models. It is argued that most functionalist models lack explanatory power
because they do not exhibit a credible causal mechanism by which the basic

needs of society could mould social institutions. The undeniable ineffi-
ciency of many social institutions in serving social needs clearly shows that
it is inadmissible to assume that existing social needs automatically create
the social institutions satisfying these needs. Likewise, conformist theories,
explaining social behavior in terms of existing social values and social
norms, are insufficient unless they can also explain these social values and
social norms themselves. In contrast, rational-choice models propose to
explain social institutions, social values and social norm in terms of the actual motives and interests of the individuals and the social groups originally
creating them and continually modifying them over time. Thus, they automatically provide the causal mechanism accounting for them.

The remaining four papers in Part II discuss game-theoretical models for
the analysis of international conflicts as well as for the explanation of social
power and of social status. Both power and status are explained in terms of
game-theoretical bargaining models. Different models are proposed for
two-person and for *n-person* power situations, and again for situations involving *unilateral* or *reciprocal* power. In analysing the power of a person
A over another person B, we have to distinguish A's *independent power*
(defined as the outcomes that A can achieve without the cooperation, or
even against the resistance, of B) and his *incentive power* (defined as the
outcomes that A can achieve only with B's cooperation but for which B's
cooperation is fully assured by the incentives, i.e., by the rewards and/or
punishments, that A can provide for B).

Like social power, social status is also interpreted as a result of bargaining between an individual and the social group (or organization) to which he
belongs. Other things being equal, each individual will be granted a higher
social status the more important the services and the disservices he can supply to the group, and the less important the services and the disservices this
group can supply to him. Of course, social status is only one of various
rewards that a social group can provide for its members. The most important
alternative reward is economic income. Whereas economic income consists
of money (or other economic resources) over which the recipient will be
given full property rights, social status consists in priority of access to resources over which the group as a whole retains these property rights. In
many social situations, it may largely consist in priority of access to certain
privileges of purely symbolic value. Nevertheless, these symbolic privileges
may be very important because they will typically indicate the group's de-

sire to retain the recipient as a valued member of the group on a permanent basis. Usually, these symbolic privileges also indicate a willingness by other members of the group to engage in friendly social intercourse with the recipient. As a result, high-status members of a group will tend to have privileged social access to other members as potential friends, business associates, potential spouses, etc. This privileged social access may very well be the most important benefit derived from high social status.

One way of interpreting the privileges associated with high status is to consider them to be simply an accentuated form of the privileges associated with ordinary group membership. Among the members of a social group, we often distinguish between full members and less-than-full members. One may argue that high-status members are those who belong to what may be called the 'inner core' of the group and, therefore, posses even fuller membership rights than ordinary rank-and-file full members do.

III

Part III of the book contains two papers, both dealing with scientific explanation. One of the two papers tries to explain, in terms of well-known mathematical properties of dynamic systems, why models of social development which use *economic variables* as explanatory variables, often possess particularly great explanatory power.

The other paper cirticizes Popper's thesis that, when scientists prefer the *simplest* hypothesis consistent with the empirical observations, this should be interpreted as preference for the intrinsically *least probable* hypothesis. Against this thesis, the paper argues that the simplest hypothesis is normally also the intrinsically *most probable* hypothesis because it involves the smallest number of unexplained independent assumptions.

I wish to express my gratitude to my wife as well as to many friends and colleagues, too numerous to list, for many helpful discussions and critical comments over the twenty-two years when these papers were written. Special thanks are due also to the National Science Foundation for its sustained support.

University of California   JOHN C. HARSANYI

REFERENCES

Samuelson, Paul A.: 'Complementarity - An Essay on the 40th Anniversary of the Hicks-Allen Revolution in Demand Theory,' J. *Econ. Lit.* **12** (1974), 1255–1289.
Theil, Henri: *Optimal Decision Rules for Government and Industry,* North-Holland and Rand McNally, Amsterdam and Chicago, 1968.

ACKNOWLEDGEMENTS

The author wishes to thank the Editors and Publishers mentioned below for permission to reprint the following papers:

'Cardinal Utility in Welfare Economics and in the Theory of Risk-Taking,' *Journal of Political Economy* **61** (1953) 434-435. Copyright 1953 by Chicago University Press.
Reprinted by permission of Chicago University Press.

'Cardinal Welfare, Individualistic Ethics, and Interpersonal Comparisons of Utility,' *Journal of Political Economy* **63** (1955) 309-321. Copyright 1955 by Chicago University Press.
Reprinted by permission of Chicago University Press.

'Ethics in Terms of Hypothetical Imperatives,' *Mind* **47** (1958) 305-316. Copyright 1958 by *Mind*.
Reprinted by permission of the Editor.

'Can the Maximin Principle Serve as a Basis for Morality? A Critique of John Rawls's Theory,' *American Political Science Review* **69** (1975) 594-606. Copyright 1975 by the American Political Science Association.
Reprinted by permission of the Editor and the American Political Science Association.

'Nonlinear Social Welfare Functions: Do Welfare Economists Have a Special Exemption from Bayesian Rationality?' *Theory and Decision* **6** (1975) 311-332. Copyright by D. Reidel Publishing Company, Dordrecht, Holland.
Reprinted by permission of the Editors and D. Reidel.

'Advances in Understanding Rational Behavior,' in *Logic, Methodology and Philosophy of Science,* the *Proceedings* of the *Fifth International Congress of Logic, Methodology and Philosophy of Science* at London,

Ontario, in August-September, 1975 (R. Butts and J. Hintikka, Editors), to be published by D. Reidel Publishing Company, Dordrecht, Holland.
Reprinted by permission of the Editors and D. Reidel.

'Rational-Choice Models of Political Behavior vs. Functionalist and Conformist Theories,' *World Politics* **21** (1969) 513-538. Copyright o 1969 by Princeton University Press.
Reprinted by permission of Princeton University Press.

'Games Theory and the Analysis of International Conflicts,' *Australian Journal of Politics and History* **11** (1965) 292-304. Copyright 1965 by Queensland University Press, Brisbane, Queensland, Australia.
Reprinted by permission of the Editor and Queensland University Press.

'Measurement of Social Power, Opportunity Costs, and the Theory of Two-Person Bargaining Games,' *Behavioral Science* **7** (1962) 67-80. Copyright 1962 by *Behavioral Science.*
Reprinted by permission of the Editors of *Behavioral Science.*

'Measurement of Social Power in n-Person Reciprocal Power Situations,' *Behavioral Science* **7** (1962) 81-91. Copyright 1962 by *Behavioral Science.*
Reprinted by permission of the Editors of *Behavioral Science.*

'A Bargaining Model for Social Status in Informal Groups and Formal Organizations,' *Behavioral Science* **11** (1966) 357-369. Copyright 1966 by *Behavioral Science.*
Reprinted by permission of the Editors of *Behavioral Science.*

'Explanation and Comparative Dynamics in Social Science,' *Behavioral Science* **5** (1960) 136-145. Copyright 1960 by *Behavioral Science.*
Reprinted by permission of the Editors of *Behavioral Science.*

'Popper's Improbability Criterion for the Choice of Scientific Hypotheses,' *Philosophy* **25** (1960) 332-340. Copyright 1960 by the Royal Institute of Philosophy, London, England.
Reprinted by permission of the Royal Institute of Philosophy.

                                                                    J.C.H.

PART A

ETHICS AND WELFARE ECONOMICS

CHAPTER 1

CARDINAL UTILITY IN WELFARE ECONOMICS
AND IN THE THEORY OF RISK-TAKING*

From most branches of economics the concept of cardinal utility has been eliminated as redundant since ordinal utility has been found to suffice for doing the job. Cardinal utility has been kept only in welfare economics to support the demand for a more equal income distribution. Recently, however, the concept of cardinal utility has been introduced also in the theory of choices involving risk.[1]

The question naturally arises whether the concepts of cardinal utility used in these two parts of economics are the same thing or not. According to Messrs. Friedman and Savage, who are among the main initiators of the use of cardinal utility in the theory of risk-taking, the two concepts have nothing to do with each other: 'It is entirely unnecessary to identify the quantity that individuals are interpreted as maximizing[in the case of choices involving risk] with the quantity that should be given special importance in public policy.'[2]

In effect, the cardinal utility function has to be invested with quite opposite properties in each case. In welfare economics the marginal utility of income is assumed to decrease with a growing income. In the theory of risk-taking on the contrary, increasing marginal utility is to be assumed to prevail over a considerable range, in view of people's willingness in the case of gambling to pay a price far above the actuarial value for a small chance of a large gain. Still, I do not think that these facts decide the matter.

It is, of course, clear that the concept of social welfare is vague enough to be compatible with quite divergent interpretations so that no particular interpretation can be proved to be logically 'necessary'. But I should like to show there is a fairly plausible interpretation of the concept of social welfare—or, more precisely, of value judgments concerning social welfare—which brings the cardinal utility concept of welfare economics very close to the cardinal utility concept used in the theory of choices involving risk.

Value judgments concerning social welfare are a special class of judgments of preference, inasmuch as they are nonegoistic impersonal judgments of preference. If somebody prefers an income distribution more favorable to the poor for the sole reason that he is poor himself, this can hardly be considered as a genuine value judgment on social welfare. But if somebody feels such a preference in spite of being wealthy himself, or if somebody who is in fact poor expresses such a preference, but does it quite independently of the fact of being poor himself, this may well be a value judgment of the required kind.

Now, a value judgment on the distribution of income would show the required impersonality to the highest degree if the person who made this judgment had to choose a particular income distribution in complete ignorance of what his own relative position (and the position of those near to his heart) would be within the system chosen. This would be the case if he had exactly the same chance of obtaining the first position (corresponding to the highest income) or the second or the third, etc., up to the last position (corresponding to the lowest income) available within that scheme.

This choice in that hypothetical case would be a clear instance of a 'choice involving risk'. Of course, in the real world value judgments concerning social welfare are usually not of this type, in that they do not presuppose actual ignorance of how a certain measure under discussion would affect one's personal interests; they only presuppose that this question is voluntarily disregarded for a moment. But they may still be interpreted as an expression of what sort of society one would prefer if one had an equal chance of being 'put in the place of' any particular member of the society, so that the cardinal utility 'maximized' in value judgments concerning social welfare and the cardinal utility maximized in choices involving risk may be regarded as being fundamentally based upon the same principle.

At the same time, this interpretation by no means excludes the possibility that the cardinal utility function may show some opposite properties in the two cases owing to a difference in the pertinent conditions.

When welfare economists compare the marginal utility of higher and of lower incomes, they have in mind people's habitual incomes. On this basis it is a reasonable assumption that the wealthy derive, from a marginal dollar, less utility than the poor do. On the contrary, gamblers compare the marginal utility of their actual income with the utility they expect from a sudden large increase in their income, which latter is certainly much higher than the utility of this higher income would be for a person long accustomed to enjoying it.

Moreover, the disutility of being a loser in a voluntary gamble, in which everybody has had the same 'fair' chance of winning, tends to be less than the disutility of being the loser in the social game envisaged by the welfare economist, in which the chances have been quite unequal from the very start. Thus there are valid reasons why gamblers should ascribe both a larger utility to a gain and a smaller disutility to a loss than might be expected on the basis of the cardinal utility function assumed in welfare economics.

At the same time, gamblers' notorious irrationality works in the same direction. Their confidence in their personal 'luck' makes them overrate their chance of winning, while their imagination makes them overestimate the subjective satisfaction they would derive from a given gain.

To sum up, the analysis of impersonal value judgements concerning social welfare seems to suggest a close affinity between the cardinal utility concept of welfare economics and the cardinal utility concept of the theory of choices involving risk. On the other hand, the differences found in the quantitative properties of the cardinal utility function in the two cases can be accounted for without difficulty.

NOTES

* *Journal of Political Economy*, **LXI** (1953), 434–435.

[1] See J. von Neumann and O. Morgenstern, *The Theory of Games and Economic Behaviour* (2d ed.; Princeton: Princeton University Press, 1947), pp. 15-31, 617-32; M. Friedman and L. J. Savage, 'The Utility Analysis of Choices Involving Risk', *Journal of Political Economy*, LVI (August, 1948), 279-304; H. Markowitz, 'The Utility of Wealth', *Journal of Political Economy*, LX (April, 1952), 151-58; M. Friedman and L. J. Savage, 'The Expected-Utility Hypothesis and the Measurability of Utility', *Journal of Political Economy*, LX (December, 1952), 463-74.

[2] Friedman and Savage, 'The Utility Analysis of Choices Involving Risk', *op. cit.*, p. 283, n. 11.

CHAPTER II

CARDINAL WELFARE, INDIVIDUALISTIC ETHICS, AND INTERPERSONAL COMPARISONS OF UTILITY*[1]

I

The naïve concept of social welfare as a sum of intuitively measurable and comparable individual cardinal utilities has been found unable to withstand the methodological criticism of the Pareto school. Professor Bergson[2] has therefore recommended its replacement by the more general concept of a social welfare function, defined as an arbitrary mathematical function of economic (and other social) variables, of a form freely chosen according to one's personal ethical (or political) value judgments. Of course, in this terminology everybody will have a social welfare function of his own, different from that of everybody else except to the extent to which different individuals' value judgments happen to coincide with one another. Actually, owing to the prevalence of individualistic value judgments in our society, it has been generally agreed that a social welfare function should be an increasing function of the utilities of individuals: if a certain situation, X, is preferred by an individual to another situation, Y, and if none of the other individuals prefers Y to X, then X should be regarded as socially preferable to Y. But no other restriction is to be imposed on the mathematical form of a social welfare function.

Recently, however, Professor Fleming[3] has shown that if one accepts one further fairly weak and plausible ethical postulate, one finds one's social welfare function to be at once restricted to a rather narrow class of mathematical functions so as to be expressible (after appropriate monotone transformation of the social welfare and individual utility indexes if necessary) as the weighted sum of the individuals' utilities. This does not mean, of course, a return to the doctrine that the existence of an additive cardinal utility function is intuitively self-evident. The existence of such a function becomes, rather, the consequence of the ethical postulates adopted and is wholly dependent on these postulates. Still, Fleming's results do in a sense involve an unexpected revival of some views of the pre-Pareto period.

In this paper I propose, first of all, to examine the precise ethical meaning of Fleming's crucial postulate and to show that it expresses an *individualistic* value judgment going definitely beyond the generally adopted individualistic postulate mentioned earlier, though it represents, as I shall argue, a value judgment perfectly acceptable according to common ethical standards (Sec. II). I shall also attempt to show that, if both social and individual preferences are assumed to satisfy the von Neumann–Morgenstern–Marschak axioms about choices between uncertain prospects, even a much weaker ethical postulate than Fleming's suffices to establish an additive cardinal social welfare function (Sec. III). In effect, it will be submitted that a mere logical analysis of what we mean by value judgments concerning social welfare and by social welfare functions leads, without any additional ethical postulates, to a social welfare function of this mathematical form (Sec. IV). Finally, I shall turn to the problem of interpersonal comparisons of utility, which gains new interest by the revival of an additive cardinal welfare concept, and shall examine what logical basis, if any, there is for such comparisons (Sec. V).

II

Fleming expresses his ethical postulates in terms of two alternative conceptual frameworks: one in terms of an '*ideal utilitarianism*' of G. E. Moore's type, the other in terms of a *preference* terminology more familiar to economists. Though he evidently sets greater store by the first approach, I shall adopt the second, which seems to be freer of unnecessary metaphysical commitments. I have also taken the liberty of rephrasing his postulates to some extent.

Postulate A (asymmetry of social preference). — If 'from a social standpoint'[4] situation X is preferred to situation Y, then Y is not preferred to X.

Postulate B (transitivity of social preference). — If from a social standpoint X is preferred to Y, and Y to Z, then X is preferred to Z.

Postulate C (transitivity of social indifference). — If from a social standpoint neither of X and Y is preferred to the other, and again neither of Y and Z is preferred to the other, then likewise neither of X and Z is preferred to the other.

These three postulates are meant to insure that 'social preference' establishes a *complete ordering* among the possible social situations, from which the existence of a social welfare function (at least of an ordinal type) at once follows. (Actually, two postulates would have sufficed if, in the postulates, 'weak' preference, which does not exclude the possibility of indifference, had been used instead of 'strong' preference.)

Postulate D (*positive relation of social preferences to individual preferences*). — If a given individual i prefers situation X to situation Y, and none of the other individuals prefers Y to X, then X is preferred to Y from a social standpoint.

As already mentioned Postulate D expresses a generally accepted individualistic value judgment.

Finally, Fleming's Postulate E states essentially that on issues on which two individuals' interests (preferences) conflict, all other individuals' interests being unaffected, social preferences should depend exclusively on comparing the relative social importance of the interests at stake of each of the two individuals concerned. In other words, it requires that the distribution of utilities between each pair of individuals should be judged separately on its own merits, independently of how utilities (or income) are distributed among the other members of the community.

Postulate E (*independent evaluation of the utility distribution[5] between each pair of individuals*).–(1) There are at least three individuals. (2) Suppose that individual i is indifferent between situations X and X' and also between situations Y and Y', but prefers situations X and X' to situations Y and Y'. Suppose, further, that individual j is also indifferent between X and X' and between Y and Y', but (unlike individual i) prefers Y and Y' to X and X'. Suppose also that all other individuals are indifferent between X and Y, and likewise between X' and Y'.[6] Then social preferences should always go in the same way between X and Y as they do between X' and Y' (that is, if from a social standpoint X is preferred to Y, then X' should also be preferred to Y'; if from a social standpoint X and Y are regarded as indifferent, the same should be true of X' and Y'; and if from a social standpoint Y is preferred to X, then Y' should also be preferred to X').

Postulate E is a natural extension of the individualistic value judgment expressed by Postulate D. Postulate D already implies that if the choice between two situations X and Y happens to affect the interests of the individuals i and j only, without affecting the interests of anybody else, social choice must depend exclusively on i's and j's interests—provided that i's and j's interests *agree* in this matter. Postulate E now adds that in the assumed case social choice must depend exclusively on i's and j's interests (and on weighing these two interests one against the other in terms of a consistent ethical standard), even if i's and j's interests are in *conflict*. Thus both postulates make social choice dependent solely on the *individual* interests directly affected.[7] They leave no room for the separate interests of a superindividual state of or impersonal cultural values[8] (except for the ideals of equity incorporated in the ethical postulates themselves).

At first sight, Postulate E may look inconsistent with the widespread habit of judging the 'fairness' or 'unfairness' of the distribution of income between two individuals, not only on the basis of these two people's personal conditions and needs, but also on the basis of comparing their incomes with the incomes of the other members of their respective social groups. Thus people's judgments on the income distribution between a given worker and his employer will also depend on the current earnings of other similar workers and employers. But the conflict with Postulate E is more apparent than real. In a society with important external economies and diseconomies of consumption, where the utility of a given income depends not only on its absolute size but also on its relation to other people's incomes, it is not inconsistent with Postulate E that, in judging the income distribution between two individuals, other people's incomes should also be taken into account. An income distribution between a given worker and a given employer, which in the original situation seemed perfectly 'fair' in terms of a given ethical standard, may require adjustment in the worker's favor, once wages have generally gone up, since the worsening of this worker's position relative to that of his fellows must have reduced him to a lower level of utility.

Postulate E requires that the distribution of *utility* between two individuals (once the utility levels of the two individuals are given) should always be judged independently of how utility and income are distributed among other members of the society. In the absence of external economies and diseconomies of consumption, this would necessarily also mean judging the distribution of *income* between two individuals independently of the incomes of others. In the presence of such economies and diseconomies, however, when the utility level of any person depends not only on his own income but also on other persons' incomes, it is not inconsistent with Postulate E that our value judgment on the distribution of income between two individuals should be influenced by the income distribution in the rest of the society—in so far as the income distribution in the rest of the society affects the utility levels of these two individuals themselves and consequently the distribution of utility between them. Postulate E demands only that, once these effects have been allowed for, the distribution of income in the rest of the society must not have any further influence on our value judgment.

III

In accordance with prevalent usage in welfare economics, Fleming's postulates refer to social or individual preferences between *sure prospects* only. However, it seems desirable to have both sorts of preferences defined for choices between *uncertain prospects* as well. More often than not, we have to choose in practice between social policies that promise given definite results only with larger or smaller probabilities. On the other hand, if we subscribe to some sort of individualistic ethics, we should like to make social attitude toward uncertainty somehow dependent on individual attitudes toward it (at least if the latter do not manifest too patent and too great an inconsistency and irrationality).

Since we admit the possibility of external economies and diseconomies of consumption, both social and individual prospects will, in general, specify the amounts of different commodities consumed and the stocks of different goods held by all individuals at different future dates (up to the time horizon adopted), together with their respective probabilities.

As the von Neumann–Morgenstern axioms[9] or the Marschak postulates[10] equivalent to them (which latter I shall adopt) are essential requirements for rational behavior, it is natural enough to demand that both social and individual preferences[11] should satisfy them. This gives us:

Postulate a.— Social preferences satisfy Marschak's Postulates I, II, III', and IV.

Postulate b.— Individual preferences satisfy the same four postulates.

In addition, we need a postulate to secure the dependence of social preferences on individual preferences:

Postulate c.—If two prospects P and Q are indifferent from the standpoint of every individual, they are also indifferent from a social standpoint.

Postulate c once more represents, of course, an individualistic value judgment — though a very weak one, comparable to Fleming's Postulate D rather than to his Postulate E.

I propose to show that Postulate c suffices to establish that the cardinal social welfare function defined by Postulate a can be obtained as a weighted sum of the cardinal individual utility functions defined by Postulate b (on the understanding that the zero point of the social welfare function is appropriately chosen).

THEOREM I.—There exists a social welfare function such that its actuarial value is maximized by choices conformable to the social preferences given. This social welfare function is unique up to linear transformation.

THEOREM II.—For each individual there exists a utility function such that its actuarial value is maximized by choices conformable to the individual's preferences. This utility function is unique up to linear transformation.

Both theorems follow from Marschak's argument.

Let W denote a social welfare function satisfying Theorem I and U denote a utility function of the i''th individual, satisfying Theorem II. Moreover, let W be chosen so that $W = 0$ if for all the n individuals $U_1 = U_2 = \ldots = U_n = 0$.

THEOREM III.—W is a single-valued function of $U_1, U_2, \ldots, U_n$. This follows, in view of Theorems I and II, from Postulate c.

THEOREM IV.—W is a homogeneous function of the first order of U_1, $U_2, \ldots, U_n$.

Proof.— We want to show that, if the individual utilities $U_1 = u_1$; $U_2 = u_2$; $\ldots$; $U_n = u_n$ correspond to the social welfare $W = w$, then the individual utilities $U_1 = k\, u_1$; $U_2 = k\, u_2$; $\ldots$; $U_n = k\, u_n$ correspond to the social welfare $W = k\, w$.

This will be shown first for the case where $0 \leqslant k \leqslant 1$. Suppose that prospect O represents $U_1 = U_2 = \ldots = U_n = 0$ for the different individuals and consequently represents $W = 0$ for society, while prospect P represents $U_1 = u_1$; $U_2 = u_2$; $\ldots$; $U_n = u_n$ for the former and $W = w$ for the latter. Moreover, let Q be the mixed prospect of obtaining either prospect O (with the probability $1 - p$) or prospect P (with the probability p). Then, obviously, Q will represent $U_1 = p\, u_1$; $U_2 = p\, u_2$; $\ldots$; $U_n = p\, u_n$ for the individuals and $W = p\, w$ for society. Now, if we write $k = p$, a comparison between the values of the variables belonging to prospect P and those belonging to prospect Q will, in view of Theorem III, establish the desired result for the case where $0 \leqslant k \leqslant 1$ (p, being a probability, cannot be < 0 or > 1).

Next let us consider the case where $k < 0$. Let us choose prospect R so that prospect O becomes equivalent to the mixed prospect of obtaining either prospect R (with the probability p) or prospect P (with the probability $1-p$). A little calculation will show that in this case prospect R will represent $U_1 = (1-1/p)u_1$; $U_2 = (1-1/p)u_2$; ...; $U_n = (1-1/p)u_n$ for the different individuals and $W = (1-1/p)w$ for society. If we now write $k = 1-1/p$, a comparison between the variables belonging to R and those belonging to P will establish the desired result for the case $k < 0$ (by an appropriate choice of the probability p, we can make k equal to any negative number).

Finally, the case where $k > 1$ can be taken care of by finding a prospect S such that prospect P becomes equivalent to the mixed prospect of obtaining either S (with a probability p) or O (with a probability $1-p$). Then this prospect S will connected with the values $U_1 = (1/p)u_1$; $U_2 = (1/p)u_2$; ...; $U_n = (1/p)u_n$ and $W = (1/p)w$. If we now write $k = 1/p$ we obtain the desired result for the case where $k > 1$ (by an appropriate choice of p we can make k equal to any number > 1).

THEOREM V.—W is a weighted sum of the individual utilities, of the form

$$W = \Sigma a_i \cdot U_i ,$$

where a_i stands for the value that W takes when $U_i = 1$ and $U_j = 0$ for all $j = i$.

Proof.—Let S_i be a prospect representing the utility U_i to the ith individual and the utility zero to all other individuals. Then, according to Theorem IV, for S_i we have $W = a_i \; U_i$.

Let T be the mixed prospect of obtaining either S_1 or S_2 or ... S_n, each with probability $1/n$. Then T will represent the individual utilities U_1/n, U_2/n, ..., U_n/n and the social welfare

$$W = \frac{1}{n} \cdot \Sigma a_i \cdot U_i .$$

In view of Theorem IV, this directly implies that if the individual utility functions take the values U_1, U_2, ..., U_n, respectively, the social welfare function has the value

$$W = \Sigma a_i \cdot U_i,$$

as desired.[12]

In the pre-Pareto conceptual framework, the distinction between social welfare and individual utilities was free of ambiguity. Individual utilities were assumed to be directly given by introspection, and social welfare was simply their sum. In the modern approach, however, the distinction is far less clear. On the one hand, our social welfare concept has come logically nearer to an individual utility concept. Social welfare is no longer regarded as an objective quantity, the same for all, by necessity. Rather, each individual is supposed to have a social welfare function of his own, expressing his own individual values—in the same way as each individual has a utility function of his own, expressing his own individual taste. On the other hand, our individual utility concept has come logically nearer to a social welfare concept. Owing to a greater awareness of the importance of external economies and diseconomies of consumption in our society, each individual's utility function is now regarded as dependent not only on this particular individual's economic (and noneconomic) conditions but also on the economic (and other) conditions of all other individuals in the community—in the same way as a social welfare function is dependent on the personal conditions of all individuals.

At the same time, we cannot allow the distinction between an individual's social welfare function and his utility function to be blurred if we want (as most of us do, I think) to uphold the principle that a social welfare function ought to be based not on the utility function (subjective preferences) of *one* particular individual only (namely, the individual whose value judgments are expressed in this welfare function), but rather on the utility functions (subjective preferences) of *all* individuals, representing a kind of 'fair compromise' among them.[13] Even if both an individual's social welfare function and his utility function in a sense express his own individual preferences, they must express preferences of different sorts: the former must express what this individual prefers (or, rather, would prefer) on the basis of impersonal social considerations alone, and the latter must express what he actually prefers, whether on the basis of his personal interests or on any other basis. The former may be called his 'ethical' preferences, the latter his 'subjective' preferences. Only his 'subjective' preferences (which define his utility function) will express his preferences in the full sense of the word as they actually are, showing an egoistic attitude in the case of an egoist and an altruistic attitude in the case of an altruist. His 'ethical' preferences (which define his social welfare function) will, on the other hand, express what can in only a qualified sense be called his 'preferences': they will, by definition, express what he prefers only in those possibly rare moments when he forces a special impartial and impersonal attitude upon himself.[14]

In effect, the ethical postulates proposed in Sections II and III—namely, Postulates D, E, and c—can be regarded as simply an implicit definition of what sort of 'impartial' or 'impersonal' attitude is required to underlie 'ethical' preferences: these postulates essentially serve to exclude nonethical subjective preferences from social welfare functions. But this aim may also be secured more directly by explicity defining the impartial and impersonal attitude demanded.

I have argued elsewhere[15] that an individual's preferences satisfy this requirement of impersonality if they indicate what social situation he would choose if he did not know what his personal position would be in the new situation choosen (and in any of its alternatives) but rather had an equal *chance* of obtaining any of the social positions[16] existing in this situation, from the highest down to the lowest. Of course, it is immaterial whether this individual does not in fact know how his choice would affect his personal interests or merely disregards this knowledge for a moment when he is making his choice. As I have tried to show,[17] in either case an impersonal choice (preference) of this kind can in a technical sense be regarded as a choice between 'uncertain' prospects.

This implies, however, without any additional ethical postulates that an individual's impersonal preferences, if they are rational, must satisfy Marschak's axioms and consequently must define a cardinal social welfare function equal to the arithmetical mean[18] of the utilities of all individuals in the society (since the arithmetical mean of all individual utilities gives the actuarial value of his uncertain prospect, defined by an equal probability of being put in the place of any individual in the situation chosen).

More exactly, if the former individual has any objective criterion for comparing his fellows' utilities with one another and with his own (see Sec. V), his social welfare function will represent the unweighted mean of these utilities, while in the absence of such an objective criterion it will, in general, represent their weighted mean, with arbitrary weights depending only on his personal value judgments. In the former case social welfare will in a sense be an objective quantity, whereas in the latter case it will contain an important subjective element; but even in this latter case it will be something very different from the utility function of the individual concerned.[19]

V

There is no doubt about the fact that people do make, or at least attempt to make, interpersonal comparisons of utility, both in the sense of comparing different persons' total satisfaction and in the sense of comparing increments or decrements in different persons' satisfaction.[20] The problem is only what logical basis, if any, there is for such comparisons.

In general, we have two indicators of the utility that *other* people attach to different situations: their preferences as revealed by their actual choices, and their (verbal or nonverbal) expressions of satisfaction or dissatisfaction in each situation. But while the use of these indicators for comparing the utilities that a *given* person ascribes to different situations is relatively free of difficulty, their use for comparing the utility that *different* persons ascribe to each situation entails a special problem. In actual fact, this problem has two rather different aspects, one purely metaphysical and one psychological, which have not, however, always been sufficiently kept apart.

The *metaphysical* problem would be present even if we tried to compare the utilities enjoyed by different persons with identical preferences and with identical expressive reactions to any situation. Even in this case, it would not be inconceivable that such persons should have different susceptibilities to satisfaction and should attach different utilities to identical situations, for, in principle, identical preferences may well correspond to different absolute levels of utility (as long as the ordinal properties of all persons' utility functions are the same[21]), and identical expressive reactions may well indicate different mental states with different people. At the same time, under these conditions this logical possibility of different susceptibilities to satisfaction would hardly be more than a metaphysical curiosity. If two objects or human beings show similar behavior in *all* their relevant aspects open to observation, the assumption of some unobservable hidden difference between them must be regarded as a completely gratuitous hypothesis and one contrary to sound scientific method.[22] (This principle may be called the 'principle of unwarranted differentiation'. In the last analysis, it is on the basis of this principle that we ascribe mental states to other human beings at all: the denial of this principle would at once lead us to solipsism.[23]) Thus in the case of persons with similar preferences and expressive reactions we are fully entitled to assume that they derive the same utilities from similar situations.

In the real world, of course, different people's preferences and their expressive reactions to similar situations may be rather different, and this does represent a very real difficulty in comparing the utilities enjoyed by different people—a difficulty in addition to the metaphysical difficulty just discussed and independent of it. I shall refer to it as the *psychological* difficulty, since it is essentially a question of how psychological differences between people in the widest sense (for example, differences in consumption habits, cultural background, social status, sex and other biological conditions, as well as purely psychological differences, inborn or acquired) affect the satisfaction that people derive from each situation. The problem in general takes the following form. If one individual prefers situation X to situation Y, while another prefers Y to X, is this so because the former individual attaches a *higher* utility to situation X, or because he attaches a *lower* utility to situation Y, than does the latter—or is this perhaps the result of both these factors at the same time? And, again, if in a given situation one individual gives more forcible signs of satisfaction or dissatisfaction than another, is this so because the former feels more intense satisfaction or dissatisfaction, or only because he is inclined to give stronger expression to his feelings?

This psychological difficulty is accessible to direct empirical solution to the extent to which these psychological differences between people are capable of change, and it is therefore possible for some individuals to make direct comparisons between the satisfactions open to one human type and those open to another.[24] Of course, many psychological variables are not capable of change or are capable of change only in some directions but not in others. For instance, a number of inborn mental or biological characteristics cannot be changed at all, and, though the cultural patterns and attitudes of an individual born and educated in one social group can be considerably changed by transplanting him to another, usually they cannot be completely assimilated to the cultural patterns and attitudes of the second group. Thus it may easily happen that, if we want to compare the satisfactions of two different classes of human beings, we cannot find any individual whose personal experiences would cover the satisfactions of both these classes.

Interpersonal comparisons of utility made in everyday life seem, however, to be based on a different principle (which is, of course, seldom formulated explicitly). If two individuals have opposite preferences between two situations, we usually try to find out the psychological differences responsible for this disagreement and, on the basis of our general knowledge of human psychology, try to judge to what extent these psychological differences are likely to increase or decrease their satisfaction derived from each situation. For example, if one individual is ready at a given wage rate to supply more labor than another, we tend in general to explain this mainly by his having a lower disutility for labor if his physique is much more robust than that of the other individual and if there is no ascertainable difference between the two individuals' economic needs; we tend to explain it mainly by his having a higher utility for income (consumption goods) if the two individuals' physiques are similar and if the former evidently has much greater economic needs (for example, a larger family to support).

Undoubtedly, both these methods of tackling what we have called the 'psychological difficulty' are subject to rather large margins of error.[25] In general, the greater the psychological, biological, cultural, and social differences between two people, the greater the margin of error attached to comparisons between their utility.

Particular uncertainty is connected with the second method, since it depends on our general knowledge of psychological laws, which is still in a largely unsatisfactory state.[26] What is more, all our knowledge about the psychological laws of satisfaction is ultimately derived from observing how changes in different (psychological and other) variables affect the satisfactions an individual obtains from various situations. We therefore have no direct empirical evidence on how people's satisfactions are affected by the variables that, for any particular individual, are *not* capable of change. Thus we can, in general, judge the influence of these 'unchangeable' variables only on the basis of the correlations found between these and the 'changeable' variables, whose influence we can observe directly. For instance, let us take sex as an example of 'unchangeable' variables (disregarding the few instances of sex change) and abstractive ability as an example of 'changeable' variables. We tend to assume that the average man finds greater satisfaction than the average woman does in solving mathematical puzzles *because*, allegedly, men in general have greater abstractive ability than women. But this reasoning depends on the implicit assumption that differences in the 'unchangeable' variables, if unaccompanied by differences in the 'changeable' variables, are in themselves immaterial. For example, we must assume that men and women equal in abstractive ability (and the other relevant characteristics) would tend to find the same satisfaction in working on mathematical problems.

Of course, the assumption that the 'unchangeable' variables in themselves have no influence is *ex hypothesi* not open to direct empirical check. It can be justified only by the a priori principle that, when one variable is alleged to have a certain influence on another, the burden of proof lies on those who claim the existence of such an influence.[27] Thus the second method of interpersonal utility comparison rests in an important sense on empirical evidence more indirect[28] than that underlying the first method. On the other hand, the second method has the advantage of also being applicable in those cases where no one individual can possibly have wide enough personal experience to make direct utility comparisons in terms of the first method.

In any case, it should now be sufficiently clear that interpersonal comparisons of utility are not value judgments based on some ethical or political postulates but rather are factual propositions based on certain principles of inductive logic.

At the same time, Professor Robbins[29] is clearly right when he maintains that propositions which purport to be interpersonal comparisons of utility often contain a purely *conventional* element based on ethical or political value judgments. For instance, the assumption that different individuals have the same susceptibility to satisfaction often expresses only the egalitarian value judgment that all individuals should be treated equally rather than a belief in a factual psychological equality between them. Or, again, different people's total satisfaction is often compared on the tacit understanding that the gratification of wants regarded as 'immoral' in terms of a certain ethical standard shall not count. But in order to avoid confusion, such propositions based on ethical or political restrictive postulates must be clearly distinguished from interpersonal comparisons of utility without a conventional element of this kind.

It must also be admitted that the use of conventional postulates based on personal value judgments may sometimes be due not to our free choice but rather to our lack of the factual information needed to give our interpersonal utility comparisons a more objective basis. In effect, if we do not know anything about the relative urgency of different persons' economic needs and still have to make a decision, we can hardly avoid acting on the basis of personal guesses more or less dependent on our own value judgments.

On the other hand, if the information needed is available, individualistic ethics consistently requires the use, in the social welfare function, of individual utilities not subjected to restrictive postulates. The imposition of restrictive ethical or political conventions on the individual utility functions would necessarily qualify our individualism, since it would decrease the dependence of our social welfare function on the actual preferences and actual susceptibilities to satisfaction, of the individual members of the society, putting in its place a dependence on our own ethical or political value judgments (see nn. 7 and 8).

To sum up, the more complete our factual information and the more completely individualistic our ethics, the more the different individuals' social welfare functions will converge toward the same objective quantity, namely, the unweighted sum (or rather the unweighted arithmetic mean) of all individual utilities. This follows both from (either of two alternative sets of) ethical postulates based on commonly accepted individualistic ethical value judgments and from the mere logical analysis of the concept of a social welfare function. The latter interpretation also removes certain difficulties connected with the concept of a social welfare function, which have been brought out by Little's criticism of certain of Arrow's conclusions.

Of course, the practical need for reaching decisions on public policy will require us to formulate social welfare functions—explicitly or implicitly—even if we lack the factual information needed for placing interpersonal comparisons of utility on an objective basis. But even in this case, granting the proposed ethical postulates (or the proposed interpretation of the concept of a social welfare function), our social welfare function must take the form of a weighted sum (weighted mean) of all individual utility functions, with more or less arbitrary weights chosen according to our own value judgments.

There is here an interesting analogy with the theory of statistical decisions (and, in general, the theory of choosing among alternative hypotheses). In the same way as in the latter, it has been shown[30] that a rational man (whose choices satisfy certain simple postulates of rationality) must act *as if* he ascribed numerical subjective probabilities to all alternative hypotheses, even if his factual information is insufficient to do this on an objective basis—so in welfare economics we have also found that a rational man (whose choices satisfy certain simple postulates of rationality and impartiality) must likewise act *as if* he made quantitative interpersonal comparisons of utility, even if his factual information is insufficient to do this on an objective basis.

Thus if we accept individualistic ethics and set public policy the task of satisfying the preferences of the individual members of the society (deciding between conflicting preferences of different individuals according to certain standards of impartial equity), our social welfare function will always tend to take the form of a sum (or mean) of individual utilities; but whether the weights given to these individual utilities have an objective basis or not will depend wholly on the extent of our factual (psychological) information.

NOTES

* *Journal of Political Economy*, **LXIII** (1955), 309–321.

[1] I am indebted to my colleagues at the University of Queensland, Messrs. R. W. Lane and G. Price, for helpful comments. Of course, the responsibility for shortcomings of this paper and for the opinions expressed in it is entirely mine.

[2] A. Bergson (Burk), 'A Reformulation of Certain Aspects of Welfare Economics', *Quarterly Journal of Economics*, LII (February, 1938), 310–34, and 'Socialist Economics', in *A Survey of Contemporary Economics*, ed. H. S. Ellis (Philadelphia, 1949), esp. pp. 412–20.

[3] M. Fleming, 'A Cardinal Concept of Welfare', *Quarterly Journal of Economics*, LXVI (August, 1952), 366–84. For a different approach to the same problem see L. Goodman and H. Markowitz, 'Social Welfare Functions Based on Individual Rankings', *American Journal of Sociology*, Vol. LVIII (November, 1952).

[4] Of course, when I speak of preferences 'from a social standpoint', often abbreviated to 'social' preferences and the like, I always mean preferences based on a given individual's value judgments concerning 'social welfare'. The foregoing postulates are meant to impose restrictions on *any* individual's value judgements of this kind, and thus represent, as it were, value judgments of the second order, that is, value judgments concerning value judgments. Later I shall discuss the concept of 'preferences from a social standpoint' at some length and introduce the distinctive term 'ethical preferences' to describe them (in Sec. IV). But at this stage I do not want to prejudge the issue by using this terminology.

[5] The more general term 'utility distribution' is used instead of the term 'income distribution',

since the utility enjoyed by each individual will, in general, depend not only on his own income but also, owing to external economies and diseconomies of consumption, on other people's incomes.

6 It is not assumed, however, that the other individuals are (like i and j) indifferent between X and X' and between Y and Y'. In effect, were this restrictive assumption inserted into Postulate E, this latter would completely lose the status of an independent postulate and would become a mere corollary of Postulate D.

7 In view of consumers' notorious 'irrationality', some people may feel that these postulates go too far in accepting the consumers' sovereignty doctrine. These people may reinterpret the terms in the postulates referring to individual preferences as denoting, not certain individuals' actual preferences, but rather their 'true' preferences, that is, the preferences they *would* manifest under 'ideal conditions', in posession of perfect information, and acting with perfect logic and care. With some ingenuity it should not be too difficult to give even some sort of 'operational' meaning to these ideal conditions, or to some approximation of them, acceptable for practical purposes. (Or, alternatively, these terms may be reinterpreted as referring even to the preferences that these individuals *ought* to exhibit in terms of a given ethical standard. The latter interpretation would, of course, deprive the postulates of most of their individualistic meaning.)

8 These postulates do not exclude, however, the possibility that such consideration may influence the relative weights given to different individuals' utilies within the additive social welfare function. Even by means of additional postulates, this could be excluded only to the extent to which the comparison of individual utilities can be put on an objective basis independent of individual value judgments (see Sec. V).

9 See. J. von Neumann and O. Morgenstern, *Theory of Games and Economic Behavior* (2d ed.; Princeton, 1947), pp. 641 ff.

10 J. Marschak, 'Rational Behavior, Uncertain Prospects, and Measurable Utility', *Econometrica*, XVIII (1950), 111–41, esp. 116–21. Marschak's postulates can be summarized as follows. *Postulate I (complete ordering)*: The relation of preference establishes a complete ordering among all prospects. *Postulate II* (continuity): If prospect P is preferred to prospect R, while prospect Q has an intermediate position between them (being preferred to R but less preferred than P), then there exists a mixture of P and R, with appropriate probabilities, such as to be exactly indifferent to Q. *Postulate III* (*sufficient number of nonindifferent prospects*): There are at least four mutually nonindifferent prospects. *Postulate IV* (*equivalence of mixture of equivalent prospects*): If prospects Q and Q' are indifferent, then, for any prospect P, a given mixture of P and Q is indifferent to a similar mixture of P and Q', (that is, to a mixture of P and Q' which has the same probabilities for the corresponding constituent prospects).

Postulate I is needed to establish the existence of even an *ordinal* utility (or welfare) function, while the other three postulates are required to establish the existence of a *cardinal* utility (or welfare) function. But, as Postulates II and III are almost trivial, Postulate IV may be regarded as being decisive for cardinality as against mere ordinality.

11 There are reasons to believe that, in actuality, individual preferences between uncertain prospects do not always satisfy these postulates of rational behavior (for example, owing to a certain 'love of danger'; see Marschak, *op. cit.*, pp. 137–41). In this case we may fall back again upon the preferences each individual *would* manifest under 'ideal conditions' (see n. 7).

12 If we want a formal guaranty that no individual's utility can be given a negative weight in the social welfare function, we must add one more postulate (for instance, Postulate D of Sec. II).

13 This principle is essentially identical with Professor Arrow's 'nondictatorship' postulate in his *Social Choice and Individual Values* (New York, 1951), p. 30 (see also n. 14).

[14] Mr. Little's objection to Arrow's nondictatorship postulate (see Little's review article in the *Journal of Political Economy*, LX [October, 1952], esp. 426–31) loses its force, once the distinction between 'ethical' and 'subjective' preferences is noted. It does, then, make sense that an individual should morally *disapprove* (in terms of his 'ethical' preferences) of an unequal income distribution which benefits him financially, and should still *prefer* it (in terms of his 'subjective' preferences) to a more egalitarian one or should even *fight* for it—behavior morally regrettable but certainly not logically inconceivable.

Arrow's distinction between an individual's 'tastes' (which order social situations only according to their effects on his own consumption) and his 'values' (which take account also of external economies and diseconomies of consumption and of ethical considerations, in ordering social situations) does not meet the difficulty, since it does not explain how an individual can without inconsistency accept a social welfare function conflicting with his own 'values'. This can be understood only if his social welfare functions represents preferences of another sort than his 'values' do. (Of course, in my terminology Arrow's 'values' fall in the class of 'subjective' preferences and not in the class of 'ethical' preferences, as is easily seen from the way in which he defines them.)

[15] See my 'Cardinal Utility in Welfare Economics and in the Theory of Risk-taking', *Journal of Political Economy*, LXI (October, 1953), 434–35.

[16] Or rather, if he had an equal chance of being 'put in the place of' any individual member of the society, with regard not only to his objective social (and economic) conditions, but also to his subjective attitudes and tastes. In other words, he ought to judge the utility of another individual's position not in terms of his own attitudes and tastes but rather in terms of the attitudes and tastes of the individual actually holding this position.

[17] *Op. cit.*

[18] Obviously, the (unweighted or weighted) *mean* of the individual utilities defines the same social welfare function as their *sum* (weighted by the same relative weights), except for an irrelevant proportionality constant.

[19] The concept of ethical preferences used in this section implies, of course, an ethical theory different from the now prevalent subjective attitude theory, since it makes a person's ethical judgments the expression, not of his subjective attitudes in general, but rather of certain special unbiased impersonal attitudes only. I shall set out the philosophic case for this ethical theory in a forthcoming publication. (For an similiar view, see J. N. Findlay, 'The Justification of Attitudes', *Mind*, N.S., LXIII [April, 1954], 145–61.)

[20] See I. M. D. Little, *A Critique of Welfare Economics* (Oxford, 1950), chap. iv. I have nothing to add to Little's conclusion on the *possibility* of interpersonal comparisons of utility. I only want to supplement his argument by an analysis of the *logical basis* of such comparisons. I shall deal with the problem of comparisons between total utilities only, neglecting the problem of comparisons between differences in utility, since the social welfare functions discussed in the previous sections contain only total utilities of individuals.

[21] Even identical preferences among uncertain prospects (satisfying the Marschak axioms) are compatible with different absolute levels of utility, since they do not uniquely determine the zero points and the scales of the corresponding cardinal utility functions.

[22] By making a somewhat free use of Professor Carnap's distinction, we may say that the assumption of different susceptibilities of satisfaction in this case, even though it would not be against the canons of *deductive* logic, would most definetely be against the canons of *inductive* logic.

[23] See Little, *A Critique of Welfare Economics*, pp. 56–57.

[24] On the reliability of comparisons between the utility of different situations before a change in one's 'taste' (taken in the broadest sense) and after it, see the first two sections of my 'Welfare Economics of Variable Tastes', *Review of Economic Studies*, XXI, (1953-54), 204–8.

[25] Though perhaps it would not be too difficult to reduce these margins quite considerably (for example, by using appropriate statistical techniques), should there be a need for more precise results.

[26] Going back to our example, for instance, the disutility of labor and the utility of income are unlikely to be actually independent variables (as I have tacitly assumed), though it may not always be clear in which way their mutual influence actually goes. In any case, income is enjoyed in a different way, depending on the ease with which it has been earned, and labor is put up with in a different spirit, depending on the strength of one's need for additional income.

[27] This principle may be called the 'principle of unwarranted correlation' and is again a principle of inductive logic, closely related to the principle of unwarranted differentiation referred to earlier.

[28] There is also another reason for which conclusions dependent on the principle of unwarranted correlation have somewhat less cogency than conclusions dependent only on the principle of unwarranted differentiation. The former principle refers to the case where two individuals differ in a certain variable X (in our example, in sex) but where there is no special evidence that they differ also in a certain other variable Y (in susceptibility to satisfaction). The latter principle, on the other hand, refers to the case where there is no ascertainable difference at all between the two individuals in any observable variable whatever, not even in X (in sex). Now, though the assumption that these two individuals differ in Y (in susceptibility to satisfaction) would be a gratuitous hypothesis in either case, obviously it would be a less unnatural hypothesis in the first case (where there is some observed difference between the two individuals) than in the second case (where there is none).

[29] See L. Robbins, 'Robertson on Utility and Scope', *Economica*, N.S., XX (1953), 99–111, esp. 109; see also his *An Essay on the Nature and Significance of Economic Science* (2d ed.; London, 1948), chap. vi; and his 'Interpersonal Comparisons of Utility', *Economic Journal*, XLIII (December, 1938), 635–41.

[30] See Marschak's discussion of what he calls 'Ramsey's norm', in his paper on 'Probability in the Social Sciences', in *Mathematical Thinking in the Social Sciences*, ed. P. F. Lazarsfeld (Glencoe, Ill., 1954), Sec. I, esp. pp. 179–87; also reprinted as No. 82 of 'Cowles Commission Papers' (N.S.).

For a survey of earlier literature see K. J. Arrow, 'Alternative Approaches to the Theory of Choice in Risk-taking Situation', *Econometrica*, XIX (October, 1951), 404–37, esp. 431–32, and the references there quoted.

CHAPTER III

ETHICS IN TERMS OF HYPOTHETICAL IMPERATIVES*

I

The affinity of moral rules—and of value judgements in general—to imperatives has often been pointed out by philosophers. It has been argued recently with admirable clarity in Mr. R. M. Hare's *The Language of Morals*. But most advocates of this view follow Kant in regarding moral rules as non-hypothetical, *i.e.* categorical, imperatives. I shall try to show that this view is mistaken, and that moral rules are in actual fact *hypothetical* imperatives. Indeed, I shall argue that on closer analysis all imperatives turn out to be hypothetical, even though their protasis is often left unexpressed.

Kant only considered hypothetical imperatives where the protasis refers to a hypothetical end while the apodosis proposes means causally conducive to this end, as is the case with technical instructions, and would also be the case with prudential rules if these were interpreted with Kant as instructions for producing happiness. However, in actual fact there are hypothetical imperatives in common use where the relation between the protasis and the apodosis is quite obviously *formal* rather than *causal*: the protasis specifies certain desired criteria whereas the apodosis suggests an object or a pattern of behaviour satisfying these criteria. For instance: 'If you want to climb a very high mountain'(or 'If you want to climb the highest mountain in Europe...'), 'climb the Mont Blanc'. 'If you want to play soccer, do not touch the ball with your hand unless you are the goalkeeper'. 'If you want to be really polite to him, call him 'Sir'.'We still may speak of ends and means if we like, but these terms now have to be taken in a looser and non-causal sense. We may say, for example, that somebody's end is to climb a very high mountain, and that he chooses to climb the Mont Blanc as a means to this end— yet the underlying idea is not that a trip to the Mont Blanc causally produces a trip to a very high mountain, but rather that a trip to the Mont Blanc already *is* a trip to a very high mountain. It may be even argued that hypothetical imperatives of the causal type themselves represent a special case of hypothetical imperatives of the formal type, *viz.* the case where the criterion to be satisfied is that of causal efficiency in producing a certain desired effect.

The existence of non-causal hypothetical imperatives removes an important objection to the view that moral rules are hypothetical imperatives. Only a strict utilitarian could maintain that moral rules prescribe means to a certain end (*e.g.* the production of pleasure). But one need not be a strict utilitarian to think that moral rules prescribe patterns of behaviour which satisfy certain formal criteria.

II

I propose first to show that non-moral imperatives are always hypothetical imperatives. Non-moral imperatives may be divided into *advices* and *demands.* By a demand I mean an imperative suggesting a certain course of action as conducive to the speaker's own ends, whether these ends are selfish or unselfish. By an advice I mean an imperative suggesting a certain course of action as conducive to the addressee's ends, again irrespective of whether these ends are selfish or unselfish. Thus the speaker is making a 'demand' if he is asking for money for his own purposes or for the purposes of some altruistic cause he is interested in. On the other hand, he is giving 'advice' if he recommends to a certain person money expenditure serving this person's own interests or serving some altruistic cause this person is attached to.

Since any advice is meant to help the advisee in furthering his own ends, it must have the form: 'If you want the end A, do X'. As a hypothetical imperative it may be equally of the causal or of the non-causal type. If my friend tells me that he wants to climb the highest mountain in Europe, it will be an 'advice' both if I tell him that in this case he must climb the Mont Blanc (non-causal) and if I tell him that in this case he must use a special sort of tourist equipment (causal-technical). Moreover, an advice will be technically a hypothetical imperative even if the speaker knows that the hypothesis is actually fulfilled. 'If you want A (as I know you do), then do X' is also a hypothetical imperative—though it is what is traditionally called an 'assertorial', rather than a 'problematical', hypothetical imperative.

At first sight it may be less obvious that demands must also always contain a reference to the addressee's ends, because their actual aim is furthering the ends of the speaker, not those of the addressee. But in fact they must make a reference to the addressee's ends to have any prospect of being effective. If the addressee can be assumed to take a spontaneous benevolent interest in furthering the speaker's ends, it may be quite sufficient to refer to this benevolent interest alone: 'If you want to do me a favour...', 'If you do not want to leave me in an awkward position . . .' etc. Requests of this type are often, though not always, hypothetical imperatives of the non-causal type: the action requested would *be* a favour rather than *produce* a favour— while it would produce a less awkward position. In other cases it will be necessary for the speaker to promise rewards or threaten with punishment, ranging from physical advantages or disadvantages to mere friendly or unfriendly feelings. In such cases demands will have the logical form: 'If you want me to do A (or refrain from B), do X (or refrain from Y)'. These are, of course, hypothetical imperatives of the causal type.

If the speaker can neither appeal to the addressee's spontaneous goodwill nor support his demand with promises or threats, he can do no more than express a mere wish. If we admit wishes to be true imperatives, we may say that wishes represent the only possible type of non-hypothetical imperatives. But I agree with Hare's view that mere wishes are not true imperatives because they are not possible answers to the question. 'What shall I do?' Therefore I prefer to say that all true imperatives are hypothetical imperatives. Of course, wishes which actually imply a request, *i.e.* a demand appealing to the addressee's benevolent attitude, *are* true imperatives. But like all demands they are hypothetical imperatives.

III

How do moral rules fit into this scheme? If we regard moral rules as possible reasons (*i.e.* rational motives) for a person to perform the acts enjoined by these rules, moral rules can also be interpreted only as hypothetical imperatives. Suppose I am told 'If you want to follow Christian ethics, do X', or 'If you want to please public opinion, do X', or 'If you want to be generous, do X', or 'If you want to gain the approval of an impartial and sympathetic observer, do X— this will be a good reason for me to do X, provided that I do want to follow Christian ethics, or to please public opinion, or to be generous, or to gain the approval of an impartial and sympathetic observer. These statements supply a good reason for my doing X because they make an appeal to an attitude which I actually entertain and suggest a pattern of behaviour corresponding to this attitude.

If moral rules were expressions only of the speaker's attitudes who utters them, as the *subjectivist* theories suggest, and did not involve an appeal to the addressee's attitudes, they would not normally represent a reason for the addressee to do some particular action. Suppose a subjectivist philosopher tells me 'Repay your debts'. If this only means that he himself wants me to repay my debts—and perhaps also that he wants other people to repay their debts—this will be a reason for me to repay my debts only if we happen to be personal friends and I am anxious to do what he wants me to do simply because he wants me to do it. (But even in this case his statement should be interpreted as a hypothetical imperative of the form 'If you want to comply with my wishes, repay your debts'.)

Similarly, if moral rules were interpreted, in accordance with the *intuitionist* theories, as statements about the non-natural qualities of certain acts, they would not furnish a reason for people to perform these acts. Intuitionist philosophers have correctly argued that even a complete description of the situation in terms of all its 'natural' characteristics cannot provide a 'reason' for me to embark upon some particular course of action: *from what there is it cannot be inferred what should be done* (to say the opposite would be committing the *naturalistic* fallacy). But this principle will still apply even if we supplement the description of the situation in terms of its natural characteristics by a list of the 'non-natural' qualities inherent in the situation. No descriptive statement in the indicative—whether it describes natural or non-natural attributes—can provide a sufficient reason for people to perform a certain act. (Shall we say that to assert the opposite would be committing the *ontologistic* fallacy?) At least, moral rules must be construed as hypothetical imperatives of the form: 'If you want to do acts which have the non-natural quality A, do X'. But, once we admit that moral rules are hypothetical imperatives, we can perfectly well do without any non-natural qualities altogether and can interpret moral rules as hypothetical imperatives of the form: 'If you want your behaviour to satisfy the criterion A (or the criteria $A_1, A_2, \ldots, A_n$), then do X'—where A or $A_1, A_2, \ldots, A_n$ stand for natural qualities or relations.

To sum up, if we want to restrict the term 'moral rule' to statements which can serve as a rational motive for people to do certain actions and to refrain from others, we can admit only hypothetical imperatives as having the full status of moral rules. Other statements (indicatives or non-hypothetical imperatives) can be called moral rules only if they are regarded as elliptical statements implying an unexpressed hypothetical imperative.

IV

Now obviously, if moral rules are hypothetical imperatives at all, they are 'advices' and not 'demands'. They do not promise rewards or threaten with punishments; nor do they ask for compliance as a favour to the speaker who utters them. Rather, they are advices for people who already have a certain moral attitude, telling them what sort of behaviour is consistent with the moral attitude they entertain.

Moreover, moral rules are hypothetical imperatives of the non-causal type. Their nearest relatives are not technical instructions, but rules of a game, rules of etiquette, or legal rules. Moral rules do not tell us what to do in order to produce certain particular results, but rather tell us what to do to make our behaviour (and the consequences of our behaviour) satisfy certain formal criteria. The criterion to be satisfied may be simply conformity to a certain historical moral code: 'If you want to follow Christian ethics, do X'. Or it may be a criterion not containing reference to any historical particular: 'If you want to be generous, do X'. On the other hand, the criterion stated or implied may be what the addressee reards as the basic criterion for morally right conduct, or may be only a derivative criterion. For instance generosity may be a moral criterion by its own right or may be accepted as a moral criterion only because of its social usefulness or because of its conformity to Christian ethics. In many cases he addressee (or the speaker, for that matter) will be quite unable to tell whether he wants to regard a certain criterion as basic or as derivative. Nor can we expect that people will be in general very consistent in applying different moral criteria. The moral philosopher, however, will be interested in finding out whether there is any self-consistent set of basic criteria for morally right conduct such as to account for his own moral attitudes and for those of his fellows.

V

In recent years a number of contemporary moral philosophers[1] have called attention to Adam Smith's moral theory, which regards moral rules as rules of behaviour that a well-informed and intelligent impartially sympathetic observer would recommend for general observance.

In what follows it is proposed to show that a particularly satisfactory theory of morals obtains if the hypothetical-imperative theory of moral rules is

combined with Adam Smith's theory of the impartially sympathetic observer. This would give moral rules the form: 'If you want to do what an impartially sympathetic observer would recommend for general observance,
do X (or refrain from Y)'. Alternatively, it may be possible to formalize the
requirements of impartiality and of sympathetic humanism (and possibly a
few other requirements) in terms of a small number of formal axioms—as
has already been done by welfare economists for a more limited field—in
which case moral rules could be put in the form: 'If you want your behaviour to satisfy axioms A_1, A_2, ..., A_n, then do X (or refrain from Y)'.

VI

In this form the present theory comes very close to Kant's, who can be interpreted as saying that moral rules have to satisfy the formal requirement or
axiom of *universalizability* and that this is the only requirement they have
to satisfy. We know now that this one requirement would be quite insufficient for determining the content of a moral code—but this does not mean
that a more extensive set of formal requirements might not achieve this
goal.

    However, there is also another difference between the present theory and
Kant's. Even if we accepted Kant's universalizability requirements as sufficient, we would still differ from him in giving moral rules a hypothetical
form. The basic difference between the hypothetical and the non-hypothetical formulations lies in the fact that the hypothetical form is addressed (in
a non-vacuous sense) only to those who already want to conform their behaviour to certain formal requirements (*e.g.* under Kant's theory, to those
who already want to act according to a maxim which could be accepted as a
general law)—while the non-hypothetical form purports to be addressed to
everybody. And precisely for this reason, Kant would certainly have objected to our hypothetical formulation. He wanted a moral law calling, by
the authority of reason, not only on those who already have a certain
moral attitude but also on those who do not have such an attitude
at all. Before Kant, moralists tried to prove that it is irrational for the sinner
to sin against the moral law, by referring to the divine punishment unfail-
ingly awaiting all sinners. Kant, who was precluded from using arguments
appealing to self-interest, tried to prove the same point by making the moral
law a Categorical Imperative. But he could not possibly succeed. It is im-

possible to prove that a certain person acts irrationally by failing to conform his behaviour to certain formal criteria, if he simply does not want to conform his behaviour to these criteria. At the same time, this fact need not have any detrimental consequences for practical morality. It will not weaken the appeal of the moral rules to whose who *do* want to conform their behaviour to the formal criteria in question. On the other hand, philosophic arguments could not be expected anyhow to impress those who *do not* want to conform their behaviour to these criteria – even if these arguments were logically valid. In practice even Kantian philosophers would use education or propaganda, and not philosophic arguments, to gain over those who do not want to follow their moral standard. The arguments of a moral philosopher cannot make us accept a certain moral standard – though they can make it clearer what sort of behaviour a given moral standard actually requires, by analysing the moral rules associated with this standard as hypothetical imperatives whose validity can be ascertained by rational methods.

VII

The present theory gives the moral rules a *content* fairly similar (though), as we shall see presently, a content not quite identical) to that which utilitarianism would give them, but gives them a *logical form* rather different. Utilitarians seem to say that moral rules are descriptive statements in the indicative (since moral terms like 'good' and 'right' as well as their opposites are to be defined by indicative phrases); but it is likely that they actually mean to say that moral rules are hypothetical imperatives of the causal type, giving quasi-technical instructions for producing certain desired consequences (say, pleasure). In contrast, the present theory makes moral rules hypothetical imperatives of the non-causal type.

There are two main points in which ordinary utilitarianism differs from common sense as to the content of the moral law: one is its hedonism and the other is its interpretation of moral obligations. I submit that what misled utilitarians on both points was their assimilating moral rules to hypothetical imperatives of the causal type, and that conclusions in better accord with common sense are reached on the basis of the present theory.

If moral rules are hypothetical imperatives of the non-causal type, we are not logically committed to the view that morally good behaviour always necessarily involves producing any particular sort of good consequences, whether pleasure or 'mental states of intrinsic worth' or anything else. Indeed, if we define moral rules with reference to an impartially sympathetic observer, we are in fact committed to a different view. The hypothetical impartially sympathetic observer must judge the consequences that a given action has for various people, 'sympathetically' in the literal sense of the term, *i.e.* in terms of the attitudes, wants, desires, preferences of these people themselves—rather than in terms of some independent standard, whether the standard of hedonism or some other. Since any moral standard is supposed to be defined in terms of the recommendations of the impartially sympathetic observer, this observer himself cannot determine what is 'good' for different persons, with reference to any pre-existing moral standard, but only with reference to the preferences of these persons themselves. The value of pleasure, or higher mental states, or anything else, to any particular person he can judge ultimately only on the basis of the importance this person himself assigns to it.

Only this theory can do full justice to the traditional principle that morality essentially consists in following the rule: 'Treat other people in the same way as you want to be treated yourself'. For, after all, *what* way do I myself want to be treated? To this question the fundamental answer—the only answer necessarily true, because tautologically true—is: 'I want to be treated in accordance with my own wants'. All other answers like 'I want to be given pleasure', etc. can be only derivative answers. Accordingly, we shall treat other people in the same way as we want to be treated ourselves, only if we make a point of it to give them what they themselves want—and not what we consider or what anybody else considers to be good for them.

This conclusion is, however, subject to an important qualification or rather clarification. Common sense does distinguish between sensible and foolish wants or preferences, and it would be absurd to suggest that our moral code should not take account of this distinction in one way or another. For instance, benevolence cannot require us to satisfy other people's obviously foolish wants and preferences in the same way as their sensible wants and preferences. Hedonism (and also the theory of 'mental states of intrinsic worth') is essentially an attempt to supply a criterion for distinguishing 'rational' preferences from 'irrational' ones: the former being preferences directed towards objects of a *real* pleasure-producing capacity (or objects with a *real* capacity of producing 'mental states of intrinsic worth') and the latter being preferences directed towards objects of the opposite sort. However, the purpose this distinction is supposed to serve can also be achieved without reference to any standard outside of the own attitudes of the persons concerned. We may define a person's *'true'* preferences as those preferences that this person himself would manifest on due reflection and in possession of all relevant information (including information on the pleasures and pains resulting from alternative courses of action), making the moral rules enjoin acts that tend to produce consequences conformable to people's 'true' preferences rather than to their actual explicit preferences (which may not always correctly represent their 'true' preferences). This rule will achieve the aim of excluding 'irrational' preferences resulting from error and ignorance, or from carelessness, rashness, strong excitement, or other conditions which hinder rational choice.

May I here add a note on terminology? I have suggested that the question of what is and what is not 'good' for other people should be judged ultimately in terms of their own 'preferences'. Perhaps it would have been in better agreement with prevalent every-day and philosophic usage to replace the term 'preferences' by such terms as 'attitudes', 'wants' or 'desires'. But I have thought it may be worth while to borrow the term 'preferences' from economics because all alternative terms tend to be misleading: they fail to indicate the important fact that a person's 'attitudes' or 'wants' or 'desires' can guide his own behaviour or the behaviour of other people sympathetic to him only if he makes up his mind and *chooses* between the conflicting attitudes or wants or desires he may have.

VIII

Common sense regards certain moral obligations as binding even if in particular cases fulfilment of these obligations has predominantly bad consequences (with the possible exception of extreme cases). In contrast, ordinary utilitarianism is committed to the view that prima-facie obligations are never binding if the consequences of fulfilling them would be predominantly bad. Moreover, ordinary utilitarianism is unable to account for the distinction which common sense makes between duties of special obligation and duties of benevolence. (Actually, in every-day language duties of benevolence are usually not called 'duties' at all.)

Mr. R. F. Harrod has shown in 'Utilitarianism Revised' (*Mind*, April, 1936) that the first difficulty of utilitarianism can be overcome if the utilitarian criterion is applied not to the consequences of each *single* act but rather to the cumulative consequences of the *general* practice of acting in a certain particular way (acting according to a certain rule) in all similar cases. This theory can also be used for distinguishing between duties of special obligation and duties of benevolence: the former are duties based on the cumulative good consequences of the general observance of certain rules while the latter are duties based on the good consequences of particular acts.

This theory of special obligations can also be put in the following form. In the case of special obligations, the immediate reason for which people are morally bound to do certain acts is not social expediency: it is rather the existence of these obligations themselves, and possibly the existence of corresponding rights on the part of other people. But the existence itself of these obligations and rights, on the other hand, has to be explained in terms of the social expediency of this system of obligations and rights. For instance, it is not a matter of social expediency but is a self-evident analytical truth that people are morally required to respect other people's morally *valid* property rights. However, it is a matter of social expediency and cannot be determined by conceptual analysis whether, and under what conditions, people should be allowed by the moral rules to acquire valid property rights (and what restrictions these property rights should be subjected to). Similarly, it is not a matter of social expediency but is a self-evident analytical truth that people are morally required to fulfil morally *binding* promises. At the same time, it is a matter of social expediency whether, and under what conditions, people should be allowed by the moral rules to enter into binding obligations by means of making promises. For instance, minors may not be allowed by the moral (and legal) rules to enter into binding obligations by making promises. Probably the self-evidence of such analytical truths as 'Other people's valid property rights ought to be respected' or 'Binding promises ought to be fulfilled' accounts for the intuitive feeling of 'fittingness' that some intuitionist philosophers claim to have on considering acts of respecting other people's property or acts of fulfilling promises, etc.

Now, interpretation of the moral rules with reference to an intelligent and sympathetic observer naturally leads to Harrod's theory of moral obligations, because an intelligent and sympathetic observer will obviously take into account not only the consequences of particular acts but also the cumulative long-run consequences of the general observance of the moral rules he recommends (and the cumulative long-run consequences of the system of obligations and rights established by these rules). On the other hand, the utilitarian theory, which makes moral rules hypothetical imperatives of the causal type, even if it is not formally inconsistent with Harrod's theory, more naturally leads, and has actually led, to the crude utilitarian theory of moral obligations, which has been criticized above.

IX

To conclude, the present theory of moral rules avoids the formidable epistemological difficulties of alternative theories. As Hare has shown (pp. 33-38), hypothetical imperatives are either *analytical* truths, or else follow from two premises of which one is a hypothetical imperative that is itself an analytical truth while the other is an empirical statement in the indicative. Accordingly, under the present theory the highest-order moral rules become analytical statements where the apodosis only enjoins what is entailed by the formal requirements stated in the protasis (*viz.* enjoins patterns of behaviour entailed by the requirement of conformity to the recommendations of an impartially sympathetic observer). On the other hand, the lower-order moral rules become the logical consequences of these analytical highest-order moral rules and of certain empirical facts. Of these empirical facts the most important ones are facts about people's 'true' preferences. (Under the present theory, facts about people's 'true' preferences have an importance similar to the importance that facts about human 'nature' had in the systems of some earlier moralists.) Thus moral rules have full *objective* validity—though in a looser sense they may be said to have only hypothetical objective validity (meaning that their apodosis has only hypothetical validity). If the moral rules enjoin a particular act under certain conditions, this means that it is an objective fact, depending on certain logical truths and possibly also on certain empirical truths, that if anybody wants to follow the recommendations which a well-informed and intelligent impartially sympathetic observer would make he *must* perform this act under the specified conditions. This fact has to be accepted by everybody, even by those who do not actually themselves want to follow the recommendations of an impartially sympathetic observer.

Of course, the same quasi-hypothetical objective validity appertains not only to the moral rules of Adam Smith's ethics of impartially sympathetic humanism, but appertains to the norms of any self-consistent code of behaviour. It is an objective fact that whoever wants to gain the approval of an impartially sympathetic observer must oppose aggressive wars—but it is equally an objective fact that whoever wants, on the contrary, to subordinate any other consideration to national self-interest must support his country's profitable-looking aggressive wars, etc.

If two codes of behaviour are equally self-consistent, the choice between them is not a matter of logic alone, but rather primarily a matter of personal attitudes. However, analysis by moral philosophy of alternative codes of behaviour can help us to make our choice more intelligent. It can make us more clearly aware of the difference among codes of behaviour based on individual egoism, on group egoism, and on disinterested attitudes; and again of the difference between *humanistic* codes based on disinterested sympathy with human interests—and *idealistic* codes based on disinterested love for certain ideals or values (such as love for truth or beauty, or for spiritual or intellectual, or even biological, 'perfection' of some sort, or for certain particular social institutions of cultural traditions, etc.), these ideals or values being sought strictly for their own sake and not for the sake of the human interests they may serve. For instance, under this terminology Nietzsche's moral code is a non-humanistic idealistic moral code based on a quasi-aesthetic admiration for strong and colourful personalities. Moral philosophy can point out the fact of fundamental importance that in ultimate analysis all non-humanistic codes of behaviour are merely expressions of contingent personal preferences—though possibly of very disinterested preferences—on the part of the people adopting these codes: whereas the code of impartially sympathetic humanism is the only one which by definition gives the same equal weight to the preferences of any other person as well. (This last statement, of course, presupposes the possibility of making operationally meaningful interpersonal utility comparisons—see my 'Cardinal Welfare, Individualistic Ethics, and Interpersonal Comparisons of Utility', *Journal of Political Economy,* August, 1955.)

I think this difference is sufficiently important to justify placing the code of impartially sympathetic humanism in a different category from any other code of behaviour, and reserving the term 'moral code' and 'moral rules' for describing this particular code and the norms associated with it—at least in systematic moral philosophy, while preferably retaining the wider usage in the social sciences and in the history of moral philosophy. But it is a point of minor significance whether this terminological policy is adopted or some other. The only important thing is that this fundamental difference between humanistic and non-humanistic standards of behaviour should be brought out in full relief for the information of those people who have to choose between them.

Yet, when all has been said, everybody has to make his own choice.

NOTE

* *Mind,* **67** (1958), 305–316.

[1] See W. Kneale, 'Objectivity in Morals', *Philosophy*, April 1950, pp. 149–166; R. Firth, 'Ethical Absolutism and the Ideal Observer', *Philosophy and Phenomenological Research*, March 1952, pp. 317–345; and J. N. Findlay, 'The Justification of Attitudes', *Mind*, April 1954, pp. 145–161.

CHAPTER IV

CAN THE MAXIMIN PRINCIPLE SERVE AS A BASIS FOR MORALITY? A CRITIQUE OF JOHN RAWLS'S THEORY*§

I. INTRODUCTION

John Rawls's *A Theory of Justice*[1] is an important book. It is an attempt to develop a viable alternative to *utilitarianism*, which up to now in its various forms was virtually the only ethical theory proposing a reasonably clear, systematic, and purportedly rational concept of morality. I shall argue that Rawls's attempt to suggest a viable alternative to utilitarianism does not succeed. Nevertheless, beyond any doubt, his book is a significant contribution to the ongoing debate on the nature of rational morality.

Rawls distinguishes two major traditions of systematic theory in post-medieval moral philosophy. One is the *utilitarian* tradition, represented by Hume, Adam Smith, Bentham, John Stuart Mill, Sidgwick, Edgeworth, and many others, including a number of contemporary philosophers and social scientists. The other is the *contractarian* (social-contract) tradition of Locke, Rousseau, and Kant. The latter has never been developed as systematically as the utilitarian tradition and clearly, one of Rawls's objectives is to remedy this situation. He regards his own theory as a generalization of the classical contractarian position, and as its restatement at a higher level of abstraction (p. 11).

Rawls argues that the 'first virtue' of social institutions (i.e., the most fundamental moral requirement they ought to satisfy) is *justice* (or *fairness*). Suppose that all members of a society—or, more precisely, all 'heads of families' (p. 128; *pace* Women's Lib!)—have to agree on the general principles that are to govern the institutions of their society. All of them are supposed to be rational individuals caring only about their own personal interests (and thoose of their own descendants). But, in order to ensure that they would reach a fair-minded agreement (p. 12), Rawls assumes that they would have to negotiate with each other under what he calls the *veil of ignorance*, i.e., without knowing their own social and economic positions, their own special interests in the society, or even their own personal talents and abilities (or their lack of them). This hypothetical situation in which all participants would have to agree on the most basic institutional arrangements of their society while under this veil of ignorance, is called by Rawls the *original position*. In his theory, this purely hypothetical—and rather abstractly defined—original position replaces the historical or semi-historical 'social contract' of earlier contractarian philosophers. He considers the institutions of a given society to be *just* if they are organized according to the principles that presumably would have been agreed upon by rational individuals in the original position (p. 17).

What decision rule would rational individuals use in the original position in deciding whether a given set of institutions was or was not acceptable to them? In the terminology of modern decision theory, the initial position would be a situation of *uncertainty* because, by assumption, the participants would be uncertain about what their personal circumstances would be under any particular institutional framework to be agreed upon.

There are two schools of thought about the decision rule to be used by a rational person under uncertainty. One proposes the *maximin principle*, or some generalization or modification of this principle, as the appropriate decision rule.[2] From the mid-'forties (when the problem first attracted wider attention) to the mid-'fifties this was the prevailing opinion. But then came a growing realization that the maximin principle and all its relatives lead to serious paradoxes because they often suggest wholly unacceptable practical decisions.[3] The other—Bayesian—school of thought, which is now dominant, proposes *expected-utility maximization* as decision rule under uncertainty.[4]

In my opinion, the concept of the original position is a potentially very powerful analytical tool for clarifying the concept of justice and other aspects of morality. In actual fact, this concept played an essential role in my own analysis of moral value judgements,[5] prior to its first use by Rawls in 1957[6] (though I did not use the term 'original position'). But the usefulness of this concept crucially depends on its being combined with a satisfactory decision rule. Unfortunately, Rawls chooses the maximin principle as decision rule for the participants in the original position. By the very nature of the maximin principle, this choice cannot fail to have highly paradoxical implications.

2. THE MAXIMIN PRINCIPLE AND ITS PARADOXES

Suppose you live in New York City and are offered two jobs at the same time. One is a tedious and badly paid job in New York City itself, while the other is a very interesting and well paid job in Chicago. But the catch is that, if you wanted the Chicago job, you would have to take a plane from New York to Chicago (e.g., because this job would have to be taken up the very next day). Therefore there would be a very small but positive probability that you might be killed in a plane accident. Thus, the situation can be represented by the following double-entry table:

	If the N.Y.-Chicago plane has an accident	If the N.Y.-Chicago plane has no accident
If you choose the N.Y. job	You will have a poor job, but will stay alive	You will have a poor job, but will stay alive
If you choose the Chicago job	You will die	You will have an excellent job and will stay alive

Tha maximin principle says that you must evaluate every policy available to you in terms of the *worst possibility* that can occur to you if you follow that particular policy. Therefore, you have to analyze the situation as follows. If you choose the New York job then the worst (and, indeed, the only) possible outcome will be that you will have a poor job but you will stay alive. (I am assuming that your chances of dying in the near future for reasons other than a plane accident can be taken to be zero.) In contrast, if you choose the Chicago job then the worst possible outcome will be that you may die in a plane accident. Thus, the worst possible outcome in the first case would be much better than the worst possible outcome in the second case. Consequently, if you want to follow the maximin principle then you must choose the New York job. Indeed, you must not choose the Chicago job *under any condition*—however unlikely you might think a plane accident would be, and however strong your preference might be for the excellent Chicago job.

Clearly, this is a highly irrational conclusion. Surely, if you assign a low enough probability to a plane accident, and if you have a strong enough preference for the Chicago job, then by all means you should take your chances and choose the Chicago job. This is exactly what Bayesian theory would suggest you should do.

If you took the maximin principle seriously then you could not ever cross a street (after all, you might be hit by a car); you could never drive over a bridge (after all, it might collapse); you could never get married (after all, it might end in a disaster), etc. If anybody really acted this way he would soon end up in a mental institution.

Conceptually, the basic trouble with the maximin principle is that it violates an important continuity requirement: It is extremely irrational to make your behavior wholly dependent on some highly unlikely unfavorable contingencies *regardless of how little probability you are willing to assign to them.*

Of course, Rawls is right when he argues that in *some* situations the maximin principle will lead to reasonable decisions (pp. 154–156). But closer inspection will show that this will happen only in those situations where the maximin principle is essentially *equivalent* to the expected-utility maximization principle (in the sense that the policies suggested by the former will yield expected-utility levels as high, or almost as high, as the policies suggested by the latter would yield). Yet, the point is that in cases where the two principles suggest policies very dissimilar in their consequences so that they are far from being equivalent, it is always the expected-utility maximization principle that is found on closer inspection to suggest reasonable policies, and it as always the maximin principle that is found to suggest unreasonable ones.

3. THE MAXIMIN PRINCIPLE IN THE ORIGINAL POSITION

In the last section I have argued that the maximin principle would often lead to highly irrational decisions in everyday life. This is already a sufficient reason for rejecting it as a decision rule appropriate for the original position. This is so because the whole point about the concept of the original position is to imagine a number of individuals ignorant of their personal circumstances and then to assume that under these conditions of ignorance they would act in a *rational manner*, i.e., in accordance with some decision rule which consistently leads to reasonable decisions under ignorance and uncertainty. But, as we have seen, the maximin principle is most definitely *not* a decision rule of this kind.

Yet, after considering the performance of the maximin principle in everyday life, I now propose to consider explicitly the more specific question of how well this principle would perform in the original position itself. In particular, do we obtain a satisfactory concept of justice if we imagine that the criteria of justice are chosen by people in the original position in accordance with the maximin principle?

As Rawls points out, use of the maximin principle in the original position would lead to a concept of justice based on what he calls the *difference principle*, which evaluates every possible institutional arrangement in terms of the interests of the *least advantaged* (i.e., the poorest, or otherwise worst-off) individual (pp. 75–78). This is so because in the original position nobody is assumed to know what his own personal situation would be under any specific institutional arrangement. Therefore, he must consider the possibility that he might end up as the worst-off individual in the society. Indeed, according to the maximin principle, he has to evaluate any particular institutional framework *as if* he were *sure* that this was exactly what would happen to him. Thus, he must evaluate any possible institutional framework by identifying with the interests of the worst-off individual in the society.[7]

Now, I propose to show that the difference principle often has wholly unacceptable moral implications. As a first example, consider a society consisting of one doctor and two patients, both of them critically ill with pneumonia. Their only chance to recover is to be treated by an antibiotic, but the amount available suffices only to treat one of the two patients. Of these two patients, individual A is a basically healthy person, apart from his present attack of pneumonia. On the other hand, individual B is a terminal cancer victim but, even so, the antibiotic could prolong his life by several months. Which patient should be given the antibiotic? According to the difference principle, it should be given to the cancer victim, who is obviously the less fortunate of the two patients.

In contrast, utilitarian ethics—as well as ordinary common sense—would make the opposite suggestion. The antibiotic should be given to A because, it would do 'much more good' by bringing him back to normal health than it would do by slightly prolonging the life of a hopelessly sick individual.

As a second example, consider a society consisting of two individuals. Both of them have their material needs properly taken care of, but society still has a surplus of resources left over. This surplus can be used either to provide education in higher mathematics for individual A, who has a truly exceptional mathematical ability, and has an all-consuming interest in receiving instruction in higher mathematics. *Or*, it could be used to provide remedial training for individual *B*, who is a severely retarded person. Such training could achieve only trivial improvements in *B*'s condition (e.g., he could perhaps learn how to tie his shoelaces); but presumably it would give him some minor satisfaction. Finally, suppose it is not possible to divide up the surplus resources between the two individuals.

Again, the difference principle would require that these resources should be spent on *B*'s remedial training, since he is the less fortunate of the two individuals. In contrast, both utilitarian theory and common sense would suggest that they should be spent on *A*'s education, where they would accomplish 'much more good', and would create a much deeper and much more intensive human satisfaction.[8]

Even more disturbing is the fact that the difference principle would require us to give *absolute* priority to the interests of the worst-off individual, *no matter what*, even under the most extreme conditions. Even if his interest were affected only in a very minor way, and all other individuals in society had opposite interests of the greatest importance, his interests would always override anybody else's. For example, let us assume that society would consist of a large number of individuals, of whom one would be seriously retarded. Suppose that some extremely expensive treatment were to become available, which could very slightly improve the retarded individual's condition, but at such high costs that this treatment could be financed only if some of the most brilliant individuals were deprived of all higher education. The difference principle would require that the retarded individual should all the same receive this very expensive treatment at any event—*no matter how many* people would have to be denied a higher education, and *no matter how strongly* they would desire to obtain one (and no matter how great the satisfaction they would derive from it).

Rawls is fully aware that the difference principle has implications of this type. But he feels these are morally desirable implications because in his view they follow from Kant's principle that people should 'treat one another not as means only but as ends in themselves' (p. 179). If society were to give priority to *A*'s interests over *B*'s on the utilitarian grounds that by satisfying *A*'s interests 'more good' or 'more utility' or 'more human satisfaction' would be produced (e.g., because *A* could derive a greater benefit from medical treatment, or from education, or from whatever else), this would amount to 'treating *B* as means only, and not as end in himself'.

To my own mind, this is a very artificial and very forced interpretation of the Kantian principle under discussion. The natural meaning of the phrase 'treating *B* as a means only, and not as end in himself' is that it refers to using *B*'s *person*, i.e., his mental or physical faculties or his body itself, as *means* in the service of other individuals' interests, without proper concern for *B*'s own interests. One would have to stretch the meaning of this phrase quite a bit even in order to include an unauthorized use of *B*'s material *property* (as distinguished from his person) in the service of other individuals.

This, however, is still not the case we are talking about. We are talking about *B*'s merely being *denied* the use of certain resources over which he has no prior property rights, and this is done on the ground that other individual have 'greater need' for the resources, i.e., can derive greater utility from them (and let us assume, as may very well be the case, that almost all impartial observers would agree that this was so). But there is no question at all of using *B*'s person or property for the benefit of other individuals. Therefore, it is very hard to understand how the situation could be described as 'treating *B* as a means only, and not as end in himself'.

In any case, even if we did accept such an unduly broad interpretation of the Kantian principle, the argument would certainly cut both ways—and indeed, it would go much more against the difference principle than in favor of it. For suppose we accept the argument that it would be a violation of the Kantian principle if we gave priority to a very important need of *A* over a relatively unimportant need of *B*, because it would amount to treating *B* as a mere means. Then, surely, the opposite policy of giving absolute priority to *B*'s *unimportant* need will be an even stronger violation of the Kantian principle and will amount *a fortiori* to treating A now as a mere means rather than as an end.

4. DO COUNTEREXAMPLES MATTER?

Most of my criticism of Rawls's theory up to now has been based on counterexamples. How much weight do arguments based on counterexamples have? Rawls himself seems to have considerable reservations about such arguments. He writes (p. 52):

Objections by way of counterexamples are to be made with care, since these may tell us only what we know already, namely that our theory is wrong somewhere. The important thing is to find out how often and how far it is wrong. All theories are presumably mistaken in places. The real question at any given time is which of the views already proposed is the best approximation overall.

To be sure, counterexamples to some minor details of an ethical theory may not prove very much. They may prove no more than that the theory needs correction in some minor points, and this fact may have no important implications for the basic principles of the theory. But it is a very different matter when the counterexamples are directed precisely against the most fundamental principles of the theory, as are the maximin principle and the difference principle for Rawls's theory. In this case, if the counterexamples are valid, it can only mean that the theory is *fundamentally* wrong.

Admittedly, all my counterexamples refer to rather special situations. It is quite possible that, in *most* everyday situations posing no special problems, Rawls's theory would yield quite reasonable practical conclusions. Indeed, it is my impression that in most situations the practical implications of Rawls's theory would not be very different from those of utilitarian theories. But of course, if we want to *compare* Rawls's theory with utilitarian theories in order to see which of the two yields more reasonable practical conclusions, we have to concentrate on those cases where they yield significantly different conclusions.

Clearly, as far as Rawls's theory often has implications similar to those of utilitarian theories, I must agree with his point that counterexamples do not prove that his theory does not have at least *approximate* validity in most cases. But my understanding is that Rawls's claims more than approximate validity *in this sense* for this theory. Though he does not claim that his theory is absolutely correct in every detail, he does explicitly claim that at the very least the basic principles of his theory yield more satisfactory results than the basic principles of utilitarian theories do. Yet, in my opinion, my counterexamples rather conclusively show that the very opposite is the case.

5. AN ALTERNATIVE MODEL OF MORAL VALUE JUDGEMENTS

All difficulties outlined in Section 3 can be avoided if we assume that the decision rule used in the original position would not be the maximin principle but would rather be the expected-utility maximization principle of Bayesian theory.

In the two papers already quoted,[9] I have proposed the following model. If an individual expresses his preference between two alternative institutional arrangements, he will often base his preference largely or wholly on his personal interests (and perhaps on the interests of his family, his friends, his occupational group, his social class, etc). For instance, he may say: 'I know that under capitalism I am a wealthy capitalist, whereas under socialism I would be at best a minor government official. Therefore, I prefer capitalism'. This no doubt would be a very natural judgment of personal preference from his own point of view. But it certainly would not be what we would call a *moral* value judgement by him about the relative merits of capitalism and socialism.

In contrast, most of us will admit that he would be making a moral value judgment if he chose between the two social systems *without knowing* what his personal position would be under either system. More specifically, let us assume that society consists of n individuals, and that the individual under consideration would choose between the two alternative social systems on the assumption that under either system he would have the same probability, $1/n$, of taking the place of the best-off individual, or the second-best-off individual, or the third-best-off individual, etc., up to the worst-off individual. This I shall call the *equi-probability assumption*. Moreover, let us assume that in choosing between the two social systems he would use the principle of expected-utility maximization as his decision rule. (This is my own version of the concept of the 'original position'.)

It is easy to verify that under these assumptions our individual would always choose that social system which, in his opinion, would yield the higher *average utility level* to the individual members of the society. More generally, he would evaluate every possible social arrangement (every possible social system, institutional framework, social practice, etc.) in terms of the average utility level likely to result from it. This criterion of evaluation will be called the *principle of average utility*.

Of course, in real life, when people express a preference for one social arrangement over another, they will often have a fairly clear idea of what their own personal position would be under both. Nevertheless, we can say that they are expressing a *moral value judgment*, or that they are expressing a *moral preference* for one of these social arrangements, if they make a serious effort to *disregard* this piece of information, and make their choice *as if* they thought they would have the same probability of taking the place of any particular individual in the society.

Thus, under this model, each individual will have two different sets of preferences: he will have a set of *personal preferences*, which may give a particularly high weight to his personal interests (and to those of his close associates); and he will have a set of *moral preferences*, based on a serious attempt to give the same weight to the interests of every member of the society, in accordance with the principle of average utility.

While Rawls's approach yields a moral theory in the contractarian tradition, my own model yields a moral theory based on the principle of average utility and, therefore, clearly belonging to the utilitarian tradition.

6. RAWLS'S OBJECTION TO USING PROBABILITIES IN THE 'ORIGINAL POSITION'

Rawls discusses my model primarily in Chapters 27 and 28 of his book. One of his critical comments is directed against my use of probabilities in the original position, in the form of the equiprobability assumption. He does not object to the equiprobability assumption as such *if* probabilities are to be used at all. He accepts Laplace's principle of indifference in the limited sense that in a situation of complete ignorance, *if* we want to use probabilities at all, *then* it is reasonable to assign equal probabilities to all possibilities (p. 169).[10] What he objects to is the very use of probabilities in the original position, in all those cases where these probabilities are not based on empirical evidence. That is, he objects to using *subjective* probabilities or even *logical* probabilities,[11] in the absence of *empirical* probabilities estimated on the basis of empirical facts. (He does not insist, however, that these empirical probabilities should be estimated on the basis of observed statistical frequencies. He is willing to accept more indirect empirical evidence.)

The need and justification for using subjective probabilities have been extensively discussed by Bayesian decision theorists.[12] But Rawls makes no attempt to refute their arguments. Here I shall make only two points.

(a) The only alternative to using subjective probabilities, as required by Bayesian theory, would be to use a decision rule chosen from the maximin-principle family; and, as I have argued (in Section 2), all these decision rules are known to lead to highly irrational decisions in important cases.

(b) Bayesian decision theory shows by rigorous mathematical arguments that any decision maker whose behavior is consistent with a few—very compelling—rationality postulates simply *cannot help* acting *as if* he used subjective probabilities. (More precisely, he cannot help acting *as if* he tried to maximize his expected utility, computed on the basis of some set of subjective probabilities.) I shall quote only two of these rationality postulates: (1) 'If you prefer A to B, and prefer B to C, then consistency requires that you should also prefer A to C'; (2) 'You are better off if you are offered a *more valuable* prize with a given probability, than if you are offered a *less valuable* prize with the same probability'. The other rationality postulates of Bayesian theory are somewhat more technical, but are equally compelling.

To illustrate that a rational decision maker simply *cannot help* using subjective probabilities, at least implicitly, suppose I offered you a choice between two alternative bets and said: '*Either*, I shall pay you $ 100 if candidate X *wins* the next election, and shall pay you nothing if he does not. *Or* I shall pay you $ 100 if he does *not* win, and pay you nothing if he does. Which of the two bets do you choose?'

First of all, it would be clearly irrational for you to refuse both bets, because *some* chance of obtaining $ 100 is surely better than no chance at all—since you can get this chance for free. So, if you are rational, you will choose one of the two bets. Now, if you choose the first bet then I can infer that (at least implicitly) you are assigning a subjective probability of $1/2$ or *higher* to Mr. X's winning the next election. On the other hand, if you choose the second bet then I can infer that (at least implicitly) you are assigning a subjective probability of $1/2$ or *lower* to Mr. X's winning the election. Thus, whichever way your choice goes, it will amount to choosing a subjective probability for Mr. X's winning the election—either a probability in the range $[1/2, 1]$, or one in the range $[0, 1/2]$.

By the same token, if a decision maker follows the maximin principle, he is not really avoiding a choice of subjective probabilities, at least implicitly. Of course, he may not think explicitly in terms of probabilities at all. But, whether he likes it or not, his behavior will really amount to assigning probability one (or nearly one) to the worst possibility in any given case. He may very well regard the task of choosing subjective probabilities as a rather burdensome responsibility: but he has no way of escaping this responsibility. For instance, if his reliance on the maximin principle results in a foolish decision because it amounts to grossly overestimating the probability of the worst possibility, then he cannot escape the consequences of this foolish decision. (He certainly cannot escape the consequences by saying that he has never explicitly assigned any numerical probability to the worst possibility at all; and that in actual fact he acted in this foolish way only because he wanted to avoid any explicit choice of numerical probabilities.)

Rawls also argues that a given individual's actions in the original position will be easier to justify to other people, including his own descendants, if these actions are based on the maximin principle, than if they are based on the equiprobability assumption (p. 169). But it seems to me that the exact opposite is the case.

As we have seen (cf. note 10), the equiprobability assumption can be justified by the principle of indifference, and also by the moral principle of assigning the same *a priori* weight to every individual's interests. On the other hand, using the maximin principle in the original position is equivalent to assigning unity or near-unity probability to the possibility that one may end up as the worst-off individual in society; and, as far as I can see, there cannot be any rational justification whatever for assigning such an extremely high probability to this possibility.

Rawls's argument becomes much more convincing if it is turned around. If the original position were an historical fact, then any person, other than the worst-off individual in society, would have a legitimate complaint against his ancestor if the latter in the original position voted for an institutional arrangement giving undue priority to the interests of the worst-off individual. (For instance, to take the examples discussed in Section 3, he would have a legitimate complaint if his ancestor's vote in the original position now had the effect of depriving him of some life-saving drug, or of a much-desired higher education, etc.)

7. DO VON NEUMANN-MORGENSTERN UTILITY FUNCTIONS HAVE ANY PLACE IN ETHICS?

In my model, every person making a moral value judgment will evaluate any institutional arrangement in terms of the average utility level it yields for the individual members of the society, i.e., in terms of the arithmetic mean of these individuals' von Neumann-Morgenstern (= vNM) utility functions.[13] This means that, under my theory, people's vNM utility functions enter into the very definition of justice and other moral values. Rawls objects to this aspect of my theory on the ground that vNM utility functions basically express people's attitudes toward risk-taking, i.e., toward gambling—and these attitudes have no moral significance. Therefore, Rawls argues, vNM utility functions should not enter into our definitions of moral values (pp. 172 and 323).

This objection is based on a misinterpretation of vNM utility functions, which is unfortunately fairly widespread in the literature. To be sure, the vNM utility function of any given individual is estimated from his choice behavior under risk and uncertainty. But this does not mean that his vNM utility function is *merely* an indication of his attitudes toward risk taking. Rather, as its name shows, it is a utility function, and more specifically, it is what economists call a cardinal utility function. This means that the primary task of a vNM utility function is *not* to express a given individual's attitudes toward risk taking; rather, it is to indicate how much utility, i.e., how much subjective *importance*, he assigns to various goals.

For example, suppose we find that a given individual is willing to gamble at very unfavorable odds—say, he is willing to pay $ 5 for a lottery ticket giving him a 1/1000 chance of winning $ 1000. This allows us the inference that his vNM utility function assigns (at least) 1000 times as much utility to $ 1000 as it assigns to $ 5. Thus, the theory of vNM utility functions suggests the following explanation for this individual's willingness to gamble at unfavorable odds: he is acting this way because he is attaching unusually *high* importance to getting $ 1000, and is attaching unusually *low* importance to losing $ 5. More generally, people are willing to gamble at unfavorable odds, if they feel they would need a large sum of money *very badly* (but do not care too much about losing a small sum of money).

Consequently, vNM utility functions have a completely legitimate place in ethics because they express the subjective importance people attach to their various needs and interests. For example, I cannot see anything wrong with a concept of justice which assigns high priority to providing university education for a given individual partly on the ground that he attaches very high *utility* to receiving such an education (i.e., wants to receive one very badly)—as shown by the fact that he would be prepared to face very considerable personal and financial *risks*, if he had to, in order to obtain a university education.

8. DO INTERPERSONAL UTILITY
COMPARISONS MAKE SENSE?

Rawls objects to the use of interpersonal utility comparisons in defining justice (p. 173). In contrast, my own model makes essential use of such comparisons in the sense that it requires any person making a basic moral value judgment to try to visualize what it would be like to be in the shoes of any other member of the society. That is, he must try to estimate what utility level he would enjoy if he himself were placed in the *objective* physical, economic, and social conditions of any other individual—and if at the same time he also suddenly acquired this individual's *subjective* attitudes, taste, and preferences, i.e., suddenly acquired his utility function.

Admittedly, the idea of evaluating another individual's personal circumstances in terms of *his* utility function, and not in terms of our own, is a difficult concept. But it is a concept we cannot avoid in any reasonable theory of morality. Clearly, if I want to judge the fairness of a social policy providing a diet very rich in fish for a given group of individuals (e.g., for students living in a certain dormitory), I obviously must make my judgement in terms of these individuals' liking or disliking for fish, and not in terms of my own.

As I tried to show in my 1955 paper,[14] the ultimate logical basis for interpersonal utility comparisons, interpreted in this way, lies in the postulate that the *preferences and utility functions of all human individuals* are *governed by the same basic psychological laws*. My utility function may be very different from yours. But, since both of our utility functions are governed by the very same basic psychological laws, if I had your personal characteristics—and, in particular, if I had your biological inheritance and had your life history behind me—then presumably I would now have a utility function exactly like yours.[15] This means that any *inter*personal comparison I may try to make between your present utility level and my own, reduces to an *intra*-personal utility comparison between the utility level *I* myself *do* now enjoy, and the utility level *I* myself *would* enjoy under certain hypothetical conditions, namely if I were placed in your physical, economic, and social position, and also had my own biological and biographical background replaced by yours.

This means that interpersonal utility comparisons have a completely specific theoretical meaning, in the sense that, 'under ideal conditions', i.e., if we had full knowledge of the psychological laws governing people's preferences and their utility functions, and also had sufficient information about other people's personal characteristics, then we could make perfectly error-free interpersonal utility comparisons. Of course, in actual fact, our knowledge of psychological laws and of other people's personal characteristics is very limited, and, therefore, interpersonal utility comparisons are often subject to considerable error—but, of course, so are many other judgments we have to make before we can reach practical decisions, whether these are moral decisions or purely pragmatic ones. Nevertheless, in many *specific* cases, we may have enough background information to be quite confident in our judgments of interpersonal utility comparison—and this confidence is often justified by the fact that in many of these cases there is a reasonable agreement between the conclusions reached by different competent observers when they try to make such comparisons.

In any case, we all make, and cannot help making, interpersonal utility comparisons all the time. We have to decide again and again which particular member of our family, or which particular friend of ours, etc., has a more urgent need for our time or our money, or could derive greater satisfaction from a present, and so on. Likewise, as voters or public officials, we have to decide again and again which particular social group would derive the greatest benefit from government help, etc. To my mind, it makes no sense to deny the legitimacy of a mental operation we all perform every day, and for which a completely satisfactory logical analysis can be provided.[16]

Rawls expresses considerable doubts about the validity of interpersonal utility comparisons (pp. 90 and 321–324). But he makes no attempt to refute my theory of such comparisons, stated in my 1955 article (and briefly summarized above). Instead, he concentrates his criticism on two highly articicial procedures suggested in the literature for making interpersonal utility comparisons (pp. 321–323). One is based on equating the smallest noticeable utility differences of different people. The other is based on equating all individuals' highest possible utility levels, and then again equating their lowest possible utility levels. Of course, he has no trouble showing that, in order to use either procedure in moral philosophy, we would have to introduce some highly arbitrary and implausible moral postulates. But none of these criticisms applies to my own theory of interpersonal utility comparisons.

This completes my discussion of Rawls's objections to my own version of utilitarian theory. I shall now discuss some objections of his to utilitarian theories in general.

9. UTILITARIANISM AND SUPEREROGATORY ACTIONS

Commonsense morality distinguishes between morally good actions we have a duty to perform, and morally good actions which go beyond the call of duty (supererogatory actions). But, as Rawls points out (p. 117), classical utilitarianism cannot accommodate this distinction because it claims that our duty is always to perform the actions likely to produce the *greatest* good for society. This would mean that, even if we were constantly engaged in the most heroic acts of altruistic self-sacrifice, we would merely do our duty, and no human action could ever be correctly described as supererogatory. I agree with Rawls that it is a serious shortcoming of classical utilitarianism that it cannot admit the existence of supererogatory actions, and draws the line between morally permissible and impermissible conduct at an absurdly high level of moral perfection.

This shortcoming, however, can be easily remedied without going beyond the principles of utilitarianism. The mistake of the classical utilitarians was to overlook the fact that people attach considerable utility to *freedom* from unduly burdensome moral obligations. It may be true (though this is by no means a foregone conclusion) that society will reach a higher level of economic prosperity and cultural excellence if its moral code requires all people all the time to act in the most public-spirited manner, and to set themselves the highest possible standards in their economic and cultural activities. But most people will prefer a society with a more relaxed moral code, and will feel that such a society will achieve a higher level of average utility—even if adoption of such a moral code should lead to some losses in economic and cultural accomplishments (so long as these losses remain within tolerable limits). This means that utilitarianism, if correctly interpreted, will yield a moral code with a standard of acceptable conduct very much below the level of highest moral perfection, leaving plenty of scope for supererogatory actions exceeding this minimum standard.

10. VAGUENESS VERSUS SIMPLEMINDEDNESS
IN MORAL PHILOSOPHY

As Rawls correctly states (p. 320), the utilitarian concept of morality inevitably shows some degree of vagueness or indeterminacy because of its dependence on—more or less uncertain—interpersonal utility comparisons.

Other authors have pointed out another source of indeterminacy, no less important, in the dependence of utilitarian morality on uncertain predictions about the short-run and long-run consequences of alternative social policies and institutional arrangements. As a result, two equally well-intentioned and well-informed, and equally intelligent utilitarians may very well disagree in many specific situations about what is socially useful or socially harmful and, therefore, also about what is right or wrong, and just or unjust, etc.

Rawls's own theory, of course, cannot completely escape such ambiguities either, but it is certainly much less affected by them than utilitarian theories are. First of all, Rawls's basic postulate, the difference principle, is much less dependent on interpersonal utility comparisons than the basic utilitarian principles (for example, the principle of average utility) are; therefore, it yields more specific practical conclusions than the latter do in many cases. In addition, Rawls supplements the difference principle by second-order rules, which are supposed to rank the major values of human life according to their relative moral importance. Thus, for example, according to Rawls, people's basic liberties should always be given absolute priority over their economic and social interests, etc. Clearly, if we are willing to accept such rigid second-order rules of priority, then they will often go a long way toward deciding our moral uncertainties in a fairly unambiguous manner.

Yet, I very much doubt that this is really an advantage. It seems to me that the uncertainties of utilitarian morality merely reflect the great complexity and the unavoidable dilemmas of real-life moral situations. Simple-minded rigid mechanical rules cannot possibly do justice to the complexity of moral problems; and they cannot resolve our moral dilemmas satisfactorily, because they cannot help choosing the wrong horn of the dilemma in many important cases.

For example, there are good reasons to believe that in an underdeveloped country in many cases economic growth cannot be set in motion without concentrating a good deal of power in the hands of the government and perhaps even without *some* curtailment of civil liberties (though this does not mean that there is any need or justification for a complete suppression of civil liberties as practiced by the arbitrary dictatorial governments now existing in many of these countries).

Who is the moral philosopher to lay down the law for these countries and tell them that no amount of economic and social development, however large, can ever justify any curtailment of civil liberties, however small? Should we not rather say, with the utilitarian philosophers, that judgments about any particular policy must always depend on the balance of the advantages and disadvantages it is likely to yield, and that the main task of the moral philosopher is to ensure that people will not overlook any major advantage or disadvantage in reaching a decision?

11. SAVING AS A MORAL DUTY TO FUTURE GENERATIONS

What proportion of national income ought to be saved as a matter of moral duty (as a matter of justice) to future generations? As Rawls rightly argues (p. 286), utilitarianism (at least as it is usually interpreted) gives an unsatisfactory answer to this question, in that it seems to require unreasonably high savings. The mathematical problem of computing the morally optimal amount of savings under utilitarian criteria was solved by Keynes's friend, the brilliant economist-philosopher Frank P. Ramsey, in 1928.[17] Of course, the numerical answer depends on the utility functions used. But Ramsey showed that, if we use reasonable-looking utility functions, then the utilitarian model may easily yield optimal savings amounting to much more than one half of national income, which is clearly an unacceptable conclusion.

How well does Rawls's own theory deal with this problem? It is easy to verify that the difference principle would suggest *zero* net savings from one generation to another. This is so because, even without any net savings, as a result of mere technological progress, future generations will be much better off than the present generation is, anyhow (provided the population explosion can be brought under control). Therefore, any positive net saving would be inconsistent with the difference principle since it would amount to a transfer of economic resources from a much poorer generation to much richer generations. Thus, while utilitarian theory seems to require unduly high savings, Rawls's difference principle would certainly require unduly low (viz., zero) savings.

Rawls is aware that the difference principle would have this undesirable implication (p. 291). Nevertheless, surprisingly enough, he seems to imply that his theory handles the saving problem much *better* than utilitarian theory does (pp. 297–298). The truth is that he can avoid the zero-savings conclusion only by giving up the difference principle altogether in dealing with the saving problem, and by replacing it with a completely *ad hoc* motivational assumption. (Whereas in all other respects he makes the participants of the original position complete egoists, in this one respect, viz., in relation to future generations, he endows them with considerable altruism.) Of course, by introducing *ad hoc* assumptions of its own, utilitarianism could just as easily avoid the unwelcome logical necessity of enjoining excessive savings.

In actual fact, in order to obtain a reasonable solution for the problem of optimal savings in terms of utilitarian principles, we have no need for *ad hoc* assumptions. All we have to do is to take a second look at Ramsey's utility functions. The utility functions he postulates seem to be reasonable enough if they are meant to measure the utility that a given individual in the present generation would derive from higher income levels (on the assumption that other people's incomes would remain more or less unchanged). But they greatly overstate the extra utility that future generations are likely to derive from higher incomes as a result of substantially increased saving and investment by the present generation. There are at least three reasons for this:

(1) The *risk effect:* there is always a considerable risk that future changes in technology and in social customs will drastically reduce the benefit that future generations would derive from investments undertaken by the present generation. (For instance, the United States and some European countries invested very large amounts of money in building canals just before the railway age. These huge investments almost completely lost their usefulness very soon thereafter as a result of railway construction.)

(2) The *relative-income effect:* a rise in a given person's income, when other people's incomes remain largely the same, will tend to increase his social status. But if his income rises as a result of a general increase in society's income then of course this effect will be lost. Therefore, in the former case the rise in his income will produce a much greater increase in his utility than it will do in the latter case.

(3) The *inherited-wealth effect:* inherited wealth often has a very powerful influence on human motivation. Some of this influence may be beneficial. (People born into very rich families often develop highly idealistic and altruistic attitudes, and may take a strong interest in social causes or in political, philanthropic, and cultural activities.) But some of this influence may be highly detrimental for a person's chances of leading a happy and so-

cially useful life. (People born into very rich families often lack all interest in serious work, including altruistic or intellectual work; and they may be offered so many opportunities to amuse themselves that they may lose all ability to enjoy the normal pleasures of human life.) It is not unreasonable to assume that if society as a whole inherits very high levels of material abundance, so that there is very little pressure on the average man to earn a living by serious work, then the negative effects are likely to predominate. (We can already see some indications of this in our own society). Therefore, the net benefit that future generations are likely to derive from increased saving and investment by the present generation may be much smaller than at first one might think.

Thus, if the likely utility of much higher incomes to future generations is reassessed in a more realistic manner then utilitarian theory will yield much lower levels of optimal savings, and in fact will furnish a completely satisfactory solution for this problem, without any need for *ad hoc* assumptions.

12. THE STABILITY OF A JUST SOCIETY

Rawls raises a very interesting problem, so far largely neglected by moral and political philosophers. Suppose there is a society with a strong sense of justice among its citizens, and with completely (or almost completely) just institutions. Would such a society be stable? He strongly argues that the answer is in the affirmative (pp. 490–504). He also suggests that a society based on his own conception of justice would be more stable than one based on a utilitarian conception (p. 498).

The just society he describes in this connection, however, is not merely an improved version of the best societies now existing; rather, it is unlike any society known to political scientists or historians or other competent observers. It is a society where citizens and legislators are never motivated by their own selfish interests or (in the case of the legislators) by the selfish interests of their constituents, but rather are always motivated by their strong sense of justice. As such, this society is almost the opposite of the society pictured in Anthony Downs's *An Economic Theory of Democracy*.[18]

Of course, Rawls is quite right in rejecting Downs's motivational assumptions as a fully realistic picture of human motivation. It is certainly not true that ordinary citizens never care about anything but their narrow economic (and perhaps other) self-interest, or that politicians never care about anything but their chances for election or reelection. Indeed, it is quite clear that under *some* conditions many rich people will strongly support legislation benefiting the poor but greatly increasing their own taxes (though it is much less clear under what conditions this will or will not happen). Again, we have all seen elected officials follow their own moral and political convictions and make highly unpopular decisions, greatly endangering their prospects for reelection (and sometimes we wished they did not, while at other times we were glad they did). Indeed, it is quite obvious that Downs does not claim that his oversimplified motivational assumptions are literally true; all he claims is that our political system operates most of the time *as if* these motivational assumptions *were* correct.

Nevertheless, the fact that Downs's motivational assumptions come so close to being true, should make us stop to think before accepting Rawls's theory of stability. Should we not take this fact as an indication that the very high levels of public-spirited motivation that Rawls assumes for his just society, would be intrinsically *unstable?* Indeed, our historical experience seems to show that whole societies can achieve such motivational states only for rather short periods (e.g., during revolutions or some very popular wars). The same experience also shows that these highly idealistic —and often highly fanatical and intolerant—motivational states of a society are far from being an unmixed blessing.

It seems to me that any healthy society needs a proper balance between egoistic and altruistic motivation. Without political leaders fighting for altruistic objectives, or without private citizens giving them political support, present-day democratic societies would not have achieved even that, no doubt imperfect, level of social justice and of good government they currently enjoy.

On the other hand, political movements based largely or wholly on well-understood self-interest are an equally essential component of any political system. Citizens pressing for their sectional economic interests may be very biased judges of the public interest, but at least they are well-informed judges in most cases. In contrast, citizens pursuing highly altruistic objectives might often fight for causes about which they know very little, or about which they have strikingly onesided information. Steelworkers pressing for their own economic interests will at least know what they are talking about. But faraway benevolent millionnaires fighting for the steelworkers' interests might have very mistaken ideas about what these steelworkers really want or need. A society where everybody neglects his own interests, and is busily looking after everybody else's interests, probably would not be a very stable society—and certainly would not be a very happy one.

Accordingly, it seems to me that a just society with a reasonable prospect for social stability would *not* be a society where ordinary citizens and legislators would be primarily motivated by their sense of justice. Rather, it would be a society where most people would be motivated by the normal mixture of egoistic and altruistic interests. Of course, it would have to be a society where people have a strong sense of justice—but this does not mean that a pursuit of justice would have to be their main and continual preoccupation. It only means that they would have to show enough respect for justice so as to stop pressing their own egoistic—and altruistic—objectives *beyond* the point where they would violate the just legal and moral rights of other people; and so as to fight for restoring these rights if they have been violated by injustices of the past.

13. CONCLUSION

To conclude, in spite of my numerous disagreements with Rawls's theory, I strongly recommend his book to all readers interested in moral and political philosophy. He raises many interesting and, to my mind, highly important problems, even though some of us may question the solutions he proposes. The author's serious concern for truth and justice is evident on every page of the book. He makes a real effort to look at both (or all) sides of every difficult or controversial problem, and to reach a fair and balanced conclusion. Where he touches on problems of topical interest, he does not hestitate for a moment to express unpopular views, for example, by pointing out the possible destabilizing effects that very widespread civil disobedience might have on democratic institutions (p. 374). In the political climate of Harvard in the late 'sixties or early 'seventies it must have required no little moral courage to express such an opinion.

We live in an age where our moral attitudes are rapidly changing, and so are many of our social institutions, with end results very hard to predict; where traditional world views are more and more replaced by a world view based on science and depriving man of his privileged position in nature; where the fast progress of technology poses very difficult moral dilemmas and is likely to pose incomparably more difficult ones in the not-too-distant future (e.g., when it may become feasible to double the present human life span, opening up new dimensions for the problem of overpopulation; or when it may become possible to undertake large-scale genetic and reproductional engineering; or when robots and computers truly competitive with humans may become available, and so on). In an age like this, any investigation into the criteria of rational choice between alternative moral codes is of much more than merely theoretical significance.

Therefore, there is no question whatever in my mind that Rawls poses problems of the greatest importance. But this is precisely the reason why I feel it is important to *resist* the solutions he proposes for these problems. We should resist any moral code which would force us to discriminate against the legitimate needs and interests of many individuals merely because they happen to be rich, or at least not to be desperately poor; or because they are exceptionally gifted, or at least are not mentally retarded; or because they are healthy, or at least are not incurably sick, etc. We should resist such a moral code, because an alternative moral code, the utilitarian one, is readily available to us; and the latter permits us to give equal *a priori* weight to every person's legitimate interests, and to judge the relative importance of any given need of a particular person in each case by its merits, as assessed by commonsense criteria—rather than forcing us to judge them according to rigid, artificial, and often highly discriminatory rules of priority.

POSTSCRIPT

This paper was written in May 1973. In the meantime, John Rawls has tried to answer some of my criticisms in a paper entitled 'Some Reasons for the Maximin Criterion'.[19] His defence to the counterexamples I have put forward against using the maximin principle as a moral principle (in Section 3 of the preceding paper) is that 'the maximin criterion is not meant to apply to small-scale situation, say, to how a doctor should treat his patients or a university its students.... Maximin is a macro not a micro principle' (p. 142). Regretfully, I must say that this is a singularly inept defense.

First of all, though my counterexamples do refer to small-scale situations, it is very easy to adapt them to large-scale situations since they have intrinsically nothing to do with scale, whether small or large. For example, instead of asking whether a doctor should use a life-saving drug in short supply for treating patient A or patient B, we can ask whether, in allocating scarce medical manpower and other resources, society should give priority to those patients who could best benefit from medical treatment, or should rather give priority to the most hopelessly sick patients—a policy problem surely affecting several hundred thousand individuals in any major country at any given time. Or, again, instead of asking whether scarce educational resources should be used for the benefit of individual A or individual B, we can ask whether, in allocating educational expenditures, society should give priority in certain cases to several hundred thousand highly gifted students, who could presumably benefit most, or to several hundred thousand seriously retarded individuals, who could derive only minor benefits from additional education, etc. I am really astonished that a distinguished philosopher like Rawls should have overlooked the simple fact that the counterexamples I have adduced (and the many more counterexamples one could easily adduce) have nothing whatever to do with scale at all.

In fact, it would be *a priori* rather surprising if, at the most fundamental level, the basic principles of morality should take different forms for large-scale and for small-scale situations. Does Rawls seriously think that there is a certain number x, such that a situation involving *more* than x people will come under moral principles basically different from a situation involving *fewer* than x people?

In any case, what moral considerations will determine this curious boundary number x itself? More fundamentally, what are the basic logical reasons that should make large-scale and small-scale situations essentially different from a moral point of view? I cannot see how anybody can propose the strange doctrine that scale is a fundamental variable in moral philosophy, without giving credible answers to these questions at the same time.

I have argued that in *most* situations Rawls's theory will have much the same policy implications as utilitarian theory does, but that there are *some* important situations where this is not the case. Moreover, I have tried to show that, in those situations where the two theories do have quite dissimilar policy implications, Rawls's theory consistently yields morally highly *unacceptable* policy conclusions whereas utilitarian theory consistently yields morally fully *acceptable* ones (Sections 3 and 4 of the preceding paper).

Arrow has expressed a similar view.[20] After saying that in the real world the maximin principle and the utilitarian principle would have very similar practical consequences, he adds: '...the maximin principle would lead to unacceptable consequences if the world were such that they [these consequences] really differed'. My only disagreement with Arrow is that I think the world is in fact so constituted that these two principles *do* have very different practical consequences in some important cases. (In effect, in some parts of his paper, Arrow himself seems to admit that much—pp. 251–252). But we do agree on the main point, viz., on the conditional statement that, *if* such differences exist, they all speak very strongly against the maximin principle.

In my opinion, if this criticism is valid, then it completely disqualifies Rawls's theory as a serious competitor to utilitarian theory. (Why should anybody choose a theory that often does much worse, and never does any better, than utilitarian theory does?) For this reason, I find it rather unfortunate that Rawls's paper does not even try to answer this criticism at all.

To be sure, the maximin principle does have its valuable uses, and we must be grateful to Rawls for calling our attention to it. Even if it cannot serve as a *basic* principle of moral *theory*, it can be used as a principle of approximate validity in practical *applications*, such as the theory of optimal income distribution or of optimal taxation. In such applications, its relative independence of detailed interpersonal utility comparisons, and of the actual mathematical form of people's von Neumann-Morgenstern utility functions for money, is an important advantage, and can be fruitfully exploited in economic studies.[21]

Of course, from the point of view of a utilitarian observer, the results of a study of, e.g., optimal income tax rates, based on the maximin principle, will have only approximate validity. For example, if the study finds that, owing to the disincentive effect of very high marginal tax rates, the marginal income tax for the highest income group should be (say) 50 per cent, then a utilitarian observer can infer that this tax rate should certainly be *no more* than 50 per cent. Indeed, he can infer that, if the study had been based on the average utility principle instead of the maximin principle, then the marginal tax rate at the top would have come out presumably a *little lower* than 50 per cent, though perhaps not very much lower. (Sensitivity analysis may even enable us to estimate the actual percentage points by which studies based on the maximin principle are likely to overestimate the optimal tax rates for various income groups.)

It is regrettable that Rawls has ever made the untenable claim that he is proposing a moral *theory* superior to utilitarian theory. This claim can only obscure the practical merits of the maximin principle as an easily applicable postulate of approximate validity. These practical merits of course do not in any way provide a reason for abandoning utilitarian moral philosophy. (Basic philosophical principles must be exactly right, and not merely approximately right.) But they do provide a reason, even for a utilitarian moral philosopher, to use the maximin principle as an admissible approximation in many cases. Had Rawls only made this more modest, but much more realistic, claim for the maximin principle, few people would have contradicted him.

One thing that all of us must have learned in the last fifty years is that we must never commit ourselves seriously to moral principles or political ideologies that are bound to lead to morally utterly *wrong* policies from time to time—however great the advantages of these principles or ideologies may be in terms of administrative convenience, ease of application, and readier understandability.

NOTES

* *American Political Science Review,* **59** (1975), 594–606.

§ This paper has been supported by Grant GS-3222 of the National Science Foundation, through the Center for Research in Management Science, University of California, Berkeley.

[1] Cambridge, Mass.: Harvard University Press, 1971.

[2] See Abraham Wald, *Statistical Decision Functions* (New York: John Wiley & Sons, 1950); Leonid Hurwicz, 'Optimality Criteria for Decision Making Under Ignorance', *Cowles Commission Discussion Paper, Statistics* No. 370 (1951, mimeographed); and Leonard J. Savage, 'The Theory of Statistical Decision', *Journal of the American Statistical Association,* **46** (March, 1951), 55–67.

[3] See Roy Radner and Jacob Marschak, 'Note on Some Proposed Decision Criteria', in R. M. Thrall, C. H. Coombs, and R. L. Davis, eds., *Decision Processes* (New York: John Wiley & Sons, 1954), pp. 61–68.

[4] See, e.g., Leonard J. Savage, *The Foundations of Statistics* (New York: John Wiley & Sons, 1954).

[5] See John C. Harsanyi, 'Cardinal Utility in Welfare Economics and in the Theory of Risk-Taking', *Journal of Political Economy,* **61** (October, 1953), 434–435; and 'Cardinal Welfare, Individualistic Ethics, and Interpersonal Comparisons of Utility', *Journal of Political Economy,* **63** (August, 1955), 309–321.

[6] John Rawls, 'Justice as Fairness'. *Journal of Philosophy,* **54** (October, 1957), 653–662; and 'Justice as Fairness', *Philosophical Review,* **67** (April, 1958), 164–194. The 1957 paper is a shorter version of the 1958 paper with the same title.

[7] In cases where a more specific principle is necessary, Rawls favors the *lexicographical* difference principle: In comparing two possible societies, first compare them from the point of view of the *worst-off* individual. If they turn out to be equally good from his point of view, then compare them from the point of view of the *second-worst-off* individual. If this still does not break the tie, then compare them from the point of view of the *third-worst-off* individual, etc.

[8] This argument of course presupposes the possibility of interpersonal utility comparisons, at least in a rough and ready sense. I shall discuss the possibility of such comparisons in Section 8.

[9] Harsanyi, 'Cardinal Utility ...,' and Harsanyi, 'Cardinal Welfare.....'.

[10] My equiprobability assumption obviously can be regarded as an application of the principle of indifference. But is also has another possible interpretation. It may be regarded as an expression of the purely *moral* principle that, in making basic moral value judgments, we must give the same *a priori* weight to the interests of all members of the society.

[11] Following Carnap, by logical probabilities I mean subjective probabilities completely determined by symmetry considerations (if appropriate symmetry postulates are added to the standard rationality postulates of Bayesian theory).

[12] See note 4.

[13] As defined by John von Neumann and Oskar Morgenstern, *Theory of Games and Economic Behavior*, 2nd ed. (Princeton, N.J.: Princeton University Press, 1947), pp. 15–31.

[14] Harsanyi, 'Cardinal Welfare....'

[15] This statement would admittedly require appropriate qualifications if the psychological laws governing people's utility functions were found to be probabilistic, rather than deterministic. But this would not affect the basic validity of my analysis, though it would necessitate its restatement in a more complicated form.

[16] For a more detailed discussion of the epistemological problems connected with interpersonal utility comparisons, see my 1955 paper cited in note 5.

[17] Frank P. Ramsey, 'A Mathematical Theory of Saving', *Economic Journal*, 38 (December, 1928), 543–559.

[18] Anthony Downs, *An Economic Theory of Democracy* (New York: Harper and Brothers, 1957).

[19] John Rawls, 'Some Reasons for the Maximin Criterion', *American Economic Review*, 64, Papers & Proc. (May, 1974), 141–146.

[20] Kenneth J. Arrow, 'Some Ordinalist-Utilitarian Notes on Rawls's Theory of Justice', *The Journal of Philosophy*, 70 (May 10, 1973), 255.

[21] Arrow, p. 259.

CHAPTER V

NONLINEAR SOCIAL WELFARE FUNCTIONS: DO WELFARE ECONOMISTS HAVE A SPECIAL EXEMPTION FROM BAYESIAN RATIONALITY?*[1]

ABSTRACT. It is argued that Bayesian decision theory is a solution of an important philosophical problem, viz. the problem of how to define rational behavior under risk and uncertainty. The author has shown in earlier papers that if we take the Bayesian rationality postulates seriously, and take an individualistic point of view about social welfare, then our social welfare function must be a linear function of individual utilities: indeed, it must be their arithmetic mean. The present paper criticizes Diamond's and Sen's contention that one of the Bayesian postulates (viz. the sure-thing principle) does not apply to social decisions, even though it may apply to individual decisions. It also criticizes Sen's proposal of making social welfare a nonlinear function of individual utilities. The social welfare function proposed by the author depends on interpersonal utility comparisons. The use of such comparisons is defended. It is also argued that anybody who feels that the utilitarian (i.e., linear) form of the social welfare function is not egalitarian enough, should reject the author's individualism axiom, instead of trying to reject the Bayesian rationality axioms. However, this would be equivalent to giving egalitarian considerations a priority in many cases over humanitarian considerations. Finally, the paper discusses the reasons why even full agreement on the mathematical form of the social welfare function would not give rise to a utopian state of moral consensus: moral controversies arising from disagreements about what predictions to make about future empirical facts would still remain.

1. INTRODUCTION

Besides problems of empirical fact, and of formal (logical and mathematical) validity, a third important class of theoretical problems are problems of finding a rigorous scientific concept α (usually, but not necessarily, a concept defined by formal axioms) as a possible replacement for a vague and unclear concept β of prescientific commonsensical discourse (Carnap, 1950, pp. 3–8). I shall describe problems of this kind as *conceptual* or *philosophical* problems. They play a major role in philosophical discussions. But they also arise in economics and in the other social sciences. Examples are the problems of how to define rational behavior under certainty, risk, and uncertainty, as well as in game situations; how to define the concept of public interest – or, more exactly, how to define a social welfare function that would adequately formalize our intuitive notion of public interest; how to define social power, or social status, etc. (As everybody familiar with modern physics knows, philosophical problems of this type also arise in the natural sciences, though their substantive focus will be obviously different.)

The Bayesian theory of rational behavior under risk and uncertainty (Bayesian decision theory) is one of the few cases where such an essentially philosophical problem has found a very specific and unambiguous solution, accepted as correct by an increasing convergence of expert opinion. (The problem of how to define rational behavior under certainty has been solved already by classical economic theory, whereas the problem of what the precise definition of rational behavior should be in game situations is still largely an open question, though perhaps some progress is now being made towards its solution (see, e.g., Harsanyi, 1975b; cf. also Harsanyi, 1966).)

I propose here to briefly summarize the arguments in support of the Bayesian position: (1) The axioms (rationality postulates) of Bayesian theory are intellectually very compelling for anybody who has taken the trouble of properly understanding them; and no argument has yet been proposed that would cast serious doubt on these axioms as sensible criteria for rational behavior.[2] (2) Bayesian theory does not seem to lead to any counterintuitive implications. (3) The main rival definitions of rational behavior under risk and uncertainty are known to have highly counterintuitive implications (Radner and Marschak, 1954).

In two earlier papers (Harsanyi, 1953 and 1955), I have argued that if we take the rationality postulates of Bayesian theory seriously, then we can obtain a clear and unambiguous solution also for the time-honored philosophical problem of defining an adequate social welfare function. In fact, it can be shown that the social welfare function must be a linear function of all individual utilities – or, more exactly, it must be defined as the arithmetic mean of the utility levels of all individuals in the society.

To establish this result, we must distinguish between two classes of preferences by any given individual. One class comprises his *personal* preferences, based on his personal taste and his personal interests (as well as on the interests of those individuals, if any, whose well-being is a matter of personal concern for him). The other class comprises his *moral* or *social* preferences, which express his views about the general interests of society as a whole, defined in terms of impersonal and impartial criteria. Assuming that both classes of his preferences satisfy certain consistency (and continuity) requirements, the personal preferences of each individual can be represented by his *utility function* whereas his moral preferences can be represented by his *social welfare function*. Thus, under this model, each individual will have a social welfare function of his own, possibly different from the social welfare functions of other individuals. (Though, as I have argued (Harsanyi, 1955, p. 320), given sufficient information about other people's utility functions, the social welfare functions of different individuals will become identical.)

In order to characterize the mathematical relationships between the social welfare function of a given individual (individual j) and the utility functions of all individuals in the society, I proposed the following postulates (Harsanyi, 1955, pp. 312–314). *Postulate a (Individual Rationality)*: The personal preferences of *all* individuals satisfy the Bayesian rationality axioms. *Postulate b (Social Rationality)*: The moral (or social) preferences of individual j satisfy the Bayesian rationality axioms. *Postulate c (Individualism)*: If all individuals are *personally* indifferent between two social situations, then individual j will be *morally* indifferent between both of them.

Obviously, Postulate a implies that the personal preferences of each individual can be represented by a von Neumann-Morgenstern utility function (i.e., by a cardinal utility function that measures the utility of any lottery by its expected utility). Likewise, Postulate b implies that the social welfare function representing j's moral preferences will have the nature of a von Neumann-Morgenstern utility function. Finally, the three postulates together imply that j's social welfare function will be a *linear combination* of individual utilities.

The same result, indeed a slightly stronger one, can be obtained by a conceptual analysis of the nature of moral preferences (moral value judgments). As I have already indicated, moral preferences differ from mere personal preferences in being based on impersonal and impartial criteria. Now suppose that a given individual j would choose between two social situations in complete *ignorance*, or at least in complete voluntary *disregard*, of what his personal position would be in either situation. More specifically, let us suppose he would make his choice under the assumption that he would have exactly the *same probability* of occupying any one of the available social positions and, indeed, of taking up the personal identity of any particular individual in the society. Clearly, under this arrangement, his choice would necessarily satisfy the requirements of impersonality and impartiality to the highest possible degree and, therefore, would fully qualify as a statement of moral preference, i.e., as a moral value judgment.

At the same time, his choice would be a choice involving *risk* (since he could make only probabilistic predictions about his personal position in either situation). Thus, according to Bayesian decision theory, he would have to choose the social situation yielding him a higher expected utility, which in this case would mean choosing the situation providing a higher *average utility level* to the individual members of the society. Hence, our model leads to the conclusion that stating a moral preference (a moral value judgment) is equivalent to expressing a preference based on the arithmetic mean of all individual utilities as one's social welfare function (Harsanyi, 1953).

In recent years my theory has been quoted with approval by some distinguished economists (see, e.g., Theil, 1968, p. 336). But it has also come under criticism (Diamond, 1967; Rawls, 1971; Sen, 1970 and 1973).[3] The most specific criticism was Diamond's, who at least clearly recognized that my theory can be rejected only if one rejects one or more of its axioms. In contrast, Rawls has never made it clear which particular axiom(s) of my theory, if any, he wishes to deny. Diamond himself has chosen to reject the sure-thing principle as applied to social decision (which amounts to rejecting my Postulate b). Sen (1970, p. 145) seems to take a similar position. Below, I shall consider Diamond's argument in some detail. I shall try to show that welfare economists are no more at liberty to reject the sure-thing principle or the other Bayesian axioms of rationality than are people following lesser professions; and I shall try to outline some of the curious implications of Diamond's (and Sen's) point of view.

I shall also argue that Sen's proposal (1973, p. 18) of making our social welfare function dependent, not only on the mean value of individual utilities, but also on some measure of inequality (dispersion) in these utility levels, is open to much the same objections as is the view that the utility of a lottery ticket should depend, not only on its expected (mean) utility, but also on some measure of risk (on some measure of dispersion in possible utility outcomes).

It is, of course, clear enough why some economists and philosophers are unhappy with the utilitarian theory entailed by using a linear social welfare function. While Robbins (1938) once objected to utilitarianism because apparently he felt that it would have all *too* egalitarian implications, in our own age most objections are likely to come from people who find utilitarianism *not* to be egalitarian *enough*. I shall argue that any person who takes the latter position should not try to tamper with the rationality postulates of Bayesian theory: this could lead only to highly counterintuitive results. Instead, he should reject the *individualism postulate* (Postulate c) of my theory (see above; and also Harsanyi, 1955, p. 313), which makes social preferences fully determined by individual preferences.

This means that anybody who wants to adopt a moral position more egalitarian than the utilitarian position already is, must admit that the well-being of the individual members of society is *not* his ultimate moral value, and that he *is* willing in certain cases to sacrifice humanitarian considerations to egalitarian objectives when there is a conflict between the two. This is the real moral issue here; and this important moral issue should not be obscured by superficially attractive, but really quite untenable, objections to the sure-thing principle or to any other rationality axiom.

2. WELFARE ECONOMICS AND THE SURE-THING PRINCIPLE

For our purposes it is sufficient to consider the sure-thing principle as stated for *risky* situations (where all probabilities are known to the decision maker). In this case the principle asserts that, other things being equal, it is always preferable to have a chance of winning a *more highly-valued prize* with a given positive probability, to having the chance of winning a *less highly-valued prize* with the same probability. A variant of this principle is the substitution principle: it makes no difference whether one has the chance of winning one prize or another with a given probability, if one regards these two prizes as being *equally valuable*. Both forms of the sure-thing principle are intellectually highly compelling requirements for rational behavior, and it is very hard to envisage any situation in which a rational individual could feel justified in violating either of them.

Diamond admits that the sure-thing principle is a sensible rule for individual choice behavior, but denies it any validity for social choices. Even on the face of it, it would be very surprising if this view were correct. Surely, when we act on behalf of other people, let alone when we act on behalf of society as a whole, we are under an obligation to follow, if anything, *higher* standards of rationality than when we are dealing with our own private affairs. If common prudence requires private individuals to follow the sure-thing principle, then government officials who are supposed to look after our common interests can hardly be absolved from doing the same. Nor can welfare economists reasonably advise these public officials against doing so. Of course, this is not a conclusive argument: after all, there *could* be some very special reasons why public officials and welfare economists would not be bound by the Bayesian standards of rationality. In order to draw firmer conclusions, we have to consider Diamond's argument in more specific terms.

Diamond envisages a hypothetical society consisting of two individuals, where the government has a choice between two alternative policies. One policy would yield the utility vector (1,0) with certainty. The other would yield the two utility vectors (1,0) and (0,1) with equal probabilities. Assuming that society would attach equal weight to the interests of the two individuals, it is easy to see that, according to the sure-thing principle (substitution principle), the two policies should be assigned the same value from a social point of view. But, in Diamond's own opinion, the second policy is in fact socially strictly preferable to the first because it would yield *both* individuals a 'fair chance' while the first would not. According to Diamond this shows that the sure-thing principle has no validity for social decisions.

In order to gain a better understanding of Diamond's argument, I propose to apply it to a couple of more specific hypothetical situations. For example, let us imagine two societies, *A* and *B*. Society *A* has an extremely unequal income distribution, so extreme in fact that even politically rather conservative observers find it absolutely revolting. Moreover, it has virtually no social mobility, and certainly no mobility based on what could be described as individual merit. Society *B* is exactly like society *A*, except for the following difference. By old social custom, all babies born in B during any given calendar month are randomly distributed by government officials among all families who had a baby during that period, so that every baby born in that month will have the same chance of ending up in any given family. (I shall assume that all families fully accept this social custom, and treat the babies randomly allocated to them completely as their own.)

Should we now say that society B would be morally less objectionable than society A, because in B all individuals would have a 'fair chance' of ending up in a rich family and, therefore, in a privileged social and economic position? By assumption, B is a society with an income distribution just as unfair as A is. In both societies, any individual's social and economic position has nothing to do with personal merit, but rather is completely a matter of 'luck'. In A it depends wholly on the accident of birth – on the 'great lottery of life' which decides who is born into what particular family. In contrast, in B it depends wholly on a government- conducted lottery. Why should we assign higher moral dignity to a lottery organized by government bureaucrats than we assign to the 'great lottery of life' which chooses a family for each of us without the benefit of government intervention? Why should a bureaucratic lottery be regarded as being a 'fairer' allocative mechanism than the great biological lottery produced by nature?

Indeed, suppose we would obtain reliable information to the effect that the families we are born into are always chosen literally by a huge heavenly lottery. Can anybody seriously assert that this metaphysical information would make the slightest difference to our moral condemnation of hereditary social and economic inequalities?

Next, let us consider another example. Suppose that the government has a choice between two policies. The first policy would consist in abolishing an obsolete and, by now, economically very harmful protective tariff. This would benefit all citizens (many of them quite substantially), except for a small group of workers and employers in the hitherto protected industry, who would suffer moderate economic losses. The second policy would result in the same vector of individual utilities as the first, except that the individual components of this vector would be randomly permuted, because now the gainers and the losers would be chosen by a government-conducted lottery. To fix our ideas, we shall assume that the second policy would actually consist in implementing the first policy (i.e., removal of the protective tariff), followed by a random redistribution of income on the basis of a lottery.

Once more, would it make any sense to assert that the second policy would be morally preferable to the first? Under the first policy, the losers would be the members of one particular industry, who presumably have entered this industry by family association or by other accidents of personal life history. Thus, being a member of the loser group would be just as much a matter of personal 'bad luck' as would be under the second policy, where the losers would be selected literally by a lottery. Again, what would make such a lottery a morally superior allocating mechanism to those historical accidents which make people enter a particular industry?

It would be easy to adduce many more examples to corroborate the same conclusion. Diamond's suggestion that economic and social privileges allocated by government policies with random components are morally more acceptable than social and economic privileges allocated by the accidents of birth and of personal life history – i.e., the suggestion that the first kind of personal 'luck' is morally superior to the second kind – is wholly without merit. Therefore, his claim that social choices are not subject to the sure-thing principle falls to the ground.

Let me add that the same conclusion applies to the allocation of biological qualities, such as intelligence, scientific and artistic talent, health, beauty, physical strength, etc. Under appropriate safeguards, techniques of genetic engineering could no doubt benefit mankind by improving the biological endowment of the average individual of future generations. But a mere redistribution of the same unimproved biological qualities by means of an official lottery (what a horrible thought!), even if it were technologically feasible, would certainly not represent any improvement over the existing situation from a moral point of view.

3. MEAN UTILITY VS. UTILITY DISPERSION

Whereas my own theory would make the social welfare function the arithmetic mean of individual utilities, Rawls (1958 and 1971) has proposed a social welfare function based on the maximin principle, and always measuring the welfare level of society by the utility level of the worst-off individual. This means mathematically that Rawls's social welfare function would always assign *infinitely more weight* to the interests of the poorest, or otherwise least fortunate, members of society than it assigns to the richer, or otherwise more fortunate, members. In contrast, my own social welfare function would always assign the *same* weight to *equally urgent* needs of different individuals, regardless of their social or economic positions. But of course since, typically, poor people have many more unfilled urgent wants than rich people do, in practice in most cases my own social welfare function will lead to similar policy decisions to Rawls's, because it will give much higher priority to poor people's needs. Only in those, rather special, cases where some rich people may have even more urgent needs than some poor people do, will my social welfare function lead to opposite policy decisions. However, precisely in these cases I feel that my social welfare function would lead to the morally right decisisons while Rawls's would lead to morally wrong ones.

For example, if a philanthropist has to decide whether to give $100 in cash, or the same value in food, or in clothing, etc., to a poor man or to a millionaire, it is clear that he should choose the poor man since the former will have a much greater need for extra cash, or for extra food, or for extra clothing, etc. But if he has to choose between giving a life-saving drug in short supply to a poor man or to a millionaire, then the only relevant consideration must be who needs it more, i.e., who could derive the greater medical benefit from it. Surely, it would be highly immoral discrimination against the millionaire to refuse him a life-saving drug, even though he has the best claim to it from a medical point of view, merely on the ground that he happens to be a millionaire. Yet, Rawls's social welfare function would force us precisely to engage in such immoral discriminatory practices in some, rather special, but perhaps not-all-too-rare, cases.[4]

In his interesting book, *On Economic Inequality*, Sen (1973) has taken a position intermediate between Rawls's and my own. He agrees with Rawls that our social welfare function should give *more weight* to poor people's than to rich people's utility functions. But, under Sen's theory, the former would be given only a *finite* number of times more weight than the latter. My own theory would make social welfare equal to the mean value of the different individuals' utility levels, so that social welfare would be a linear function of the individual utilities. In contrast, Sen's theory would make social welfare depend, not only on the mean, but also on some measure of *inequality*, i.e., of *dispersion*, among the different individuals' utility levels (Sen, 1973, p. 18).[5] This means that social welfare would have to be a nonlinear function of the individual utilities.[6] For easier reference, this argument for a nonlinear social welfare function I shall describe as the utility-dispersion argument about social welfare.

Unfortunately, Sen's theory is open to the same objection as Rawls's theory is: it would give rise to unfair discrimination against people enjoying relatively high utility levels, much the same way as – though less often than – Rawls's theory does. Moreover, the utility-dispersion argument about social welfare, which underlies Sen's theory, shows a close formal similarity to what I shall call the utility-dispersion argument about lotteries, viz. to the view that the utility of a lottery ticket should depend, not only on its *expected (mean) utility*, but also on some measure of *risk*, i.e., on some measure of *dispersion* among its possible utility outcomes. Therefore, so the argument runs, the utility of a lottery ticket must be a nonlinear function of these possible utility outcomes.

Yet, the utility-disperson argument about lotteries is known to be mistaken (see Luce and Raiffa, 1957, p. 32; or see any textbook on decision theory). To be sure, a similar argument would be perfectly valid if all references to the *utilities* of the possible outcomes (prizes) were replaced by references to their *money values*. It is certainly true that, for most decision makers, the value of a lottery ticket is not determined solely by the *expected (mean) money income* associated with it. Rather, it strongly depends also on the *risk* involved, i.e., on the *dispersion* in the possible money incomes.

This argument, however, cannot be extended from the possible money incomes to their utilities. The basic reason for this lies in the fact that the utility of any possible money income is measured by the decision maker's von Neumann-Morgenstern utility function, which already makes appropriate allowance for his attitude toward risk. For instance, if he has a negative attitude toward risk, then his utility function will display decreasing marginal utility for money (i.e., it will be strictly concave in money). Thus, his risk aversion will already be fully reflected in the utilities he assigns to various possible incomes and, therefore, also in his expected utility associated with the lottery ticket. Hence, it would be *unnecessary* and *inadmissible* double-counting if we made an allowance for the decision maker's risk aversion for a second time, and made his utility for a lottery ticket dependent, not only on its expected utility, but also on the dispersion in achievable utilities.

Indeed, such a procedure would not only be unnecessary; it would be *logically inconsistent*. This is so because it can be shown that, if the decision maker follows the rationality postulates of Bayesian theory, then he *must* measure the utility of a lottery ticket by its expected utility (assuming that all utilities are expressed in von Neumann-Morgenstern utility units). This means that he simply *cannot* make his utility dependent on the dispersion in possible utility outcomes, and cannot make it a non-linear function of the latter.

I now propose to show that Sen's utility-dispersion argument about social welfare succumbs essentially to the same objection as the utility-dispersion argument about lotteries does: it is an illegitimate transfer of a mathematical relationship from money amounts, for which it does hold, to utility levels, for which it does not hold. It is certainly true that social welfare cannot be equated with average income per head, and cannot be even a function of this variable *alone*. Rather, if income per head is kept constant, then, as most of us will surely agree, social welfare will increase with a more equal distribution of income. This means that social welfare is a nonlinear (indeed, presumably a strictly concave) function of individual incomes.

This is so because, if we can costlessly redistribute income, and can transfer $100 from a rich man to a poor man, then normally the damage (disutility) done to the former will be considerably less than the benefit (utility) accruing to the latter. This follows from the law of decreasing marginal utility for money for each individual[7] (together with the assumption that different individuals will have reasonably similar utility functions for money, so that the law of decreasing marginal utility for money will affect them in a similar way). Of course, this argument makes sense only if the utility gains and utility losses of different individuals are *comparable*. In Harsanyi (1955, pp. 316–321), I have set out my reasons for believing in the possibility of interpersonal utility comparisons. (I think Sen agrees with me on this point (Sen, 1973, p. 14).) I shall come back to this problem below (Section 4).

Yet, even if social welfare is a nonlinear function of individual *incomes*, it does not follow at all that it is a nonlinear function also of individual *utilities*. If we decrease a rich man's utility level by 100 utility units and simultaneously increase a poor man's utility level by 100 utility units, then (assuming that we have measured utility in the same units in both cases) the utility loss suffered by the former will be exactly the *same* as the utility gain accruing to the latter. It makes very good sense to assume a law of decreasing marginal utility for *money* (or for commodities); but it would make no sense whatever to assume a law of decreasing marginal utility for *utility*. (It would be surely nonsensical to assert that a utility increase from 1 000 000 units to 1 000 100 units is a smaller utility increment than a utility increase from 200 units to 300 units is. By describing both as 100-unit increments, we are committed to assuming their equality.)

What is at stake here, of course, is not a (rather trivial) point in simple mathematics. Rather, as I have already argued in discussing Rawls's theory, we are dealing with an important *moral* issue. When we are assigning the same quantitative measure to utility changes affecting two different individuals (e.g., when we describe both of them as 100-unit changes), then we are implicitly asserting that these utility changes for both individuals involve human needs of *equal urgency*. But, this being so, it would be highly unfair – and, in many cases, quite inhumane – discrimination to claim that, as a matter of principle, satisfaction of one man's needs hould have a lower social priority than satisfaction of the other man's needs should have. Though I have illustrated this point by an example (involving a life-saving drug), I shall now propose a second example because this will give me a chance to discuss some other aspects of the problem.

Suppose there are two five-year-old boys in my neighborhood. One of them, *A*, is a child of very lucky temperament, who seems to be very happy most of the time, and who can derive great joy from minor presents. The other boy, *B*, has a rather unlucky temperament. He looks unhappy most of the time, and minor presents seem to give him only little satisfaction. I happen to have a little present in my pocket. Which boy should I give it to?

Utilitarian theory supplies a clear answer to this question: the present should go to that boy who is likely to derive more utility from it. Presumably, this means that it should go to *A*, who can be expected to get more immediate enjoyment out of it. (But this conclusion would have to be reversed, should I feel there was reasonable hope that receiving presents and other signs of attention might have a large enough beneficial long-run effect on *B*'s unfavorable personality.)

In contrast, Rawls's theory would *always* favor giving the present to *B*, who is obviously the less fortunate of the two boys. Finally, Sen's theory would suggest that it should be given either to *A* or *B*, depending on the actual distance between the two boys' utility levels: if *B*'s utility level is *not* very much below *A*'s, then *A*'s higher marginal utility for the present will be the deciding factor, and the little present should go to *A*; whereas if *B*'s utility level *is* very much below *A*'s, then this difference in their utility levels will be the deciding factor, and the little present should go to *B*.

Once more, the issue is this. In case I come to the conclusion that, everything considered, I could create more human happiness by giving the present to *A*, am I permitted to do so? Or, am I required under certain conditions to discriminate against *A* and give the present to *B*, even though I know that *A* would make better use of it – merely because *A* is already a pretty happy fellow?

As things are, *A* has a rather high utility level while *B* has a rather low one. This situation is not of my own making: it had already existed when I first appeared on the scene. The question is what obligations this state of affairs imposes on me. Sen and I agree that one obligation I have is to create as much human happiness as I can in this situation. But Sen seems to hold that I am also under a second obligation (which in some cases may override the first) of *compensating B* for his low utility level as such. In my opinion, the question of compensating *B* does not arise at all. Of course, I would certainly owe *B* a fair compensation if his low utility level were a result of my own culpable actions in the past. But, under our assumptions, this is not the case. Therefore, unwarranted *guilt* feelings about *B*'s low utility level should have no influence on my behavior. (Nor should my behavior be influenced, of course, by any irrational *resentment* against people who, like *A*, are lucky enough to enjoy high utility levels, achieved without any recourse to morally objectionable activies.) Rather, my only obligation in this situation is to pursue the basic goal of all morally good actions, viz. to create as much happiness as possible in this world.

To conclude, we have found not only that Sen's utility-dispersion argument about social welfare represents an illegitimate extension of a mathematical relationship from incomes to the corresponding utilities, much the same way as the utility-dispersion argument about lotteries does. We have also found that the reasons why this extension is illegitimate are very similar in both cases. The basic reason is that, given the non-linearity – concavity or near-concavity – of individual utility functions in terms of money and of commodities (i.e., their tendency to display decreasing marginal utility), poor people's needs will normally have a much higher social priority than rich people's, even if we use a linear social welfare function. Therefore, it is quite *unneccesary* and, indeed, it is *morally inadmissible*, to make the social welfare function itself nonlinear in the inidividual utilities – just as it is unnecessary and inadmissible to make the utility of a lottery ticket nonlinear in the possible utility outcomes.

Indeed, such a nonlinear social welfare function would also be *logically inconsistent*, at least for people who believe in the Bayesian rationality postulates as well as in a humanistic-individualistic moral philosophy. For, as I have shown (Harsanyi, 1955, pp. 312–314), the Bayesian rationality postulates, together with an individualism axiom (Postulate *c*), logically entail the use of a linear social welfare function.

4. INTERPERSONAL UTILITY COMPARISONS

The Bayesian rationality postulates and the individualism axiom only imply that our social welfare function must be linear in individual utilities: but they say nothing about the weights we should give to the various individuals' utility functions. Yet, it is natural to supplement this theory by adding a symmetry axiom, which requires that the social welfare function should treat different individuals' utility functions in a similar manner, and should assign the same weight to each of them.[8]

This requirement, in turn, implies that our social welfare function must be based on *interpersonal utility comparisons*. For, in order to assign the same weight to the various individuals' utility functions, we must be able to express all of them in the same utility unit. Of course, when we first define a von Neumann-Morgenstern utility function for each individual in the usual way, we shall normally choose an independent utility unit for each individual. But, then, we must engage in interpersonal utility comparisons in order to estimate *conversion ratios* between the different individuals' utility units. (For example, we may first choose, for each individual, as utility unit his utility for an extra $1. But then we must try to estimate how different individuals' marginal utilities for an extra $1 compare with one another.)

This dependence of linear social welfare functions, and of utilitarian theory in general, on interpersonal utility comparisons has given rise to a good deal of misunderstanding. Most of this misunderstanding could have been avoided if more attention had been paid to the close similarity between the role that subjective probabilities play in Bayesian decision theory and the role that interpersonal utility comparisons (interpersonal utility conversion ratios) play in utilitarian moral theory.

More specifically, since in uncertain situations expected utility is defined in terms of subjective probabilities, Bayesian decision theory requires us to assign subjective probabilities to alternative contingencies. Obviously, this requirement is not based on assuming that human decision makers are necessarily very good at assessing these probabilities. Indeed, in situations where they have insufficient information to guide their probability judgments, these judgments are bound to be of rather poor quality. Nevertheless, Bayesian theory suggests that we should make our decisions on the basis of such probabilitity assessments, even in situations of very insufficient information, because:

(1) If our behavior is consistent with the Bayesian rationality postulates, then we simply *cannot avoid* making such probability assessments, at least implicitly. For example, suppose I have to choose between two bets. Bet A would make me win $100 if candidate X wins a particular election, and would make me lose $100 if he loses; whereas bet B would exactly reverse these two contingencies. Then, by choosing either bet, I will make an implicit probability judgment about the chances of his winning or losing the election. I simply cannot avoid making such a judgment.

(2) Since we have to make such probability judgments at least implicitly, we shall be better off if we make them explicitly: this will enable us to avoid damaging inconsistencies in our probability judgments, and will enable us also to make the fullest possible use of the information actually available to us – however much or however little this information may be in any given case.

In the same way, utilitarian theory requires us to use a social welfare

function based on interpersonal utility comparisons. However, this requirement in no way presupposes that human decision makers are particularly
good at making such comparisons. Presumably, when we know two individuals (or two groups of indivuals) reasonably well, and have good
knowledge of the situations they are in, then we can compare the utilities
they would derive from given commodity baskets (or even from less
tangible benefits), with a tolerable accuracy. (For example, I think I can
tell with some assurance which friend of mine would derive the highest
utility from a Mozart opera, or from a good dinner at a French restaurant,
etc.) On the other hand, utility comparisons between two individuals with
social and cultural backgrounds unfamiliar to us must be subject to wide
margins of error. But, in any case, utilitarian theory suggests that we
should make our moral decisions on the basis of such interpersonal
utility comparisons, because:

(1) If we follow the axioms of utilitarian theory (and, in everyday
life, all of us behave as utilitarians, at least some of the time), then we
simply *cannot avoid* making interpersonal utility comparisons, at least
implicitly. For example, when we have to decide whether we want to give
a particular present to A or to B, then one of the important considerations
(though perhaps not the only important consideration) will be whether
A or B is likely to derive a higher utility from it.

(2) Since we have to make such interpersonal utility comparisons anyhow, we are under a moral obligation to make them with the greatest
possible care, and with the fullest use of all relevant information available
to us – at least when they will serve as a basis for an important moral
decision. Any attempt to avoid such interpersonal comparisons, owing
to some philosophical prejudice against them, can only lead to careless
and irresponsible moral decisions.

As I have argued elsewhere (Harsanyi, 1955, pp. 316–321; and 1975a,
Section 8), there is nothing mysterious in our undeniable ability to make
such comparisons, with various degrees of accuracy, depending on the
situation. Any such comparison is logically equivalent to a prediction of
what our own choice behavior and our own emotional reactions would be
in certain hypothetical situations – possibly in situations very different
from anything we have experienced so far. Trying to assess the utilities that
another individual of a very different personality and social background
would derive from various commodity baskets amounts to the same thing

as trying to assess the utilities I myself would derive from various commodity baskets if my income, social position, personal situation, or emotional attitudes were exactly like his. Thus, it amounts to much the same thing as assessing the utilities I would derive from various commodity baskets if my personal situation and personal characteristics suddenly underwent a specific change.

Nobody claims that such assessments are always very reliable. All we claim is that in many cases we are under a moral obligation to make such assessments and, indeed, to make them as carefully and as knowledgeably as we possibly can – just as, in many cases, we are under a prudential (pragmatic) obligation to make probability judgments, and to make them as carefully and as knowledgeably as we possibly can.

5. SUPER-EGALITARIAN SOCIAL WELFARE FUNCTIONS

Owing to the great cogency of the Bayesian rationality postulates, it seems to me that it is a rather hopeless undertaking to build up a moral theory on a rejection of these postulates either for individual or for social choices (i.e., on a rejection of my Postulate a or b). Any such theory could only give rise to highly counterintuitive implications. Rather, anybody who wanted to construct a *super-egalitarian* theory, i.e., a theory more egalitarian than the utilitarian theory already is, would have to deny, or at least substantially weaken, my individualism axiom (Postulate c).

One possible approach would be this. Suppose that individual j wants to construct a social welfare function for society X. I shall here assume that i himself is an outside observer and is himself not a member of society X. (The model can be easily extended to the case where j is in fact a member.) Then, j may start with specifying his own political preferences about the income and utility distribution he would like to see in society X. For easier reference, I shall describe these as j's *egalitarian preferences*. (These preferences may depend on the variance of individual utilities and or individual incomes in society X, or may depend on some more complicated function of individual utilities and/or incomes.) In view of my preceding argument, it will be desirable to assume that j's egalitarian preferences satisfy the Bayesian axioms of rationality (e.g., Marschak's (1950) postulates). Then, j may replace my Postulate c by a less individualistic Postulate c^*: "If two alternatives are indifferent from the standpoint of each individual i in society X, and are also indifferent from the standpoint of my (j's) egalitarian preferences, then they are indifferent from a social standpoint as well."

By a slight modification of the proof given in my paper (Harsanyi, 1955, pp. 312–314), it is easy to verify that these axioms imply the following theorem:

THEOREM. The social welfare function W of individual j must be of the following mathematical form

$$W = t \sum_{i=1}^{n} a_i U_i + (1 - t) V_j, \quad \text{with} \quad 0 \leq t \leq 1,$$

where $U_1, ..., U_i, ..., U_n$ are the utility functions of the various individual members of society X; V_j is a von Neumann-Morgenstern utility function defined in terms of j's egalitarian preferences; whereas t and $a_1, ..., a_n$ are constants.

If j so desires, then he can choose $t = 0$, and can choose to make V_j quite independent of the utility functions $U_1, ..., U_n$: in this case, of course, W will lose all connection with individual preferences. But, even if he does not go quite as far as this, the mathematical form of W will clearly indicate that the well-being of the individual members of society X is not his overriding consideration, and that he is willing to sacrifice their well-being, at least in some cases, to his own egalitarian preferences when the two conflict with each other.

Personally, I would find such a theory of ethics or of welfare economics highly objectionable from a *moral* point of view. To my mind, humanitarian considerations should never take a second place to any other considerations, including egalitarian ones. Indeed, at a deeper level of philosophical analysis, I think such a theory would be highly *irrational*, because individual j cannot have any rational motive for wanting to impose his own political preferences on the members of society X (whether he himself is a member of society X or not). But rationality is a concept of many dimensions: the theory I have described would at least be consistent with the most conspicuous requirements of rationality, by conforming to the Bayesian rationality postulates – even if it violated some standards of rationality at deeper levels.

6. Linear Social Welfare Functions and the Problem of Moral Consensus

I have argued that there are rather compelling reasons for using social welfare functions linear in individual utilities – at least for people believing in an individualistic-humanistic moral philosophy. Among the people accepting this point of view, one source of moral disagreements will disappear: they will agree at least on the proper mathematical form of the social welfare function.

Of course, another rather obvious source of possible disagreements will remain: such people may still differ on how to compare the utilities of different individuals. Yet, one should not exaggerate the likely practical importance of this problem. In this respect, conventional treatments of welfare economics give a rather misleading impression. A little reflection will show that very few real-life policy controversies actually arise from disagreements about interpersonal utility comparisons.

This, of course, does not mean that agreement on the mathematical form of the social welfare function (even if this were accompanied by reasonably close agreement on interpersonal utility comparisons in all important cases) would bring us much nearer to a utopian state of moral consensus – just as full acceptance of Bayesian decision theory would not bring us much nearer to a consensus on purely pragmatic policy problems (i.e., on those involving no controversial moral issues of any significance).

In my opinion, the most important sources of moral disagreements are disagreements about what conditional or unconditional predictions – whether deterministic or probabilistic predictions – to make about future empirical facts. For example, we cannot expect a moral consensus in our society as long as we strongly disagree on what the likely effects of the conventional anti-inflationary policies will be in somewhat unusual economic situations, for which no real historical precedents may exist; or on what the long-run effects of continuing inflation will be on our social institutions; or on how our children will be affected in the long run by an increased emphasis on 'creativity', and a decreased emphasis on 'intellectual excellence', in our schools; or on whether a greater pressure on certain despotic regimes will speed up or rather slow down their hoped-for liberalization and democratization, etc. No doubt, further progress in human psychology, in the social sciences, and, in some cases, in the natural sciences, will give clearer answers to some of these problems than now are available to us. But open problems of this type will always remain with us – partly because the very solution of some of these problems will give rise to new ones. By solving some of these problems a radically new historical situation is created, and even if we have learned how to make predictions in the old situation, this may not help us very much in making predictions in the new one. Keynesian economics has enabled us to make much better predictions about the effects of various economic policies in conditions of mass unemployment. By this means, it has also enabled us to eliminate these very conditions, and to create a completely novel economic situation of continuing high employment, in which Keynesian predictions may no longer work. [9,10]

Nevertheless, even if an agreement on the mathematical form of our social welfare function will not cure our most important moral disagreements – as long as we keep on disagreeing in our predictions about future empirical facts – such an agreement is an objective very much worth striving for. What a good formal theory of the social welfare function can do for us in the field of moral, political, and economic decisions is much the same as what Bayesian decision theory can do for us in the field of purely pragmatic decisions: It can help us in organizing our analysis of the situation, in clarifying what we do know and what we do not know, and what the implicit assumptions we are making are; and, most important of all, it can help us in bringing a large number of – often quite heterogeneous – pieces of information together in one coherent and systematic decision-making process.

In actual fact, even if we disregard its possible practical uses, it seems to be a philosophically rather interesting proposition, should it be true, that our basic criteria of rationality, together with an individualistic-humanistic moral philosophy, leave us no other option but defining our social welfare function as a linear combination of individual utilities and, indeed, as their arithmetic mean.

NOTES

* *Theory and Decision* **6** (1975), 311–332.
1 The author wishes to thank the National Science Foundation for supporting this

research through Grant GS-3222 to the Center for Research in Management Science, University of California, Berkeley. Thanks are due also to the Institute of Mathematical Economics, University of Bielefeld, where the author has been Visiting Professor in 1973–74; as well as to Professor Reinhard Selten, of the University of Bielefeld, to Professor Amartya K. Sen, of the London School of Economics, and to Professors Louis Gevers and Robert Deschamps, both of the University of Namur, for helpful discussions.

[2] The postulates of Bayesian theory have a very clear meaning in all situations where the utility of each 'prize' is independent of the probability of attaining it. (Virtually all situations important for welfare economics belong to this category.) Difficulties of interpretation arise only when this is not the case, e.g., when part of the attraction of mountain climbing lies in its inherent danger (i.e., in the fact that the probability of safe arrival at the top is less than one (cf. Marschak, 1950)). But even in such cases the postulates retain their formal validity if the 'prizes' are properly defined (e.g., mountain climbing must be defined so as to include the presence of danger, or, more exactly, the joy of danger successfully overcome). However, this means that in such cases the behavioral implications of the Bayesian postulates will become somewhat ambiguous unless these postulates can be supplemented by a psychological theory predicting how the utilities of the prizes will quantitatively depend on their probabilities.

[3] In this paper I shall mainly discuss the criticisms of Professors Diamond and Sen, since I have already considered Professor Rawls's theory elsewhere (Harsanyi, 1975a).

[4] For a much more detailed discussion of Rawls's view, the reader is referred to Harsanyi (1975a).

[5] Sen also considers inequality measures that do not establish a complete ordering among alternative income distributions (utility distributions), but only establish a partial ordering (Sen, 1973, pp. 55–65).

[6] Any social welfare function linear and symmetric in the individual utilities is essentially the same as their arithmetic mean, apart from a possible multiplicative and a possible additive constant. Therefore, if we want our social welfare function to depend on some measure of the inequality (dispersion) among the individual utility levels, we have to make it nonlinear in the individual utilities.

[7] The force of this argument will not significantly decrease even if we accept Friedman and Savage's [1948] contention that people's utility functions may have some – relatively short – ranges of increasing marginal utility for money. Globally, these functions will still display an overall tendency to decreasing marginal utility for money.

[8] Alternatively, to establish this equal-weights requirement, we could also use my equiprobability model for moral preferences (moral value judgments). See Section 1 above; and also Harsanyi (1953).

[9] On deeper analysis, disagreements about interpersonal utility comparisons, also, are disagreements about predictions in certain hypothetical situations – such as disagreements about what the preferences and the emotional reactions of certain individuals would be if their incomes, social positions, education levels, cultural attitudes, and even their personalities, were different from what they actually are.

[10] Most contemprary philosophers divide declaratory statements in two main classes, viz. logical-mathematical statements and empirical statements. Of course, this leaves no proper room for philosophical (conceptual) statements, which cannot be really subsumed under either category (see Section 1 above). Moreover, this classification also pays insufficient attention to the special problems connected with statements

about future empirical facts, which obviously cannot be verified in the same way as statements about present or past empirical facts can, but which are major ingredients to some of our most important value judgments.

BIBLIOGRAPHY

Carnap, Rudolf, *Logical Foundations of Probability*, University of Chicago Press, Chicago, 1950.

Diamond, Peter, 'Cardinal Welfare, Individualistic Ethics, and Interpersonal Comparisons of Utility: A Comment', *Journal of Political Economy* **75** (1967) 765–766.

Friedman, Milton and Savage, Leonard J., 'The Utility Analysis of Choices Involving Risk', *Journal of Political Economy* **56** (1948) 279–304.

Harsanyi, John C., 'Cardinal Utility in Welfare Economics and in the Theory of Risk-Taking', *Journal of Political Economy* **61** (1953) 434–435.

Harsanyi, John C., 'Cardinal Welfare, Individualistic Ethics, and Interpersonal Comparisons of Utility', *Journal of Political Economy* **63** (1955) 309–321.

Harsanyi, John C., 'A General Theory of Rational Behavior in Game Situations', *Econometrica* **34** (1966) 613–634.

Harsanyi, John C., 'Can the Maximin Principle Serve as a Basis for Morality: A Critique of John Rawls's Theory', *American Political Science Review* **69** (1975a) 594–606.

Harsanyi, John C., 'The Tracing Procedure: A Bayesian Approach to Defining a Solution for *n*-Person Noncooperative Games', *International Journal of Game Theory* **4** (1975b) 61–94.

Luce, R. Duncan and Raiffa, Howard, *Games and Decisions*, John Wiley, New York, 1957.

Marschak, Jacob, 'Rational Behavior, Uncertain Prospects, and Measurable Utility', *Econometrica* **18** (1950) 111–141.

Radner, Roy and Marschak, Jacob, 'Notes on Some Proposed Decision Criteria', in Robert M. Thrall *et al.* (eds.), *Decision Processes*, John Wiley, New York, 1954.

Rawls, John, 'Justice as Fairness', *Philosophical Review* **67** (1958) 164–194.

Rawls, John, *A Theory of Justice*, Harvard University Press, Cambridge, Mass., 1971.

Robbins, Lionel, 'Interpersonal Comparisons of Utility', *Economic Journal* **48** (1938) 635–641.

Sen, Amartya K., *Collective Choice and Social Welfare*, Holden-Day, San Francisco, 1970.

Sen, Amartya K., *On Economic Inequality*, Clarendon Press, Oxford, 1973.

Theil, Henri, *Optimal Decision Rules for Government and Industry*, North-Holland and Rand McNally, Amsterdam and Chicago, 1968.

PART B

RATIONAL-CHOICE AND GAME THEORETICAL MODELS OF SOCIAL BEHAVIOR

CHAPTER VI

ADVANCES IN UNDERSTANDING
RATIONAL BEHAVIOR*

ABSTRACT. It will be argued that economic theory, decision theory and some recent work in game theory, make important contributions to a deeper understanding of the concept of rational behavior. The paper starts with a discussion of the common-sense notion of rational behavior. Then, the rationality concepts of classical economics and of Bayesian decision theory are described. Finally, some (mostly fairly recent) advances in game theory are briefly discussed, such as probabilistic models for games with incomplete information; the role of equilibrium points in non-cooperative games, and the standard game-theoretical approach to the prisoner's dilemma problem; the concept of perfect equilibrium points; the use of non-cooperative bargaining models in analyzing cooperative games; and the Harsanyi-Selten solution concept for non-cooperative games.

1. INTRODUCTION[1]

The concept of rational behavior (or of practical rationality) is of considerable philosophical interest. It plays an important role in moral and political philosophy, while the related concept of theoretical rationality is connected with many deep problems in logic, epistemology, and the philosophy of science. Both practical and theoretical rationality are important concepts in psychology and in the study of artificial intelligence. Furthermore, rational-behavior models are widely used in economics and, to an increasing extent, also in other social sciences. This fact is all the more remarkable since rationality is a normative concept and, therefore, it has been claimed (incorrectly, as I shall argue) that it is out of place in non-normative, empirically oriented studies of social behavior.

Given the important role that the concept of rationality plays in philosophy and in a number of other disciplines, I have thought it may be of some interest to this interdisciplinary audience if I report on some work in decision theory and in game theory that holds out the prospect of replacing our common-sense notion of rational behavior by a much more general, much more precise, and conceptually very much richer notion of rationality. I feel that successful development of an analytically clear, informative, and intuitively satisfactory concept of rationality would have significant philosophical implications.

I shall first discuss the common-sense notion of rational behavior. Then, I shall briefly describe the rationality concepts of classical economic theory and of Bayesian decision theory. Finally, I shall report on some, mostly very recent, results in game theory, which, I believe, are practically unknown to non-specialists. Of course, within the space available, I cannot do more than draw a sketchy and very incomplete picture of the relevant work – a picture no doubt strongly colored by my own theoretical views.

2.   THE MEANS-ENDS CONCEPT OF RATIONAL BEHAVIOR

In everyday life, when we speak of 'rational behavior', in most cases we are thinking of behavior involving a choice of the best *means* available for achieving a given *end*. This implies that, already at a common-sense level, rationality is a *normative* concept: it points to what we *should* do in order to attain a given end or objective. But, even at a common-sense level, this concept of rationality does have important *positive* (non-normative) applications: it is used for *explanation*, for *prediction*, and even for mere *description*, of human behavior.

Indeed, the assumption that a given person has acted or will act rationally, often has very considerable explanatory and predictive power, because it may imply that we can explain or predict a large number of possibly very complicated facts about his behavior in terms of a small number of rather simple hypotheses about his goals or objectives.

For example, suppose a given historian comes to the conclusion that Napoleon acted fairly rationally in a certain period. This will have the implication that Napoleon's actions admit of explanation in terms of his political and military objectives – possibly in terms of a rather limited number of such objectives – and that other, often less easily accessible, psychological variables need not be used to any major extent to account for his behavior. On the other hand, if our historian finds that Napoleon's behavior was not very rational, then this will imply that no set of reasonably well-defined policy objectives could be found that would explain Napoleon's behavior, and that any explanation of it must make use of some 'deeper' motivational factors and, ultimately, of some much more specific assumptions about the psychological mechanisms underlying human behavior.

Yet, we do make use of the notion of rationality also in cases where we are not interested in an explanation or prediction of human behavior, but are merely interested in providing an adequate *description* of it. For instance, any historical narrative of Napoleon's political and military decisions will be seriously incomplete, even at a descriptive level, if it contains no discussion of the rationality or irrationality or these decisions. Thus, it will not be enough to report that, in a particular battle, Napoleon attacked the enemy's right wing. Rather, we also want to know whether, under the existing conditions, this attack was a sensible (or perhaps even a brilliant) tactical move or not.

Philosophers, and social scientists outside the economics profession, have often expressed puzzlement about the successful use of the normative concept of rational behavior in positive economics – and, more recently, also in other social sciences[2] – for explanation and prediction, and even for mere description, of human behavior. But there is really nothing surprising about this. All it means is that human behavior is mostly *goal-directed*, often in a fairly consistent manner, in many important classes of social situations. For example, suppose that people are *mainly* after money in business life (even if they do also have a number of other objectives), or are mainly after election or re-election to public office in democratic politics, or are mainly after social status in many social activities, or are mainly after national self-interest in international affairs – at least that these statements are true as a matter of reasonable first approximation. Then, of course, it is in no way surprising if we can explain and sometimes even predict, and can also meaningfully describe, their behavior in terms of the assumption that they are after money, or after public office, or after social status, or after national self-interest.

Even if the subject matter of our investigation were not human behavior, but rather the behavior of goal-pursuing robots, a model of 'rational' (i.e. goal-pursuing) robot behavior would be a very valuable analytical tool. Of course, just as in the case of human beings, such a rationalistic model would only work with highly 'rational' (i.e. with very well-functioning) robots. To explain the behavior of a robot with a faulty steering mechanism, we would need a more complicated model, based on fairly detailed assumptions about the robot's internal structure and operation.

To be sure, while we could at least conceive of a perfectly well-constructed goal-pursuing robot, completely consistent and completely single-minded in working for his pre-established goal, human beings are seldom that consistent. In some situations, they will be deflected from their objectives by Freudian-type emotional factors, while in others they will fail to pursue any well-defined objectives altogether. Moreover, even if they do aim at well-defined objectives, their limitations in computing (information-processing) ability may prevent them from discovering the most effective strategies (or any reasonably effective strategies) for achieving these objectives. (Of course, any robot of less than infinite structural complexity will be subject to similar computational limitations. But he may not be subject to anything resembling emotional problems.)

Obviously, this means that in *some* situations models of rational behavior will not be very useful in analyzing human behavior – except perhaps after substantial modification (e.g. along the lines suggested by Simon's (1960) theory of limited rationality). Clearly, it is an empirical question what types of social situations lend themselves, and to what extent, to analysis in terms of rational-behavior models. But recent work in political science, in international relations, and in sociology, has shown that a much wider range of social situations seems to admit of rationalistic analysis than most observers would have thought even ten years ago.[3]

3.   THE RATIONAL-BEHAVIOR MODEL OF ECONOMIC THEORY

Even at a common-sense level, the means-ends model is not the only model of rational behavior we use. Another, though perhaps less important, model envisages rational behavior as choosing an object (or a person) satisfying certain stipulated formal (possibly non-causal) *criteria.* For instance, if my aim is to climb the highest mountain in California, then it will be rational for me to climb Mount Whitney, and it will be irrational for me to climb any other mountain. But we would not normally say that climbing Mount Whitney is a *means* to climbing the highest mountain in California, because my climbing of Mount Whitney does not causally *lead* to a climbing of the highest mountain. Rather, it already *is* a climbing of the highest mountain. It is a rational action in the sense of being an action (and, indeed, the only action) satisfying the stipulated criterion.[4]

Thus, it would be rather artificial to subsume criterion-satisfying behavior under the means-ends model of rationality. It is more natural to do the converse, and argue that looking for a means to a given end is a special case of looking for an object satisfying a particular criterion, viz. the criterion of being causally effective in attaining a given end.

This implies that the means-ends concept of rational behavior is too narrow because it fails to cover criterion-satisfying behavior. An even more important limitation of this concept lies in the fact that it restricts rational behavior to a choice among alternative *means* to a given end, and fails to include a rational choice among alternative *ends*. Therefore, it cannot explain why a given person may shift from one end to another.

To overcome this limitation, already 19th and early 20th century economists introduced a broader concept of rationality which defines rational behavior as a choice among alternative ends, on the basis of a given set of *preferences* and a given set of *opportunities* (i.e. a given set of available alternatives). If I am choosing a given end (or a given set of mutually compatible ends, which can be described as a unique composite end), then typically I have to give up many alternative ends. Giving up these alternative ends is the *opportunity cost* of pursuing this particular end. Thus, under this model, rational behavior consists in choosing one specific end, after careful consideration and in full awareness of the opportunity costs of this choice.

This model will often enable us to explain why a given individual has changed over from pursuing one objective to pursuing another, even if his basic preferences have remained the same. The explanation will lie in the fact that the opportunity costs of various possible objectives (i.e. the advantages and the disadvantages associated with them) have changed, or at least the information he has about these opportunity costs has done so.

For example, a given person may seek admission to a particular university, but then may change his mind and fail to attend. He may do so because the tuition fees or other monetary costs have increased; or because the studies he would have to undertake have turned out to be harder or less interesting than he thought they would be; or because he has received unfavorable information about the hoped-for economic advantages of a university degree, etc. All these explanations are compatible with the assumption that, during the whole period, his basic preferences remained the same, and that only the situation (i.e. his opportunity costs), or his information about the situation, have changed.[5]

It is easy to verify that the preferences-opportunities model includes both the means-ends model and the criterion-satisfaction model as special cases.

An important result of economic theory has been to show that, if a given person's preferences satisfy certain consistency and continuity axioms, then these preferences will admit of representation by a well-defined (and, indeed, continuous) utility function. (For proof, see Debreu, 1959, pp. 55–59.) Accordingly, for such a person, rational behavior – as defined by the preferences-opportunities model – will be equivalent to *utility-maximization* (utility-maximization theorem).

4. BAYESIAN DECISION THEORY

Classical economic theory was largely restricted to analyzing human behavior under *certainty*, i.e. under conditions where the decision maker can uniquely predict the outcome of any action he may take (or where one can assume this to be the case at least as a matter of first approximation). It has been left to modern decision theory to extend this analysis to human behavior under risk and under uncertainty.

Both risk and uncertainty refer to situations where the decision maker cannot always uniquely predict the outcomes of his action. But, in the case of *risk*, he will know at least the objective probabilities associated with all possible outcomes. In contrast, in the case of *uncertainty*, even some or all of these objective probabilities will be unknown to him (or may even be undefined altogether).

The utility-maximization model provides a satisfactory characterization of rational behavior under certainty, but fails to do so under risk and under uncertainty. This is so because it is not sufficient to assume that any given lottery (whether it is a 'risky' lottery involving known probabilities, or is an 'uncertain' lottery involving unknown probabilities) will have a well-defined numerical utility to the decision maker. Rather, we need a theory specifying *what value* this utility will have, and how it will depend on the utilities associated with the various prizes. This is exactly what decision theory is trying to specify.

The main conclusion of decision theory is this. If the decision maker's behavior satisfies certain consistency and continuity axioms (a larger number of axioms than we needed to establish the utility-maximization theorem in the case of certainty), then his behavior will be equivalent to *maximizing his expected utility*, i.e. to maximizing the mathematical expectation of his cardinal utility function. In the case of *risk*, this expected utility can be defined in terms of the relevant objective probabilities (which, by assumption, will be known to the decision maker). On the other hand, in the case of *uncertainty*, this expected utility must be defined in terms of the decision maker's own subjective probabilities whenever the relevant objective probabilities are unknown to him (expected-utility maximization theorem).[6]

This result leads to the *Bayesian* approach to decision theory, which proposes to define rational behavior under risk and under uncertainty as expected-utility maximization.[7]

Besides the axioms used already in the case of certainty, we need one additional consistency axiom to establish the expected-utility maximization theorem in the cases of risk and of uncertainty. This axiom is the *sure-thing principle*, which can be stated as follows. "Let X be a bet[8] that would yield a given prize x to the decision maker if a specified event E took place (e.g. if a particular horse won the next race). Let Y be a bet that would yield him another prize y, which he *prefers* over x, if this event E took place. There are no other differences between the two bets. Then, the decision maker will consider bet Y to be *at least as desirable* as bet X." (Actually, unless he assigns zero probability to event E, he will no doubt positively *prefer* bet Y, which would yield the more attractive prize y, if event E took place. But we do not need this slightly stronger assumption.)

In my opinion, it is hard to envisage any rational decision maker who would knowingly violate the sure-thing principle (or who would violate the – somewhat more technical – continuity axiom we need to prove the expected-utility maximization theorem). This fact is, of course, a strong argument in favor of the Bayesian definition of rational behavior. Another important argument lies in the fact that all alternative definitions of rational behavior (and, in particular, all definitions based on the once fashionable maximin principle and on various other related principles) can be shown to lead to highly irrational decisions in many practically important situations. (See Radner and Marschak, 1954; also Harsanyi, 1975a.)

In the case of risk, acceptance of Bayesian theory is now virtually unanimous. In the case of uncertainty, the Bayesian approach is still somewhat controversial, though the last two decades have produced a clear trend toward its growing acceptance by expert opinion. Admittedly, support for Bayesian theory is weaker among scholars working in other fields than it is among decision theorists and game theorists. (I must add that some of the criticism directed against the Bayesian approach has been rather uninformed, and has shown a clear lack of familiarity with the relevant literature.)

5. A GENERAL THEORY OF RATIONAL BEHAVIOR

Whatever the merits of the rationality concept of Bayesian decision theory may be, it is still in need of further generalization, because it does not adequately cover rational behavior in *game situations*, i.e. in situations where the outcome depends on the behavior of two or more rational individuals who may have partly or wholly divergent interests. Game situations may be considered to represent a special case of uncertainty, since in general none of the players will be able to predict the outcome, or even the probabilities associated with different possible outcomes. This is so because he will not be able to predict the strategies of the other players, or even the probabilities associated with their various possible strategies. (To be sure, as we shall argue, at least in principle, game-theoretical analysis does enable each player to discover the solution of the game and, therefore, to predict the strategies of the other players, provided that the latter will act in a rational manner. But the point is that, prior to such a game-theoretical analysis, he will be unable to make such predictions.)

Game theory defines rational behavior in game situations by defining solution concepts for various classes of games.

Since the term 'decision theory' is usually restricted to the theory of rational behavior under risk and under uncertainty, I shall use the term *utility theory* to describe the broader theory which includes both decision theory and the theory of rational behavior under certainty (as established by classical economic theory).

Besides utility theory and game theory, I propose to consider *ethics*, also, as a branch of the general theory of rational behavior, since ethical theory can be based on axioms which represent specializations of some of the axioms used in decision theory (Harsanyi, 1955).

Thus, under the approach here proposed, the *general theory of rational behavior* consists of three branches:

(1) *Utility theory*, which is the theory of *individual* rational be-
     havior under certainty, under risk, and under uncertainty. Its
     main result is that, in these three cases, rational behavior
     consists in *utility maximization* or *expected-utility maximiza-
     tion.*

(2) *Game theory*, which is the theory of rational behavior by *two or
     more* interacting rational individuals, each of them determined
     to maximize his own interests, whether selfish or unselfish, as
     specified by his own utility function (payoff function). (Though
     some or all players may very well assign high utilities to clearly
     altruistic objectives, this need not prevent a conflict of interest
     between them since they may possibly assign high utilities to
     quite *different*, and perhaps strongly conflicting, altruistic objec-
     tives.)

(3) *Ethics*, which is the theory of rational moral value judgments,
     i.e. of rational judgments of preference based on impartial and
     impersonal criteria. I have tried to show that rational moral
     value judgments will involve *maximizing* the *average utility
     level* of all individuals in society. (See Harsanyi, 1953, 1955,
     1958, 1975a, and 1975b.)

Whereas game theory is a theory of possibly conflicting (but not necessarily selfish) *individual* interests, ethics can be regarded as a theory of the *common* interests (or of the general welfare) of society as a whole.

6.   GAMES WITH INCOMPLETE INFORMATION

We speak of a game with *complete information* if the players have full information about all *parameters* defining the game, i.e. about all variables fully determined *before* the beginning of the game. These variables include the players' payoff functions (utility functions), the strategical possibilities available to each player, and the amount of information each player has about all of these variables. We speak of a game with *incomplete information* if some or all of the players have less than full information about these parameters defining the game.

This distinction must not be confused with another, somewhat similar distinction. We speak of a game with *perfect information* if the players always have full information about the *moves* already made in the game, including the *personal moves* made by the individual players and the *chance moves* decided by chance. Thus, perfect information means full information about all game events that took part *after* the beginning of the game. We speak of a game with *imperfect information* if some or all players have less than full information about the moves already made in the game.

It was a major limitation of classical game theory that it could not handle games with *incomplete* information (though it did deal both with games involving perfect and imperfect information). For, many of the most important real-life game situations are games with incomplete information: the players may have only limited knowledge of each other's payoff functions (i.e. of each other's real objectives within the game), and may also know very little about the strategies as well as the information available to the other players.

In the last few years we have discovered how to overcome this limitation. How this is done can be best shown in an example. Suppose we want to analyze arms control negotiations between the United States and the Soviet Union. The difficulty is that neither side really knows the other side's true intentions and technological capabilities. (They may have reasonably good intelligence estimates about each other's weapon systems in actual use, but may know very little about any new military inventions not yet used in actual weapon production.) Now we can employ the following model. The American player, called A, and the Russian player, called R, both can occur in the form of a number of different possible 'types'. For instance, the Russian player could be really R_1, a fellow with very peaceful intentions but with access to very formidable new weapon technologies; and with the expectation that the American player will also have peaceful intentions, yet a ready access to important new technologies. Or, the Russian player could be R_2, who is exactly like R_1, except that he expects the American player to have rather aggressive intentions. Or, the Russian player could be R_3, who shows still another possible combination of all these variables, etc.

Likewise, the American player could be of type A_1 or A_2 or A_3, etc., each of them having a different combination of policy objectives, of access to new technologies, and of expectations about Russian policy objectives and about Russian access to new technologies. (We could, of course, easily add still further variables to this list.)

The game is played as follows. At the beginning of the game, nature conducts a lottery to decide which particular types of the American player and of the Russian player (one type of each) will actually participate in the game. Each possible combination (A_i, R_j) of an American player type and of a Russian player type have a pre-assigned probability p_{ij} of being selected. When a particular pair (A_i, R_j) has been chosen, they will actually play the game. Each player will know his own type but will be ignorant of his opponent's actual type. But, for any given type of his opponent, he will be able to assign a numerical probability to the possibility that his opponent is of this particular type, because each player will know the probability matrix $P = (p_{ij})$.

What this model does is to reduce the original game with *incomplete* information, G, to an artificially constructed game with *complete* information, G^*. The *incomplete* information the players had in G about the basic parameters of the game is represented in the new game G^* as *imperfect* information about a certain chance move at the beginning of the game (viz. the one which determines the types of the players). As the resulting new game G^* is a game with complete (even if with imperfect) information, it is fully accessible to the usual methods of game-theoretical analysis.

The model just described is not the most general model we use in the analysis of games with incomplete information. It makes the assumption that all players' expectations about each other's basic characteristics (or, technically speaking, all players' subjective probability distributions over all possible types of all other players) are sufficiently consistent to be expressible in terms of one basic probability matrix $P = (p_{ij})$. We call this the assumption of *mutually consistent expectations*. In many applications, this is a natural assumption to make and, whenever this is the case, it greatly simplifies the analysis of the game. (See Harsanyi, 1967–68.)

There are, however, cases where this assumption seems to be inappropriate. As Reinhard Selten has pointed out (in private communication – cf. Harsanyi, 1967–68, pp. 496–497), even in such cases, the game will admit of analysis in terms of an appropriate probabilistic model, though a more complicated one than would be needed on the assumption of consistent expectations.

7. NON-COOPERATIVE GAMES AND EQUILIBRIUM POINTS: THE PRISONER'S DILEMMA PROBLEM

We have to distinguish between *cooperative* games, where the players can make fully binding and enforceable commitments (fully binding promises, agreements, and threats, which absolutely *have* to be implemented if the stipulated conditions arise), and *non-cooperative* games, where this is not the case. In real life, what makes commitments fully binding is usually a law-enforcing authority. But in some cases prestige considerations (a fear of losing face) may have similar effects.

Nash (1950 and 1951), who first proposed this distinction, defined cooperative games as games with enforceable commitments *and* with free communication between the players. He defined non-cooperative games as games without enforceable commitments *and* without communication. These were somewhat misleading definitions. Presence or absence of free communication is only of secondary importance. The crucial issue is the possibility or impossibility of binding and enforceable agreements. (For example, in the prisoner's dilemma case, as I shall argue below, the cooperative solution will be unavailable to the players if no enforceable agreements can be made. This will be true regardless of whether the players can talk to each other or not.)

In a cooperative game, the players can agree on any possible combination of strategies since they can be sure that any such agreement would be kept. In contrast, in a non-cooperative game, only self-enforcing agreements are worth making because only self-enforcing agreements have any real chance of implementation.

A self-enforcing agreement is called an equilibrium point. A more exact definition can be stated as follows. A given strategy of a certain player is called a *best reply* to the other players' strategies if it maximizes this player's payoff so long as the other players' strategies are kept constant. A given combination of strategies (containing exactly one strategy for each player) is called an *equilibrium point* if every player's strategy is a best reply to all other players' strategies. The concept of an equilibrium point, also, is due to Nash (1950, 1951).

For example, suppose that the following two-person game is played as a non-cooperative game, so that no enforceable agreements can be made:

	B_1	B_2
A_1	2, 2	0, 3
A_2	3, 0	1, 1

This type of game is called a prisoner's dilemma. (For an explanation of this name, see Luce and Raiffa, 1957, pp. 94–95.)

In this game, the strategy pair (A_2, B_2) is an equilibrium point, because player 1's best reply to B_2 is A_2, whereas player 2's best reply to A_2 is B_2. Indeed, the game has no other equilibrium point. If the two players use their equilibrium strategies A_2 and B_2, then they will obtain the payoffs $(1, 1)$.

Obviously, both players would be better off if they could use the strategies A_1 and B_1, which would yield them the payoffs $(2, 2)$. But these two strategies do not form an equilibrium point. Even if the two players explicitly *agreed* to use A_1 and B_1, they would not do so, and would *know* they would not do so. Even if we assumed for a moment that the two players did expect the strategy pair (A_1, B_1) to be the outcome of the game, *this very expectation would make them use another strategy pair* (A_2, B_2) instead. For instance, if player 1 expected player 2 to use strategy B_1, he himself would not use A_1 but would rather use A_2, since A_2 would be his best reply to player 2's expected strategy B_1. Likewise, if player 2 expected player 1 to use A_1, he himself would not use B_1 but would rather use B_2, since B_2 would be his best reply to player 1's expected strategy A_1.

Of course, if the game were played as a cooperative game, then agreements would be fully enforceable, and the two players would have no difficulty in agreeing to use strategies A_1 and B_1 so as to obtain the higher payoffs $(2, 2)$. Once they agreed on this, they could be absolutely sure that this agreement would be fully observed.

Thus, we must conclude that, if the game is played as a non-cooperative game, then the outcome will be the equilibrium point (A_2, B_2), which is often called the *non-cooperative solution*. On the other hand, if the game is played as a cooperative game, then the outcome will be the non-equilibrium point strategy pair (A_1, B_1), which is called the *cooperative solution*.

More generally, the solution of a non-cooperative game must always be an equilibrium point. In other words, each player's solution strategy must be a best reply to the other players' solution strategies. This is so because the solution, by definition, must be a strategy combination that the players can rationally *use*, and that they can also rationally *expect* one another to use. But, if any given player's solution strategy were *not* his best reply to the other players' solution strategies, then the very expectation that the other players would use their solution strategies would make it rational for this player *not* to use his solution strategy (but rather to use a strategy that was a best reply to the solution strategies he expected the other players to use). Hence, the alleged 'solution' would not satisfy our definition of a solution.

This argument does not apply to a cooperative game, where each player can irrevocably commit himself to using a given strategy even if the latter is *not* a best reply to the other players' strategies. But it does apply to any non-cooperative game, where such a commitment would have no force.

This conclusion is accepted by almost all game theorists. It is, however, rejected by some distinguished scholars from other disciplines, because it seems to justify certain forms of socially undesirable non-cooperative behavior in real-life conflict situations. Their sentiments underlying this theoretical position are easy to understand and deserve our respect, but I cannot say the same thing about their logic. I find it rather hard to comprehend how anybody can deny that there is a fundamental difference between social situations where agreements are strictly enforceable and social situations where this is not the case; or how anybody can deny that, in situations where agreements are wholly unenforceable, the participants may often have every reason to distrust each other's willingness (and sometimes even to distrust each other's very ability) to keep agreements, in particular if there are strong incentives to violate these agreements.

To be sure, it is quite possible that, in a situation that *looks like* a prisoner's dilemma game, the players will be able to achieve the cooperative solution. Usually this will happen because the players are decent persons and therefore attach considerable disutility to using a non-cooperative strategy like A_2 or B_2 when the other player uses a cooperative strategy like A_1 or B_1. Of course, if the players take this attitude, then this will change the payoff matrix of the game. For instance, suppose that both players assign a disutility of 2 units to such an outcome. This will reduce the utility payoff that player 1 associates with the outcome (A_2, B_1) to $3-2=1$. Likewise, it will also reduce the utility payoff that player 2 associates with the outcome (A_1, B_2) to $3-2=1$. (If the players assigned a special disutility to violating an agreement, and then actually agreed to use the strategy pair (A_1, B_1), this would have similar effects on the payoff matrix of the game.) Consequently, the game will now have the following payoff matrix:

	B_1	B_2
A_1	2, 2	0, 1
A_2	1, 0	1, 1

This new game, of course, is no longer a prisoner's dilemma since now *both* (A_1, B_1) *and* (A_2, B_2) are equilibrium points. Hence, even if the game remains formally a non-cooperative game without enforceable agreements, the players will now have no difficulty in reaching the outcome (A_1, B_1), which we used to call the cooperative solution, so as to obtain the payoffs $(2, 2)$. This conclusion, of course, is fully consistent with our theory because now (A_1, B_1) *is* an equilibrium point.

This example shows that we must clearly distinguish between two different problems. One is the problem of whether a game that *looks like* a prisoner's dilemma *is* in fact a prisoner's dilemma: does the proposed payoff matrix of the game (which would make the game a prisoner's dilemma) correctly express the players' true payoff functions, in accordance with their real preferences and their real strategy objectives within the game? This is *not* a game-theoretical question, because game theory regards the players' payoff functions as *given*. It is, rather, an empirical question about the players' psychological make-up. The other question *is* a game-theoretical question: it is the question of how to define the solution of the game, once the payoff matrix has been correctly specified. A good deal of confusion can be avoided if these two questions are kept strictly apart.

As a practical matter, social situations not permitting enforceable agreements often have a socially very undesirable incentive structure, and may give rise to many very painful human problems. But these problems cannot be solved by arguing that people should act as if agreements were enforceable, even though they are not; or that people should trust each other, even though they have very good reasons to withhold this trust. The solution, if there is one, can only lie in actually providing effective incentives to keep agreements (or in persuading people to assign high utility to keeping agreements, even in the absence of external incentives). What we have to do, if it can be done, is to *change* non-cooperative games into cooperative games by making agreements enforceable, rather than pretend that we live in a make-believe world, where we can take non-cooperative games as they are, and then analyze them simply as if they were cooperative games, if we so desire.

I have discussed at some length the principle that the solution of a non-cooperative game must be an equilibrium point, because this principle will play an important role in the game-theoretical investigations I am going to report on.

8. PERFECT EQUILIBRIUM POINTS

After Nash's discovery of the concept of equilibrium points in 1950, for many years game theorists were convinced that the only rationality requirement in a non-cooperative game was that the players' strategies should form an equilibrium point. But in 1965 Reinhard Selten proposed counterexamples to show that even equilibrium points might involve irrational behavior (Selten, 1965). He has suggested that only a special class of equilibrium points, which he called *perfect* equilibrium points, represent truly rational behavior in a non-cooperative game.

Since the difference between perfect and imperfect equilibrium points is obscured in the normal-form representation,[9] let us consider the following two-person non-cooperative game, given in extensive form (game-tree form):

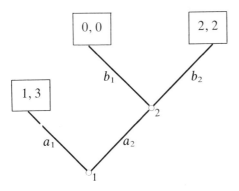

In this game, the first move belongs to player 1. He can choose between moves a_1 and a_2. If he chooses a_1, then the game will end with the payoffs $(1, 3)$ to the two players, without player 2 having any move at all. On the other hand, if player 1 chooses move a_2, then player 2 has a choice between moves b_1 and b_2. If he chooses the former, then the game will end with the payoffs $(0, 0)$; while if he chooses the latter, then the game will end with the payoffs $(2, 2)$. The normal form of this game is as follows:

	B_1	B_2
A_1	1, 3	1, 3
A_2	0, 0	2, 2

The players' strategies have the following interpretation. Strategy A_1 (or A_2) means that player 1 will choose move a_1 (or a_2) at the beginning of the game. On the other hand, strategy B_1 (or B_2) means that player 2 will choose move b_1 (or b_2) *if player 1 chooses move a_2* (while if player 1 chooses move a_1, then player 2 will do nothing). Player 2's strategies can be described only in terms of these *conditional* statements since he will have a move only if player 1 chooses move a_2.

A look at the normal form will reveal that the game has two pure-strategy equilibrium points, *viz.* $E_1 = (A_1, B_1)$ and $E_2 = (A_2, B_2)$. E_2 is a perfectly reasonable equilibrium point. But, as I propose to show, E_1 is not: it involves irrational behavior, and irrational expectations by the players about each other's behavior.

In fact, player 1 will use strategy A_1 (as E_1 requires him to do) only if he expects player 2 to use strategy B_1. (For if player 2 used B_2, then player 1 would be better off by using A_2.) But it is *irrational* for player 1 to expect player 2 to use strategy B_1, i.e. to expect player 2 to make move b_1 should player 1 himself make move a_2. This is so because move b_1 will yield player 2 only the payoff 0, whereas move b_2 would yield him the payoff 2.

To put it differently, player 2 will obviously prefer the outcome (A_1, B_1), yielding him 3 units of utility, over the outcome (A_2, B_2), yielding him only 2 units. Therefore, player 2 may very well try to induce player 1 to use strategy A_1, i.e. to make move a_1: for instance, he may threaten to use strategy B_1, i.e. to punish player 1 by making move b_1, should player 1 counter his wishes by making move a_2. But the point is that this would *not* be a credible threat because, by making move b_1, player 2 would not only punish player 1 but rather would just as much punish himself. This is so because move b_1 would reduce *both* of their payoffs to 0 (while the alternative move b_2 would give both of them payoffs of 2 units).

To be sure, if player 2 could irrevocably *commit* himself to punish player 1 in this way, and could do this *before* player 1 had made his move, then it would be rational for player 2 to make such a commitment in order to deter player 1 from making move a_2. But, in actual fact, player 2 cannot make such a commitment because this is a non-cooperative game. On the other hand, if player 2 is *not* compelled by such a prior commitment to punish player 1, then he will have no incentive to do so since, once player 1 has made his move, player 2 cannot gain anything by punishing him at the cost of reducing his own payoff at the same time.

To conclude, $E_1 = (A_1, B_1)$ is an irrational equilibrium point because it is based on the unreasonable assumption that player 2 would punish player 1 if the latter made move a_2 – even though this punishing move would reduce not only player 1's payoff but also player 2's own payoff. Following Selten's proposal, we shall call such unreasonable equilibrium points *imperfect* equilibrium points. In contrast, equilibrium points like $E_2 = (A_2, B_2)$, which are not open to such objections, will be called *perfect* equilibrium points.

The question naturally arises how it is possible that an equilibrium point should use a highly irrational strategy like B_1 as an equilibrium strategy at all. The answer lies in the fact that, as long as the two players follow their equilibrium strategies A_1 and B_1, player 2 will never come in a position *where he would have to make the irrational move b_1* prescribed by strategy B_1. For, strategy B_1 would require him to make move b_1 only if player 1 made move a_2. But this contingency will never arise because player 1 follows strategy A_1 (which requires him to make move a_1 rather than a_2).[10]

In other words, strategy B_1 would require player 2 to make move b_1 only if the game reached the point marked by 2 on our game tree[11] (since this is the point where he had to choose between moves b_1 and b_2). But, so long as the players follow the strategies A_1 and B_1, this point will never be reached by the game.

This fact suggests a mathematical procedure for eliminating imperfect equilibrium points from the game. All we have to do is to assume that, whenever any player tries to make a specific move, he will have a very small but positive probability ε of making a 'mistake', which will divert him into making another move than he wanted to make, so that *every* possible move will occur with some positive probability. The resulting game will be called a *perturbed game*. As a result of the players' assumed 'mistakes', in a perturbed game every point of the game tree will always be reached with a positive probability whenever the game is played. It can be shown that, if the game is perturbed in this way, only the perfect equilibrium points of the original game will remain equilibrium points in the perturbed game, whereas the imperfect equilibrium points will lose the status of equilibrium points. (More exactly, we can find the perfect equilibrium points of the original game if we take the equilibrium points of the perturbed game, and then let the mistake probabilities ε go to zero.)

Thus, in our example, suppose that, if player 1 tries to use strategy A_1, then he will be able to implement the intended move a_1 only with probability $(1 - \varepsilon)$, and will be forced to make the unintended move a_2 with the remaining small probability ε. Consequently, it will not be costless any more for player 2 to use strategy B_1 when player 1 uses A_1. This is so because now player 1 will make move a_2 with a positive probability and, therefore, player 2 will have to counter this by making the costly move b_1, likewise with a positive probability. As a result, strategy B_1 will no longer be a best reply to A_1, and (A_1, B_1) will no longer be an equilibrium point.

The difference between perfect and imperfect equilibrium points can be easily recognized in the extensive form of a game but is often hidden in the normal form. This implies that, contrary to a view that used to be the commonly accepted view by game theorists, the normal form of the game in general fails to provide all the information we need for an adequate game-theoretical analysis of the game, and we may have to go back to the extensive form to recover some of the missing information.

On the other hand, if the normal form often contains too little information, the extensive form usually contains far too much, including many unnecessary details about the chance moves and about the time sequence in which individual moves have to be made. For this reason, Reinhard Selten and I have defined an intermediate game form, called the *agent normal form*, which omits the unnecessary details but retains the essential information about the game. (We obtain the agent normal form if we replace each player by as many 'agents' as the number of his information sets in the game, and then construct a normal form with these agents as the players.) For a more extensive and more rigorous discussion of perfect equilibrium points and of the agent normal form, see Selten (1975).

9. NON-COOPERATIVE BARGAINING MODELS FOR COOPERATIVE GAMES

Ever since 1944 (the year when von Neumann and Morgenstern first published the *Theory of Games and Economic Behavior*), most research in game theory has been devoted either to a study of the mathematical properties of saddle points in *two-person zero-sum* games, or to a construction and study of solution concepts for *cooperative* games. Many very interesting cooperative solution concepts were proposed. But this work on cooperative games showed little theoretical unity: taken as a group, the different solution concepts that were suggested shared few common theoretical assumptions, and no clear criteria emerged to decide under what conditions one particular solution concept was to be used and under what conditions another.

Part of the problem is that the authors of the different solution concepts have seldom made it sufficiently clear what institutional arrangements (negotiation rules) each particular solution concept is meant to assume about the bargaining process among the players, through which these players are supposed to reach an agreement about the final outcome of the game. Yet, it is well known that the very same cooperative game may have quite different outcomes, depending on the actual negotiation rules governing this bargaining process in any particular case. The nature of the agreements likely to arise will be often quite sensitive to such factors as who can talk to whom and, in particular, who can talk to whom *first*, ahead of other people; the degree to which negotiations are kept public, or can be conducted in private by smaller groups if the participants so desire; the conditions that decide whether any agreement remains open to repeal and to possible re-negotiation, or is made final and irrevocable; the possibility or impossibility of unilaterally making binding promises and/or threats, etc.

As a simple example, consider the following three-person cooperative game (called a three-person majority game). Each player, acting
alone, can only achieve a zero payoff. Any coalition of two players can
obtain a joint payoff of $100. The three-person coalition of all three
players can likewise obtain a joint payoff of $100. Obviously, in this
game, if pairs of players can meet separately, then the two players who
manage to meet first are very likely to form a two-person coalition,
and to divide the $100 in a ratio 50:50 between them. In contrast, if
the negotiation rules disallow pairwise meetings, and if the negotiation
time permitted is too short for forming any two-person coalition during
the three-person negotiating session, then the likely outcome is a
three-person coalition, with payoffs $33\frac{1}{3}:33\frac{1}{3}:33\frac{1}{3}$. Finally, under most
other negotiation rules, both two-person and three-person coalitions
will arise from time to time, and the probability of either outcome will
depend on the extent to which these rules tend to help or hinder
two-person agreements.

Another limitation of most cooperative solution concepts is this.
Their application is basically restricted to fully cooperative games, and
does not extend to that very wide range of real-life game situations
which have a status intermediate between fully cooperative games and
fully non-cooperative games – such as social situations where some
kinds of agreements are enforceable while others are not, or where
different agreements may be enforceable to different extents and with
different probabilities; or where enforceable agreements are possible
among some particular players but are impossible among other
players; or where enforceable agreements cannot be concluded at
some stages of the game but can be concluded at other stages, etc. In
many contexts, it is particularly regrettable that most of these cooperative solution concepts are inapplicable to games possessing a strongly
sequential structure, making the emergence of agreements a very
gradual process, later agreements being built on earlier agreements
and extending the former in various ways.

Yet, John Nash, when he introduced the very concepts of cooperative and of non-cooperative games, also suggested what, in my opinion,
is a possible remedy to these deficiencies in the theory of cooperative
games (Nash, 1951, p. 295). He suggested that an analysis of any

cooperative game should start with constructing a precisely defined formal bargaining model (bargaining game) to represent the bargaining process among the players. Of course, this bargaining model must provide a mathematical representation, in the abstract language appropriate to such models, for the negotation rules we want to assume, whether on empirical or on theoretical grounds, to govern this bargaining process. Then, according to Nash's proposal, this bargaining model should be analyzed as a *non-cooperative* game, by a careful study of its equilibrium points.

Nash's suggestion is based on the assumption that close cooperation among the players in a cooperative game usually requires a prior agreement about the payoffs, which, in most cases, can be achieved only by bargaining among the players. But this bargaining itself must have the nature of a non-cooperative game, unless we want to assume that the players will agree in an even earlier subsidiary bargaining game on how they will act in the main bargaining game – which would be not only a rather implausible assumption but would also lead to an infinite regress.

Nash's proposal, if it can be successfully implemented, will enable us to unify the whole theory of cooperative games, because it provides a uniform method of analysis for all cooperative games. Of course, even under Nash's proposal, it will remain true that any given cooperative game may have a number of different solutions, depending on the details of the bargaining process assumed to occur among the players. But, as we have argued, this is how it should be, since in real life different bargaining methods do lead to different outcomes. Yet, the game-theoretical analysis of this bargaining process can be based on the same theoretical principles in all cases.[12]

Indeed, Nash's approach will result in a unification of *both* the theory of cooperative games *and* of the theory of non-cooperative games, because it essentially reduces the problem of solving a cooperative game to the problem of solving a non-cooperative bargaining game. Moreover, it can be easily extended to games which have any kind of intermediate status between fully cooperative games and fully non-cooperative games (including games of a sequential nature, mentioned before).

10. A BAYESIAN SOLUTION CONCEPT
FOR NON-COOPERATIVE GAMES

Nash's proposal, however, runs into a very basic difficulty – the same difficulty, which, up to very recently, also prevented the emergence of any really useful theory of non-cooperative games. This difficulty lies in the fact that almost any interesting non-cooperative game – including almost any interesting non-cooperative bargaining game – will have a great many, and often infinitely many, very different equilibrium points. (This remains true even if we restrict ourselves to perfect equilibrium points.) This means that, if all we can say is that the outcome of the game will be an equilibrium point (or even that it will be a perfect equilibrium point), then we are saying little more than that almost anything can happen in the game.

For instance, consider the very simplest kind of two-person bargaining game, in which the two players have to divide $100. If they cannot agree on how to divide it, then both of them will receive zero payoffs. This game can be analyzed by means of the following formal bargaining model. Both players name a number between 0 and 100. Let the numbers named by players 1 and 2 be x_1 and x_2. (Intuitively, these numbers represent the two players' payoff demands.) If $x_1 + x_2 \leq 100$, then player 1 will obtain $\$x_1$ and player 2 will obtain $\$x_2$. On the other hand, if $x_1 + x_2 > 0$, then both players will get $0.

If we assume that money can be divided in any possible fractional amount, then this game has infinitely many equilibrium points, since any pair (x_1, x_2) of payoff demands is an equilibrium point so long as $x_1 + x_2 = 100$. (Of course, by the rules we have assumed for the game, we must also have $0 \leq x_i \leq 100$ for $i = 1, 2$.) But even if we assumed that money can be divided only in amounts corresponding to whole numbers of dollars, the game will still have 101 equilibrium points. (Of these, 99 equilibrium points will even be perfect equilibrium points. Only the two 'extreme' equilibrium points giving one player $100 and giving the other player $0 turn out to be imperfect.) The situation will be even worse if we study more interesting, and therefore inevitably more complicated, bargaining games.

In view of these facts, several years ago Reinhard Selten and I decided to look into the possibility of defining a new solution concept for non-cooperative games, which will always select *one* particular equilibrium point as the solution for the game. This research project proved to be much more difficult than we had anticipated. But in 1974 we did find such a solution concept which seems to satisfy all intuitive and mathematical requirements. Conceptually, it amounts to an extension of the Bayesian approach, so successful in the analysis of one-person decision situations, to an analysis of non-cooperative games. The definition of this solution concept is based on the disturbed agent normal form of the game (see Section 8 above).

Let me introduce the following notation. We shall assume that a given player i $(i = 1, 2, ..., n)$ has K_i different pure strategies. Therefore, a mixed strategy s_i of player i will be a probability vector of the form $s_i = (s_i^1, s_i^2, ..., s_i^{K_i})$, where s_i^k $(k = 1, 2, ..., K_i)$ is the probability that this mixed strategy s_i assigns to the kth pure strategy of player i.

A strategy combination of all n players will be denoted as $s = (s_1, s_2, ..., s_n)$. Let $\bar{s}_i$ denote the strategy combination we obtain if we omit player i's strategy s_i from the strategy combination s. Thus, $\bar{s}_i$ is a strategy combination of the $(n - 1)$ players *other* than player i. We can write $\bar{s}_i = (s_1, ..., s_{i-1}, s_{i+1}, ..., s_n)$.

Our solution is defined in two steps. As a first step, we construct a *prior probability distribution* p_i, over the pure strategies of each player i $(i = 1, 2, ..., n)$. The second step involves a mathematical procedure which selects one specific equilibrium point $s^* = (s_1^*, s_2^*, ..., s_n^*)$ as the solution of the game, on the basis of these n prior probability distributions $p_1, p_2, ..., p_n$.

Each prior probability distribution p_i over the pure strategies of a given player i has the form of a probability vector $p_i = (p_i^1, p_i^2, ..., p_i^{K_i})$, where each component p_i^k $(k = 1, 2, ..., K_i)$ is the initial *subjective* probability that every other player j $(j \neq i)$ is assumed to assign to the possibility that player i will use his kth pure strategy in the game. Consequently, the prior probability distribution p_i is a probability vector of the same mathematical form as is any mixed strategy s_i of player i. But, of course, p_i has a very different game-theoretical interpretation. Whereas a mixed strategy s_i expresses the *objective* probabilities s_i^k that player i *himself* chooses to associate with his various pure strategies as a matter of his own strategical decision, the prior probability distribution p_i expresses the *subjective* probabilities p_i^k

that the *other* players are assumed to associate with player i's various pure strategies, simply because they do not know in advance which particular strategy player i is going to use.

The numerical prior probability p_i^k our theory assigns to a given pure strategy of each player i is meant to express the theoretical probability that a rational individual, placed in player i's position, will actually use this particular pure strategy in the game. More specifically, p_i^k is meant to express the theoretical probability that player i will find himself in a situation where his best reply is to use this particular pure strategy. (This theoretical probability p_i^k, of course, is not directly given, but can only be obtained from a suitable probabilistic model about the players' behavior in the game.)

For convenience, I shall write the n-vector consisting of the n prior probability distributions as $p = (p_1, p_2, ..., p_n)$. I shall write the $(n-1)$-vector consisting of the $(n-1)$ prior probability distributions associated with the $(n-1)$ players other than player i as $\overline{p}_i = (p_1, ..., p_{i-1}, p_{i+1}, ..., p_n)$. Thus, $\overline{p}_i$ is the $(n-1)$-vector we obtain if we omit the ith component p_i from the n-vector p.

The second step in defining our solution involves a mathematical procedure, based on Bayesian ideas, for selecting one particular equilibrium point s^* as solution, when the vector p of all prior probability distributions is given. The simplest Bayesian model would be to assume that each player i would use a strategy s_i that was his best reply to the prior probability distribution vector $\overline{p}_i$ he would associate with the other $(n-1)$ players' pure strategies, and then to define the solution as the strategy combination $s = (s_1, s_2, ..., s_n)$. But this simple-minded approach is unworkable because in general this best-reply strategy combination s will not be an equilibrium point of the game.

Accordingly, our theory uses a mathematical procedure, called the *tracing procedure*, which takes this best-reply strategy combination s as a starting point, but then systematically modifies this strategy combination in a continuous manner, until it is finally transformed into an equilibrium point s^*, which will serve as the solution of the game.

This mathematical procedure is meant to model the psychological process, to be called the *solution process*, by which the players' expectations converge to a specific equilibrium point as the solution of the game. At the beginning, the players' initial expectations about the other players' strategies will correspond to the subjective probability distributions (prior distributions) p_i, and their initial reaction to these expectations will be an inclination to use their best-reply strategies s_i. Then, they will gradually modify their expectations and their tentative strategy choices until in the end *both* their expectations and their strategy choices will converge to the equilibrium strategies s_i^* corresponding to the solution s^*. (See Harsanyi, 1975.)

Of course, within the confines of this paper, I could do no more than sketch the barest outlines of our solution concept for non-cooperative games and, more generally, could draw only a very incomplete picture of some recent work in game theory. But I feel my paper has achieved its purpose if it has induced a few people from other disciplines to take some interest in the results of Bayesian decision theory and in some recent developments in game theory, and in the implications both of these may have for a deeper understanding of the nature of rational behavior.

NOTES

* From *Logic, Methodology and Philosophy of Science*, (ed. by R. Butts and J. Hintikka), D. Reidel, Dordrecht, Holland, to be published.
[1] The author wishes to express his thanks to the National Science Foundation for supporting this research by Grant GS-3222 to the Center for Research in Management Science, University of California, Berkeley.
[2] For references, see Harsanyi (1969, p. 517, footnote 9).
[3] See footnote 2.
[4] The concept of criterion-satisfying behavior is probably not very important in everyday life. But it is very important in ethics (see Harsanyi, 1958).
[5] Of course, in many cases, when a person has changed his goals, the most natural explanation will be that his preferences themselves have changed. In such cases, the model of rational behavior will be inapplicable, or at least will have to be supplemented by other explanatory theories, e.g. by learning theory, etc.
[6] A very simple proof of this theorem for *risk* is given by Luce and Raiffa (1957, pp. 23–31). But note that their Assumptions 1 and 5 could be easily stated as one axiom, whereas Assumption 6 could be omitted because it follows from the other axioms. (Of course, the use of extra axioms was intentional and made it possible for the authors to simplify their statement of the proof.) Note also that their substitutability axiom (Assumption 4) could be replaced by a form of the sure-thing principle (see below).

A simple proof of the theorem for *uncertainty* is found in Anscombe and Aumann (1963).

[7] The term 'Bayesian approach' is often restricted to the proposal of using expected-utility maximization as a definition of rational behavior in the case of *uncertainty*, where expected utility must be computed in terms of *subjective* probabilities.

[8] The terms 'bet' and 'lottery' will be used interchangeably.

[9] For a non-technical explanation of the terms 'normal form' and 'extensive form', see Luce and Raiffa (1957, Chapter 3).

[10] From a logical point of view, strategy B_1 does satisfy the formal criteria for an equilibrium strategy because, in applying these criteria, the conditional statement defining strategy B_1 ('player 2 would make move b_1 if player 1 made move a_2') is interpreted as *material implication*. In contrast, B_1 fails to satisfy our informal criteria for a 'rational' strategy because, in applying these latter criteria, the same conditional statement is automatically interpreted as a *subjunctive conditional*.

[11] We say that a given point of the game tree is *reached* by the game if it either represents the starting position in the game or is reached by a branch representing an actual move by a player or by chance. Thus, in our example, the point marked by 1 is always reached whereas the point marked by 2 is reached only if player 1 chooses to make move a_2 (rather than move a_1).

[12] While Nash's proposal has many advantages, it certainly does not provide an easy routine method for solving cooperative games because, except in the very simplest cases, finding a suitable formal bargaining model for any given game – just as a modeling of any other complicated dynamic process – may be a very difficult task, requiring a good deal of insight and ingenuity, and subject to no mechanical rules.

BIBLIOGRAPHY

Anscombe, F. J. and Aumann, R. J.: 1963, 'A Definition of Subjective Probability', *Annals of Mathematical Statistics* **34**, 199–205.

Debreu, G.: 1959, *Theory of Value*, John Wiley & Sons, New York.

Harsanyi, J. C.: 1953, 'Cardinal Utility in Welfare Economics and in the Theory of Risk-taking', *Journal of Political Economy* **61**, 434–435.

Harsanyi, J. C.: 1955, 'Cardinal Welfare, Individualistic Ethics, and Interpersonal Comparisons of Utility', *Journal of Political Economy* **63**, 309–321.

Harsanyi, J. C.: 1958, 'Ethics in Terms of Hypothetical Imperatives', *Mind* **47**, 305–316.

Harsanyi, J. C.: 1967–68, 'Games with Incomplete Information Played by 'Bayesian' Players', *Management Science* **14**, 159–182, 320–334, and 486–502.

Harsanyi, J. C.: 1969, 'Rational-Choice Models of Political Behavior vs. Functionalist and Conformist Theories', *World Politics* **21**, 513–538.

Harsanyi, J. C.: 1975, 'The Tracing Procedure: A Bayesian Approach to Defining a Solution for *n*-Person Non-cooperative Games', *International Journal of Game Theory* **4**, 61–94.

Harsanyi, J. C.: 1975a, 'Can the Maximin Principle Serve as a Basis for Morality? A Critique of John Rawls's Theory', *American Political Science Review* **59**, 594–606.

Harsanyi, J. C.: 1975b, 'Nonlinear Social Welfare Functions', *Theory and Decision* **7**, 61–82.

Luce, R. D. and Raiffa, H.: 1957, *Games and Decisions*, John Wiley & Sons, New York.

Nash, J. F.: 1950, 'Equilibrium Points in *n*-Person Games', *Proceedings of the National Academy of Sciences, U.S.A.* **36**, 48–49.

Nash, J. F.: 1951, 'Non-cooperative Games', *Annals of Mathematics* **54**, 286-295.

Radner, R. and Marschak, J.: 1954, 'Note on Some Proposed Decision Criteria', in R. M. Thrall *et al.*, *Decision Processes*, John Wiley & Sons, New York, 1954, pp. 61–68.

Selten, R.: 1965, 'Spieltheoretische Behandlung eines Oligopolmodells mit Nachfrageträgheit', *Zeitschrift für die gesamte Staatswissenschaft* **121**, 301–324 and 667–689.

Selten, R.: 1975, 'Reexamination of the Perfectness Concept for Equilibrium Points in Extensive Games', *International Journal of Game Theory* **4**, 25–55.

Simon, H. A.: 1960, *The New Science of Management Decision*, Harper & Brothers, New York.

von Neumann, J. and Morgenstern, O.: 1944, *Theory of Games and Economic Behavior*, Princeton University Press, Princeton, N.J.

RATIONAL-CHOICE MODELS OF
POLITICAL BEHAVIOR vs. FUNCTIONALIST
AND CONFORMIST THEORIES*

I. INTRODUCTION

After a virtual neglect for several decades, in the last twenty years renewed interest has been shown in a general theory of social behavior. Most of this theoretical work has depended on two main postulates. One is the *functionalist* (sometimes called structural-functional) approach to the explanation of social institutions, based on the assumption that the *social institutions* of a given society can best be understood in terms of their *social functions,* that is, in terms of the contributions they make to the maintenance of social systems as a whole. For lack of an established technical term, we shall call the other postulate the *conformist* approach to the explanation of *individual behavior.* it is based on the assumption that uniformities of individual behavior in a given society can best be understood in terms of certain commonly accepted *social values*, which most members of the society tend to internalize during their socialization process.

The most elaborate and best known theoretical framework based on these two postulates is that of Talcott Parsons,[1] but the theoretical work of a number of other social scientists has also been based on similar assumptions.[2]

However, even though functionalist and conformist theories have enjoyed considerable popularity in recent years, they have also provoked widespread criticism.[3] Most critics agree on the following points:

(1) These theories overstate the degree of consensus and social integration found in empirical societies, and overlook the important role that conflicts of interest and disagreements over social values play in social life, and particularly in the political process as we know it.

(2) These theories have an unduly static and conservative bias: at best they are static theories of social equilibrium, rather than dynamic theories of social change.

(3) As Homans[4] has pointed out about Parsons' approach (but the same

is true about other functionalist and conformist theories in their present form), Parsons' theory is not a 'theory' at all in the sense in which this term is used in the empirical sciences, such as the natural sciences, economics, and behavioral psychology. In these sciences 'theory' means a *hypothetico-deductive theory* explaining (and possibly predicting) a large number of empirical facts from a few relatively simple theoretical assumptions or axioms. From a logical point of view, such a theory is a set of propositions, all derivable from a few axioms by strict logical (and possibly mathematical) reasoning. In contrast, Parsons' theory is a set of concepts and definitions, rather than a set of propositions; and obviously it is-even less a set of propositions forming a hypothetico-deductive system.

We shall discuss these and some other criticisms of functionalist and conformist theories in greater detail. But of course it is not enough to show that these theories have some important analytical and empirical deficiencies. The real question is whether there is any alternative theoretical approach not open to similar objections. Our main purpose in this paper is to show that such an alternative approach is in fact provided by theories based on the concept of rational choice (rational behavior, or rational decision-making) – borrowed from economics, but appropriately generalized for the analysis of noneconomic behavior.

Unlike functionalist theories, theories of rational behavior have a natural tendency to take a hypothetico-deductive form, and to explain a wide variety of empirical facts in terms of a small number of theoretical assumptions (such as assumptions about the actual objectives of people's behavior, about the resources and the information available to them, etc.). Again, unlike functionalist theories, rational-behavior theories can account for social stability and for social change with equal facility; and, by drawing on the resource of modern game theory, they can readily analyze both social conflict and social cooperation, and even those uneasy mixtures of the two that characterize most empirical social situations.[5]

II. THE CONCEPT OF RATIONAL BEHAVIOR

On the commonsense level the concept of rational behavior usually refers to choosing the appropriate means for achieving some given end. For example, we say that it will be rational for me to take a jet if my goal is to get from New York to London within a few hours, and that it would be irrational for me to go by ship because that way I could not achieve my goal.

Already at this commonsese level the concept of rational behavior has very considerable explanatory power. For instance, my wanting to make a trip from New York to London will explain a long sequence of actions I have undertaken in order to achieve this goal.

However, classical economics has substantially increased the explanatory power of the concept of rational behavior, by extending it from choices between alternative means to a given end, to choices between alternative ends. Under this more general concept, a person's behavior will be rational if he chooses among different goals according to a consistent scale of preferences, that is, according to the relative importance or utility he assigns to each particular goal.

Once we adopt this broader concept of rationality, we are no longer restricted to the analysis of human behavior in pursuing some fixed goals, but can extend our analysis to changes in people's goals. For instance, we can explain why a person will change his plans and will decide against a trip to London if the attraction of this trip significantly decreases, or if the attraction of alternative ways of spending his time and money significantly increases.

Significant further generalizations of the concept of rational behavior have been achieved by modern decision theory and game theory – by the former in relation to rational behavior under risk and uncertainty, and by the latter in relation to rational behavior in situations involving strategic interaction with other rational opponents.[6]

Finally, we have to mention the important developments in the theory of rational behavior associated with Herbert A. Simon's name.[7] Normative theories of rational choice, from classical economics to modern game theory, ignore the limited information-processing ability of human decision-makers, and so cannot be expected to make fully realistic predictions about the human decision-making process. In contrast, Simon's theory of *limited* rationality is a theory of rational behavior that tries to take full account of the limitations of human information-processing ability. Moreover, unlike normative theories of rationality, it is not merely a theory of rational choice among given alternatives. Rather, it is also a theory of how specific *new* decision-problems actually emerge and attract the attention of the relevant decision-makers; and it is also a theory of how *new* alternatives (new policy proposals) are invented and come to be considered in the decision-making process.

III. RATIONAL-CHOICE MODELS OF POLITICAL BEHAVIOR

Of course the suggestion of using rational-choice models in the analysis of noneconomic social behavior is not a novelty. Indeed, we might very well argue that at least two important strands of thought in traditional political philosophy, viz., the interest-group theory of internal politics and the national-interest theory of international politics, are in effect imprecise and unformalized versions of some kind of rational-choice approach. The same may be argued about Marxist theories of class interest.

To be sure, the family resemblance between these traditional 'interest theories' and rational-choice theories in a modern sense should not be overstated. Precisely because of the use of ill-defined concepts and of imprecisely stated theoretical assumptions, these traditional theories have never made full use of the intellectual resources of the rational-choice approach, and have left a number of important analytical questions unanswered. For example, the very concept of 'interest', so basic to these theories, has never been made sufficiently precise. In particular, there has been no real attempt to clarify the relationship between people's economic and noneconomic interests, between their short-run and long-run interests, between individual and group interests, and again between individual or group interests and more general social interests on a national or international level. There has been no theoretical analysis of the conditions leading to peaceful compromise agreements, or of those leading to social conflicts of various scopes and intensities. There has been no attempt to specify the laws governing coalition formation among different social groups, or to understand the general factors determining the relative bargaining power of various groups.[8]

However, in recent years there have also been a number of attempts, some of them in my opinion very successful, to use more rigorous and more precisely stated rational choice models in the analysis of noneconomic social behavior, and particularly of political behavior.[9]

Yet, before rational-choice models can achieve reasonably wide use in the social sciences outside economics, we shall have to solve a number of important theoretical problems.

IV. THE CHOICE OF MOTIVATIONAL ASSUMPTIONS

One such problem is what motivational assumptions to use in our analysis of noneconomic social behavior. In technical terms, this amounts to asking what assumptions to make about the nature of people's utility functions – about the goals they are trying to achieve, and about the relative importance they attach to each particular goal.

The explanatory power of any rational-behavior theory depends on its ability to explain a wide variety of possibly quite complex empirical facts about people's behavior in terms of a few relatively simple motivational assumptions. If we make our motivational assumptions complicated enough, we can 'explain' any kind of behavior – which of course means that we are explaining absolutely nothing. To take an extreme example, we could 'explain' any conceivable action of a given individual simply in terms of some desire (or preference) on his part to act in this particular way. Obviously this would be a completely useless tautological explanation.

One important reason for the remarkably great explanatory power of classical economic theory lies precisely in the extreme simplicity of its motivational assumptions, which make economic self-interest virtually the only motivating force of human behavior, at least in economic activities.[10]

Downs has proposed a theory of political behavior based on very similar motivational assumptions.[11] According to his theory, both the professional politicians and the voters are motivated by self-interest, and indeed largely by economic self-interest. The main objective of each politician is to be elected or reelected to office at the next election, whereas that of each voter is to elect a government whose policies will favor his own economic (and other) interests. As far as Downs' theory really succeeds in explaining people's actual political behavior in terms of these strikingly simple motivational assumptions, it again represents a very powerful theory of human behavior, whose explanatory power approaches that of economic theory.

Of course, nobody denies that this one-motive theory of human motivation, which makes economic self-interest the only important objective of human behavior, represents a very drastic and unrealistic oversimplification of human motivation as we know it. It is really quite surprising – yet it is a clearly established and very important empirical fact – that a major segment of real-life economic and political behavior *can* actually be reasonably well explained in terms of this simplistic motivational assumption.

Nevertheless, in my opinion it is an equally clearly established empirical fact that many important aspects of everyday economic and political behavior *cannot* be explained in terms of this over-simple theory of human motivation. Even in economic life, many aspects of people's behavior cannot be explained without recognizing that many individuals are motivated partly by noneconomic and/or nonegoistic motives.

In political life, noneconomic and/or nonegoistic motives seem to be even more important. Self-interest cannot explain even the very basic fact that many people choose to vote at election time at the cost of some personal inconvenience, even though their chances of obtaining personal benefits, let alone economic benefits, as a result of their voting are virtually nil. Likewise, for better or worse, voluntary party workers often seem to be motivated primarily by ideological considerations rather than by self-interest (or even by their party's interest in winning the next election). Indeed, even some professional politicians do not seem to be wholly immune to the temptation of sacrificing self-interest to ideology. No less obvious is the importance of noneconomic and nonegoistic motives in social activities outside the economic and political fields.

In order to do justice to these empirical facts, in my opinion we have to replace the one-motive theory of purely egoistic economic motivation with less restrictive motivational assumptions. To be sure, this means replacing an extremely simple motivational theory by a somewhat more complicated one. But the justification of this move is that at the cost of a small amount of additional complexity in our motivational assumptions we shall obtain a theory explaining a much broader range of empirical facts about people's actual behavior. At the same time, this move will also have the result of bringing our formal assumptions about human motivation much closer to what common observation and introspection tell us about the psychological forces actually motivating human behavior.

V. THE PROBLEM OF RELATIVE UTILITY WEIGHTS

Of course, as soon as we introduce several distinct motives into our theory, instead of postulating economic self-interest as the only motivating force, we are immediately faced with the question of what the relative strength will be of each of these motives in different social situations. Analytically this amounts to asking what relative utility weights people's utility functions will assign to various economic and noneconomic objectives. Conceptually this is completely analogous to asking what relative utility weights (marginal utility rations) people's utility functions will assign to various economic commodities.

The difficulty is that for the time being we cannot predict on the basis of theoretical considerations, or can do so only to a very limited extent, what these utility weights will be. To make such predictions in a systematic manner, we would need a theory specifying the mathematical form and the basic parameters of people's utility functions for economic commodities and for noneconomic values of various sorts. Sooner or later a theory of this kind may be developed, but at this point no such theory is available. Hence, for the time being all we can do is to *infer* these utility weights from people's own observed behavior in different social situations.

Yet, one reason why many social scientists other than economists oppose the use of rational-choice models is that they find this procedure objectionable from the viewpoint of scientific methodology. They argue that if we estimate the parameters of utility functions from observed behavior, and then try to explain this behavior in terms of utility functions estimated in this way, our explanation will be circular and will have no scientific value.

In actual fact, it is very common practice in the natural sciences and in economics to estimate the parameters of a given theory from the empirical facts, and then to explain these very same facts in terms of this theory, after assigning to all parameters the numerical values obtained from the empirical data. According to the accepted standards of scientific and statistical methodology, this procedure is perfectly sound and does not involve a vicious circle, so long às the number of theoretical parameters estimated from the empirical facts is significantly *smaller* than the number of independent empirical facts that the theory can explain.[12]

To sum up, we have tried to show that it is perfectly legitimate to explain people's behavior in terms of utility functions involving several distinct motives (several distinct objectives possessing positive utility) – provided that the number of distinct motives postulated by our theory is kept reasonably small. This is true even though the actual utility weights that people assign to different motives (to different objectives) usually will have to be inferred from their own behavior, instead of being predicted on the basis of more general theoretical considerations.

At the same time, our analysis also shows that we must definitely resist the temptation of postulating more than a very few basic motives in our theory, whether for the sake of 'greater realism' or for any other reason. This is so because a theory involving a *large* number of distinct motives, and therefore involving a *large* number of parameters to be estimated from the empirical facts, cannot be used to explain these empirical facts without inadmissible circularity. This is of course just another way of saying that if our theory is to have any real explanatory power then our motivational assumptions must be kept at a very low level of complexity – even if they do not have to be made quite as simple as to postulate economic self-interest as the *only* important motive of human behavior.

VI. FOUR MOTIVATIONAL POSTULATES

It seems to me that the simplest motivational theory accommodating non-economic and nonegoistic motives must involve at least the following four postulates.

(1) *Postulate of 'low-cost' impartiality and public spirit.* People tend to follow their own personal interests (or the interest of other persons, social groups, or organizations they are closely attached to) in situations where these interests are strongly affected by their behavior. But in situations where these interests are involved only weakly or not at all, people are quite able and willing to let their behavior be governed by impartial criteria and by more general social considerations. (In other words, people tend to be impartial and public-spirited when it *costs little* to be impartial or to be public-spirited.)

For example, we have conflict-of-interest laws because we do not trust the impartiality of judges and public officials in social situations where their own personal interests or those of their closest relatives and associates are significantly affected. But in other cases we do expect them to act with a reasonable degree of impartiality. If this expectation were often grossly disappointed, our judicial and governmental institutions could hardly survive.

(2) *Postulate of interest-aggregation by impartial sympathetic third parties.* In a conflict situation each party involved will tend to judge all issues from its own one-sided point of view. But, according to Postulate (1), third parties whose interests are not directly affected will find it natural to assess the situation in terms of more general impartial criteria. Formally, the behavior of such third parties will often amount to trying to maximize some 'social-welfare function' representing some sort of 'fair compromise' among the interests of the parties directly involved – or even among the interests of all members of the society.

This model can be used to explain the emergence of interest-aggregation concepts of various sorts, such as the notions of 'group interest' and of 'social interest' (or 'public interest'). Indeed, the concept of morality itself can be explained in a similar way. Conceptually, the moral point of view is the point of view of an impartial observer, sympathetic to all human interests involved in the situation but free of biases favoring any one of them in particular.[13] Once people get used to applying moral criteria to various issues, or to judging them by such standards as group interest or social interest, they may come to use moral criteria or interest-aggregation concepts – that is, they may choose to take the point of view of an outside observer – even in situations where their own interests are directly involved. But analytically we can best understand the concepts of morality or group interest and social interest as originally representing the point of view of third parties with no personal interests in the situation.

If we leave the purely philosophical importance of these concepts on one side, we see that from a social-science viewpoint the importance of these concepts is that the outcome of social conflicts is often decided largely by the stand taken by disinterested third parties; and in many cases the latter's behavior will be governed principally by their notions of morality, or by their definitions of 'group interest' or of 'social interest'.

(3) *Postulate of acquiring personal commitments by rational choice.* At any given moment, the area in which people are free to follow their rational choice and to select the course of action yielding the highest utility to them is restricted by personal commitments to their family, their close friends, and certain social organizations or non-organized social groups they are attached to. These commitments will often require them to act in a more altruistic manner than they would choose to do in the absence of these commitments.

How do people acquire such commitments in the first place? It seems reasonable to assume that normally such commitments are acquired by *rational choice*, by comparing the advantages and the disadvantages associated with any commitment (including advantages and disadvantages of a purely subjective psychological nature). For instance, people will normally decide in terms of their own (and their family's) interests, both economic and noneconomic, whether they should take on a given job and should in this way commit themselves to serving the interests of a particular employer in certain specified ways. Again, in deciding whether to adopt a child and thus commit themselves to look after him, they will weigh the satisfaction they derive from close association with children against the costs and the inconvenience involved, etc. Of course, once a person has entered into such a commitment he will be under social pressure to abide by it, and his own feelings of obligation will act in the same direction. On the basis of these considerations we state our Postulate (3) as follows: at any given moment people's free rational choice is *restricted* by personal commitments undertaken at earlier periods. But undertaking such a commitment tends to be itself a matter of rational choice.

(4) *Postulate of economic and social-acceptance motivation.* Our first three postulates have dealt with the relationship between selfish and unselfish motivation. Our last postulate will deal with the goal-objects people want to obtain for themselves (and presumably also for those other individuals whose interests they are concerned with). One way to formulate this postulate would be to say that people's behavior can be largely explained in terms of two dominant interests: economic gain and social status. But in another paper we have argued that the desire for social status is to a large extent a desire for social acceptance, for easier social access to other people as potential friends, partners in private social intercourse, business associates, marriage partners, etc.[14] Thus we now propose to formulate the postulate as follows: People's behavior can be largely explained in terms of two dominant interests: economic gain and social acceptance. (Of course, economic gain is usually not desired for its own sake but rather as a means to other goals, and the same may also be true, to a much smaller extent, of social acceptance. But for our present purposes it is not necessary to explain these two interests in terms of more fundamental phychological motivations.)

The purpose of these four postulates is to describe the main motivational variables we propose to use and to indicate in general terms the role that each of these variables is assumed to play in motivating human behavior. But, for reasons already stated (in section V), our postulates make no attempt to offer very specific predictions about the relative importance that people's utility functions will assign to the various motives under different conditions.

For example, Postulate (1) makes only the prediction that people usually can resist weak temptations, but cannot resist strong temptations, to put personal and sectional interests above general social interests. Yet the postulate does not try to specify where the dividing line has to be drawn between 'weak' and 'strong' temptations in different social situations. Where this line has to be drawn in each particular field (e.g., in the field of voting behavior) must be inferred in each case from the relevant empirical facts.

Likewise, Postulate (4) merely asserts that economic gain and social status (or social acceptance) are the two main goal-objects of human behavior, but does not try to specify their relative importance as motivating forces of human actions in different fields. This again must be inferred from the empirical data.

It is not unreasonable to expect that, as we learn more about human motivation and go on experimenting with alternative motivational assumptions, we shall be able to replace these motivational postulates by postulates making more specific predictions. Our four postulates surely do not represent the last word in the search for appropriate motivational assumptions. But we do feel that even in their present form they are a significant improvement over the economic self-interest theory of human motivation.

VII. 'IRRATIONAL' BEHAVIOR

A major challenge for any rational-choice theory of social behavior is the question of how to interpret what is, or at least appears to be 'irrational behavior'. Actually the term 'irrational behavior' is rather misleading because it seems to prejudge the issue of whether or not such behavior serves any useful purpose. A more appropriate descriptive term is *symbolic* or *expressive* behavior.

Phychologists of different schools do not agree on the specific psychological mechanisms involved, but two psychological facts are reasonably clear:

(1) If people attach strong positive or negative emotions to a given person or object, they will often extend the same positive or negative emotions to persons and objects associated with the former by similarity or by contiguity in space or time.

(2) People often derive considerable psychological satisfaction from symbolic actions, i.e., actions directed towards these secondary targets of their emotions.

Given these two facts, there is *per se* nothing 'irrational' in performing such symbolic actions. What does however require further explanation is that people sometimes indulge in such symbolic actions at very significant costs to themselves, which seem to be quite out of proportion to the psychological satisfactions they can possibly obtain this way. In many cases such behavior may be merely a result of neurotic or psychotic conditions. But in other cases this does not seem to be the explanation, or at least does not seem to be the whole explanation.

Sometimes, what appears to be excessive preoccupation with symbolic actions is a way of making social commitments. For example, opposition parties may organize a protest demonstration against government policies even though they do not expect it to have any effect on the government's actions – because it will give an opportunity for the participants to commit themselves to support the anti-government camp. (Such a commitment will be particularly effective if the names of the demonstrators are likely to become publicly known, making it very hard for them to rejoin the ranks of government supporters.)

In other cases, preoccupation with symbolic actions can be explained essentially as an act of desperation: it may simply mean that people have given up all hope of achieving their goals by reality-oriented instrumental activities, and so feel they have nothing to lose by turning to magic, ritual, ideology, and other forms of symbolic behavior. Such attitudes seem to underlie a wide variety of social movements, from some messianistic cults to some extremist political groups.

However, it may be noted that 'irrational' social policies – if by this we mean highly inefficient and self-defeating policies – do not necessarily result from 'irrational' behavior on the part of the individual participants. For example, some countries have been known to combine a tough foreign policy, amounting to continual provocation of their adversaries, with a defense policy involving very low expenditures on armaments, for reasons of economy. From a national point of view this clearly involves choosing the worst of all possible worlds. But from the point of view of the political leaders responsible for this policy it may have represented the politically most convenient compromise between the supporters of a tough foreign policy line (who presumably favored high defense expenditures) and the supporters of budget economies (who presumably would have been willing to follow a less provocative foreign policy).

VIII. DYNAMIC EXPLANATIONS

Using this basic theoretical framework, we now propose to discuss the theoretical status of the concept of social values, and of the whole conformist model of social behavior.

The concept of social values has obvious utility at a descriptive level, as a shorthand reference to certain uniformities of social behavior in a particular society. But if our aim is to *explain* social behavior rather than merely to describe it, then statements about the social values of a given society will merely pose problems of explanation for us, instead of providing solutions to such problems. For example, the statement that Americans tend to attach very high value to success in business activities (perhaps more than do people in most other societies) is a useful summary of a certain class of empirical facts about people's behavior (including their verbal behavior) in the United States. But it does not 'explain' these facts, except in a very trivial and almost tautological sense. On the other hand, this statement does refer to an important feature of American society that is itself very much in need of explanation.

In contrast, the conformist model of social behavior treats social values as basic explanatory variables (independent variables) themselves apparently not requiring further explanation. Or at any rate the proponents of this model have never really faced up to the question of how to explain the social values of various societies – though in my opinion this is one of the most important and most interesting theoretical questions we must answer about social behavior.

At this point we must introduce an important distinction between two types of theoretical explanation. We shall speak of *static explanation* if a given social variable is explained wholly in terms of variables belonging to the same period. In contrast, we shall speak of *dynamic explanation* when at least some of the explanatory variables we use belong to an earlier period than the variable to be explained.

As we have tried to show in an earlier paper,[15] most social variables require a dynamic explanation because of a certain 'inertia' associated with them. Social values are certainly variables belonging to this category. When the social conditions change, value attitudes do not fully adjust to these new conditions at once. Even if these new conditions were to persist forever without any further change, it would presumably take a long time before the value attitudes reached a new equilibrium with full adjustment.

Thus, in a changing society the existing social conditions can never explain people's social values without reference to the social values of an earlier period. What the existing social conditions as such can explain are only the *changes* in these social values from one period to the next. For example, to understand the high value that present-day Americans ascribe to business as compared with nonbusiness occupations we must know that one or two generations ago business ranked at least as high as it does today, and probably even higher. Hence what really requires explanation are the changes that have taken place in American values, notably the increased prestige now associated with certain nonbusiness occupations, such as scientist, writer, academician, artist, politician, union leader, etc.

To put it differently, since social values require a dynamic explanation it follows that explaining social values really amounts to explaining changes in these values over time. It really amounts to specifying the basic incentives for people to change their own values, and to encourage or to discourage changes in the values of others.

IX. THE COGNITIVE-UTILITARIAN MODEL OF SOCIAL VALUES

We speak of social values when we find certain uniformities of behavior in a given society or social group. Thus social values change basically for the same reasons that human behavior in general does: they change because there is a shift, real or apparent, in the balance of the advantages and the disadvantages associated with alternative forms of behavior. Social values change because people find that they will be better off by not conforming to the old social values than they would be by conforming to them. For example, social values favoring large families will tend to change when urbanization decreases the economic benefits associated with large families and increases the costs and the inconvenience associated with them; and of course the decreased costs and easier availability of contraceptives will work in the same direction.

In technical terms, such changes in social values can be explained by means of a rational-choice model. That is, we need not postulate any changes in people's basic *utility functions* (or in their preference scales underlying these utility functions). Rather, our explanation can be based completely on changes in the objective consequences of alternative courses of action (and on changes in people's information about these consequences). Thus, the economic and social consequences of opting for a large family (or for a small family) will be different under modern conditions from what they used to be before. But we need not postulate any changes in the utility values as such that people assign to any given set of economic and social consequences. For example, one element of our explanation is that under modern conditions the objective economic costs of education are much higher than they used to be. But we need not assume that the subjective disutility that people now assign to a given educational expenditure (as measured, e.g., in units of constant purchasing power) is necessarily different from what it was before.

To be sure, changes in the objective conditions will induce changes in people's behavior only when people become *aware* of these changes, which may occur only after some time lag.

More important is that when people choose between persisting in their customary behavior and adopting a new way of doing things, they will usually have a reasonably good idea of the advantages and disadvantages associated with the former, but may have only the vaguest notions of those associated with the latter. Any innovation, however desirable in itself, involves the possibility of unanticipated side effects – many of them undesirable – on the natural environment and on society itself. But very often these dangers are greatly overrated by the people opposing a proposed change. The history of social reforms is full of cases in which the earlier opponents had to admit after implementation of these reforms that few or none of the dire consequences they had predicted for themselves or for society as a whole have materialized.

Indeed, it is not an overstatement to say that a very considerable part of the social values of most societies is based on *sheer ignorance*. People regard their existing customs as superior to alternative patterns of behavior because they have little reliable information about what it really would be like to live with any of these alternatives. In most cases we simply cannot tell which pattern of behavior they would choose if they actually had this missing information.

One of the reasons why the example of others is so important in encouraging changes in people's values and behavior is that it tends to dispel some groundless fears about the dismal consequences that such changes might entail. Another reason is of course that people can more easily face the possible hostility of the supporters of the old values if they are not alone in making the change.

X. THE CONFORMIST MODEL OF SOCIAL VALUES

In the last section we have argued that the basic incentives to changes in social values are shifts in the real or assumed benefits and costs associated with the existing social practices and with their possible alternatives. Now we have to consider the main disincentives to changes in social values.

Obviously an important disincentive is expected opposition, and possibly even actual sanctions, from some other members of the society. But it is essential to recognize that in most cases different members of the society will display very unequal degrees of active opposition to any proposed change. Usually the main opposition will come from individuals whose personal interests would suffer from a shift to new values and new patterns of behavior; from individuals whose social roles give them personal responsibility for maintaining the old values of the society; and more generally from people whose background and experience have made them especially aware of the social benefits connected with the old values, and who perhaps are also especially insensitive to the social benefits likely to result from the new values.

Often the very same group of individuals will belong to all of these categories. For example, the members of any profession will tend to fight changes in social values that would reduce the importance society attaches to their work. By opposing such changes they will protect their own economic interests and their own social status, but they will also feel they are discharging a social obligation in protecting the social interests served by their profession; and their opposition will be reinforced by their extensive specialized knowledge of the various benefits that society derives from their professional activities, which will enable them to defend the interest of their profession in good faith.

Another possible obstacle to changes in social values is that in many cases people will be unable to take full advantage of these changes unless certain further conditions are met. If this is not the case, their incentives to undertake these changes will be greatly reduced.

One of these conditions may be possession of certain skills. Consider a society where cooperation and friendship are traditionally restricted to the members of the same kinship group, or at least to people who have known each other intimately since early childhood. Now suppose that certain economic changes take place that would make it desirable for this society to

adopt somewhat more universalistic value-attitudes and to establish friendly business relationships with people outside these narrow social groups.
Clearly this will not be easy to accomplish. One problem may be that people will simply lack the social skills needed to establish friendly relationships with strangers they have known for only a fairly short period.

Conversely, people not used to living in large extended families may be
unwilling to join such a family group, in spite of possible strong economic
incentives, because they will usually lack the social skills required to get
along with so many relatives at close quarters.

Again, in many cases a crucial condition will be whether a sufficient
number of other people in the society are simultaneously changing their
own values and their own behavior in a similar manner. For example, in a
society where particularistic value-attitudes are widespread, even employers whose own value-attitudes are universalistic may be unwilling to fill positions of trust with persons having no kinskip (or tribal or religious, etc.)
ties with them, because they will feel that in the absence of such particularistic ties they cannot expect loyal and reliable service. Thus a change-over
to more universalistic attitudes will be extremely slow until people become
convinced that a sizable proportion of their society has already made the
change.

XI. CONCLUDING REMARKS ON THE EXPLANATION
OF SOCIAL VALUES

To sum up our discussion of the last three sections, the theory of social values we have arrived at may be described as a combination of two different
models. One model corresponds to the assumption that the main incentive
to entertain a given set of social values lies in the belief that under existing
conditions conformity to these values will serve their own interests,
whether selfish or unselfish, more effectively than would conformity to any
alternative set of values. We may call this a *cognitive* model because it explains the common acceptance of certain social values by a uniformity of
cognitive beliefs – beliefs concerning the consequences of the existing patterns of social behavior as compared with the likely consequences of alternative patterns.

Alternatively, this model could also be called a *utilitarian* model of social
values because it assumes that people will choose among different patterns
of social behavior in terms of their presumed utility for achieving personal

goals (both selfish and unselfish). Thus, under this model, people's motives for following a particular set of social values are basically similar to their motives for following a particular technology. (This similarity can be further increased if we extend this model to incorporate the fact that successful implementation of a particular set of social values – like successful implementation of a given technology – often depends on the possession of certain special skills that cannot be easily acquired in societies where the existing social practices do not require these skills).

The other model we have used as a basic ingredient of our theory can be regarded as a modified version of what we have called the *conformist* model of social values. It corresponds to the assumption that people's main incentive to entertain a given set of social values lies not so much in the real or assumed intrinsic advantages of conformity with these values, but rather lies simply in the fact that most other people in their social environment support these values and are likely to disapprove of and resist any significant deviation from them.

We have argued that this model in itself cannot provide a satisfactory theory of social values because it cannot explain changes in them. But it does contain an important element of truth since the pressure for conformity it assumes is no doubt present to varying degrees in all known societies and so is an essential ingredient of any satisfactory theory. On the other hand, no realistic account can overlook the fact – disregarded by the conformist model in its usual form – that active opposition to any given form of deviant behavior or to any proposed change in social values is in most cases very unequally distributed over society, and tends to come primarily from individuals whose active concern is motivated by personal interests, special social responsibilities, or special background and experience.

However, if we incorporate this fact into the conformist model, and then combine it with the cognitive-utilitarian model, we shall obtain a theory of social values that can explain social stability and social change with equal ease. Formally we can combine the two models into one by making use of the fact that technically the conformist model is a special case of the cognitive-utilitarian model. This is so because possible social sanction against nonconformity is simply one of the many elements a rational individual will have to include in his cost-and benefit calculus when he is choosing between acceptance of some new values and loyalty to the old.

XII. SOCIAL FUNCTIONS:
THE COLLECTIVISTIC INTERPRETATION

Most of the points we have made about the problem of explaining social values also apply to the problem of explaining social institutions. Like the former, the latter also require a dynamic explanation because we cannot expect that they will instantaneously achieve full adjustment to changing conditions. Consequently, explaining social institutions essentially amounts to explaining *changes* in these institutions. On the other hand, these changes themselves must be ultimately explained in terms of personal incentives for some people to change their behavior. They must be explained by the fact that, as a result of certain changes in the society or in its natural environment or in its relations with its external social environment, some people have decided that their interests would be better served by a new type of institutional arrangement. (Of course, different individuals and different social groups will tend to have different interests in relation to institutional changes. Thus the outcome will be a result of conflicting social pressures and can be fully explained only in game-theoretical terms.)

If we define the term 'social function' broadly enough, we may say that this theory explains social institutions in terms of their 'social functions'. But then the 'social function' of an institution must be defined as all the benefits that various individual members of society derive from its operation.[16] This may be called the individualistic concept of social function. For example, the social function of the shoe industry in this sense is to produce shoes for consumers – as well as to provide jobs and wages for its employees, dividends for its shareholders, a market for its suppliers, etc. Similarly, the social function of educational institutions is to provide education for their students, to provide help for parents in discharging their educational responsibilities to their children, to provide educated potential employees for prospective employers, to provide jobs and salaries for teachers and other employees, etc.

In contrast, functionalists usually define the social function of a given institution in terms of its contribution to the maintenance of the social system *as a whole*. This may be called the collectivistic concept of social function.

Little argument is required to show that the individualistic concept of social function has incomparably greater explanatory power than has the collectivistic concept. First of all, the very concept of social function in a collectivistic sense gives rise to insoluble problems of definition and of empirical identification.

(A) We cannot define what is meant by 'the maintenance of the social system as a whole' without making quite arbitrary distinctions between those characteristics of a social system that are and are not essential for maintaining its identity as 'the same social system'. For example, how are we to decide how large are the changes that could be made in the political or economic institutions of American society without turning it into a 'different social system' altogether?

(B) Even if we could agree on some such definition, in many cases we simply do not know enough about the empirical laws governing the operation of social systems to be able to tell whether an institution does or does not make any significant contribution to maintaining these 'essential characteristics' of the relevant social system, as specified by our definition. In other words, we just cannot tell how seriously these essential characteristics of the society would be endangered by complete elimination or substantial impairment of the social institution in question.

For example, suppose we decide that political democracy (in some precisely stated sense of this term) is an 'essential characteristic' of the American social system. Then the question will arise how seriously the survival of democracy would be endangered, say, by elimination of private ownership of all television stations. It seems to me that on the basis of our present knowledge we simply cannot answer a question like this with any real assurance.

Second, even if we assume that these problems could be solved in some way, the collectivistic concept of social functions, could at best explain only the very grossest features of the society's institutional framework. All it could explain would be the mere existence[17] of the most important social institutions, but not anything more specific about the structure and operation of these institutions; and it could not explain even the mere existence of any minor social institution.

This is so because in all probability a social system could not survive the destruction of any of its major institutions; but presumably it could survive many structural and operational changes in these institutions, and even a complete destruction of minor social institutions, without losing its 'essential characteristics' under any reasonable definition of the latter. Thus the very existence of its major institutions may admit of explanation in terms of the contributions they make to the survival of the society; but many of their structural and operational properties do not admit of such explanation, nor does the existence of minor social institutions.

For example, the very existence of the American school system may conceivably admit of explanation in terms of its important contributions to the maintenance of American society, but many of its specific properties cannot be explained in these terms. In the case of the American shoe industry even its existence cannot be explained in this way because its disappearance would hardly endanger the survival of American society or of its essential characteristics.

Finally, if it can be shown that a social institution makes a significant contribution to the survival of the social system as a whole, this fact can 'explain' the existence of the institution only in a very limited sense – unless the advocates of such 'collectivistic' functional explanations can specify the *causal mechanisms* by which the survival needs of the society are translated into individual behavior ensuring the existence of the required institutions. In fact, the advocates of such explanations have made no serious attempt to specify the nature of these causal mechanisms.

XIII. SOCIAL FUNCTIONS:
AN INDIVIDUALISTIC INTERPRETATION

In contrast, the individualistic concept of social functions does not raise any major problem of definition and empirical identification. For example, it is not hard to ascertain the benefits that various social groups (e.g., consumers, employees, shareholders, etc. – or again, students, parents, teachers, etc.) derive from the operation of the American shoe industry or from the operation of various American educational institutions.

The benefits accruing to different social groups from the operation of various institutions not only explain the mere existence of the few major institutions, but also explain the structure and operation of all institutions, both major and minor, in considerable detail. More particularly, *changes* in social institutions can be explained as resulting from interaction among various social groups trying to maximize the net benefits they expect to obtain from the operation of these institutions. (Of course, as the social groups in question will tend to have different interests, full understanding of this interaction can be achieved only in game-theoretical terms.)

For example, if we use this approach we can explain not only the mere existence of the American school system, but can also explain many specific details in its structure and operation – such as the highly decentralized nature of education in this country, the rather high school-leaving age, the emphasis on mass education rather than elite education, etc. Both the original adoption of these institutional arrangements and their persistence ever since (as well as the changes they have undergone over time) must surely admit of explanation in terms of the balance of power among the various social groups pressing for the arrangements most favorable to their own interests (including their possible altruistic interests). At least this is the type of explanation that any social historian or social scientist would look for in his empirical research.

Finally, if we use the benefits that people obtain or expect to obtain as our basic explanatory variables, then the question of how these variables are getting translated into individual behavior does not arise – because the assumption that they are motivated by their desire to maximize these benefits is in itself a sufficient explanation of their behavior.

XIV. A DYNAMIC THEORY OF SOCIAL INSTITUTIONS

As our discussion in Sections XII and XIII shows, one of the reasons for the difficulties of functionalist theories is their undue concentration on the needs of the social system as a whole, at the expense of the interests of the individual members of the society. This leads to difficulties because explaining social facts always comes down to explaining the behavior of the individuals involved, who are always motivated by their individual interests (which by our definition may include all sorts of altruistic considerations). It also leads to an inability to understand the importance of conflicts of interest among individuals and social groups.

Another important reason for the difficulties of functionalist theories is their preoccupation with the factors contributing to the *maintenance* of the existing social system, at the expense of the factors responsible for *social change*. We have argued that the basic theoretical problem of the social sciences is to explain social change resulting from the dynamic nature of most social variables.[18] We may add that for policy-making purposes their basic problem is again to predict the social changes likely to result from alternative policies available to us, including the policy of doing nothing. (Social change of course includes the constancy of certain social variables as a special case, corresponding to social change at a rate close to zero. Thus any theory of social change automatically includes the theory of social constancy as a part. The basic objection to functionalism is the fact that the converse is not true at all: if our purpose is to explain social change then a static theory of social constancy will be normally of very little help.)

Consequently, the preoccupation of functionalist theories with the *maintenance* of the social system in its present form means adopting precisely the wrong emphasis, both for theoretical and for policy-making purposes. So it is not surprising if it leads, as we have tried to show, to asking the wrong questions again and again.

XV. RATIONAL-CHOICE MODELS AND HUMAN VALUES

In recent years many social scientists and social philosophers have complained about what they have felt to be an increasing elimination of human values and of the humanistic point of view from the social sciences. This complaint has often been combined with the assertion that this 'dehumanization' of the social sciences is connected with the increasing use of more rigorous 'scientific' techniques borrowed from the natural sciences, ranging from more carefully controlled methods of empirical observation and of statistical evaluation to the use of mathematical models in theoretical analysis.

Whatever the justification of this complaint and of the implied contrast between the humanistic and the scientific approaches may have been in the past, one of the important advantages of rational-choice theories is that they combine a 'scientific' emphasis on rigorous analytical (and possibly mathematical) models with a strong theoretical focus on human values.

First of all, rational-choice theories use human values – in the form of human preferences, interests, and objectives – as the basic explanatory and predictive variables of human behavior. In this they differ from many psychological theories of 'scientific' inspiration and from related social-science theories, which use stimulus-response or quasi-physiological terminology in describing their explanatory variables of human behavior.

On the other hand, unlike other 'scientific' theories in the social sciences, rational-choice models not only have explanatory-predictive interpretations, but also have normative interpretations. For example, the rational-choice models of economic theory can be interpreted as models of 'positive economics' but also as models of normative 'welfare economics'. The former try to explain and predict real-life economic behavior, whereas the latter try to define economic behavior possessing certain desirable normative criteria, such as Pareto-optimality or social-welfare maximization. Rational-choice models referring to noneconomic (e.g., political) behavior can likewise have both explanatory-predictive and normative interpretations. For example, an analytical model of a democratic political system may be meant to represent some real-life democracy with all its imperfections, or it may be meant to represent various kinds of 'ideal' democracies possessing various properties desirable from a normative point of view.

Such rigorous normative models can be just as important for the purpose of clarifying our normative political, economic, and social values as rigorous explanatory-predictive theories are for the purpose of clarifying our causal theories of society. These normative theories demonstrate the fact – if it still requires demonstration – that there is no incompatibility of any kind between clear and precise thinking in the best traditions of the mathematical sciences on the one hand, and a deep concern for human values in the best traditions of the humanities and of classical political philosophy on the other hand.

Perhaps the most important single contribution that normative rational-choice models can make to clearer thinking is their emphasis on the fact that in most situations we cannot realize all our social values at the same time so that a *choice* among different values is necessary. For example, economists know that we usually cannot decrease unemployment without increasing inflation and conversely; thus we have to choose between a little more employment and a little more price stability, as we can have one only at the expense of the other.

Similar choices seem to be necessary in other fields. If we give greater political participation to the electorate in political decisions (e.g., by popular initiative, referendum, etc.) then we probably decrease the protection given to minority rights or to the right of dissent. Thus one democratic value (popular participation) can be increased only at the expense of other democratic values (minority rights or the right of dissent). Again, we may have to choose.

It can of course also happen that we have to choose between political values and economic values. For example, an underdeveloped country may be able to increase its rate of economic growth only at the expense of some decrease in democratic freedoms, etc.

Such choices are never pleasant to make, but no intelligent policy decisions are possible without recognizing that such choices have to be made whenever the situation requires them.

However, the traditional attitude among social scientists in general has not been very favorable to recognizing this. Rather, the implicit assumption usually has been that 'all good things come together', all desirable factors have positive correlation with one another. Greater popular praticipation can only make the political system 'more democratic' in all respects; greater democracy can only increase the rate of economic development; more freedom and more permissiveness for the child can only improve his academic progress, etc.

We shall call this implicit assumption the Positive Correlation Fallacy. It has been one of the main obstacles to clear thinking among social scientists, and is probably responsible for a high proportion of the bad policy recommendations we have made. Extensive use of rational-choice models in analyzing our own values and in making policy recommendations is no doubt the surest way of avoiding this fallacy.

NOTES

* *World Politics,* **21** (1969), 513–538.
The author wishes to express his gratitude to the National Science Foundation, which has supported this research by grant GS-722, administered through the University of California Center for Research in Management Science. This paper was presented at the annual meeting of the American Political Science Association in Chicago, September, 1967. The author wishes to express his thanks for the comments received.

[1] Talcott Parsons, *The Structure of Social Action* (Glencoe, Ill. 1949); *The Social System* (Glencoe, Ill. 1951); *Essays in Sociological Theory* (Glencoe, Ill. 1954); *Structure and Process in Modern Societies* (Glencoe, Ill. 1961).
[2] See Gabriel Almond, 'Comparative Political Systems', *Journal of Politics,* XVIII, (Aug. 1956), 391-409; Marion J. Levy, Jr., *The Structure of Society* (Princeton1952); R. K. Merton, *Social Theory and Social Structure* (New York 1957); William C. Mitchell, *The American Polity* (New York 1962) and *Sociological Analysis and Politics* (Englewood Cliffs, N.J. 1967); A. R. Radcliffe-Brown, *Structure and Function in Primitive Society* (Glencoe, Ill. 1952), etc.
[3] See, e.g., James S. Coleman, 'Comment on 'On the Concept of Influence," *The Public Opinion Quarterly,* XXVII (Spring 1963), 63-92; Ralf Dahrendorf, 'Out of Utopia: Toward a Reorientation of Sociological Analysis', *American Journal of Sociology,* LXIV (September

1958), 115-27; *Class and Class Conflict in Industrial Society* (Stanford 1959); Alvin Gouldner, 'Some Observations on Systematic Theory, 1945-55', in Hans L. Zetterberg, ed., *Sociology in the United States* (Paris, 1956); 'Reciprocity and Autonomy in Functional Theory', in Llewellyn Gross, ed., *Symposium on Sociological Theory* (New York 1959); John C. Harsanyi, 'Explanation and Comparative Dynamics in Social Science', *Behavioral Science,* V (April 1960), 136-45, 'A Bargaining Model for Social Status in Informal Groups and Formal Organizations', *Behavioral Science* XI (September 1966), 357-69, 'Individualistic versus Functionalistic Explanations in the Light of Game Theory', in I. Lakatos and A. Musgrave, eds., *Problems in the Philosophy of Science* (Amsterdam 1967); Carl G. Hempel, 'The Logic of Functional Analysis', in Llewellyn Gross, ed., *Symposium on Sociological Theory* (New York 1959); George C. Homans, 'Contemporary Theory in Sociology', in Robert E. L. Faris, ed., *Handbook of Modern Sociology* (Chicago 1964); David Lockwood, 'Some Remarks on 'The Social System,'' *British Journal of Sociology* VII (June 1956), 134-46; John Rex, *Key Problems of Sociological Theory* (London 1961).

[4] *Ibid.*

[5] Dahrendorf, 127, has argued that we cannot use the same theoretical model to analyze social conflicts and to analyze social consensus or cooperation. In actual fact, as modern game theory has shown in analyzing games with mixed interests (where the players' interests are similar in some respects and are dissimilar in other respects), the same theoretical model can handle both conflict and cooperation without any difficulty.

[6] The von Neumann-Morgenstern approach to game theory does not yield determinate predictions for two-person non-zero-sum games and for n-person games, the two game classes most important for social science applications. John von Neumann and Oskar Morgenstern, *Theory of Games and Economic Behavior* (Princeton 1944). But later work has overcome this difficulty. See, e.g. John C. Harsanyi, 'Bargaining and Conflict Situations in the Light of a New Approach to Game Theory', *American Economic Review*, LV (May 1965), 447-57 and 'A General Theory of Rational Behavior in Game Situations', *Econometrica*, XXXIV (July 1966), 613-34.

[7] See e.g., Herbert A. Simon, *Administrative Behavior* (New York 1957), *Models of Man* (New York 1957), 'The Executive as Decision Maker', in H. A. Simon, *The Shape of Automation* (New York 1965), 'Political Research: The Decision-Making Framework', in David Easton, ed., *Varieties of Political Theory* (Englewood Cliffs, N.J. 1966).

[8] In fairness to traditional 'interest theories', before the emergence of modern game theory the analytical tools needed for answering some of these questions were simply not available.

[9] For example, Duncan Black, *The Theory of Committees and Elections* (Cambridge 1958); James M. Buchanan and Gordon Tullock, *The Calculus of Consent* (Ann Arbor 1962); James S. Coleman, 'Collective Decisions', *Sociological Inquiry*, XXXIV (Spring 1964), 166-81; John C. Harsanyi, 'Measurement of Social Power, Opportunity Costs, and the Theory of Two-Person Bargaining Games', *Behavioral Science,* VII (January 1962), 67-80, 'Measurement of Social Power in n-Person Reciprocal Power Situations', *Behavioral Science,* VII (January 1962), 81-91, 'Models for the Analysis of the Balance of Power in Society', in the *Proceedings of the 1960 International Congress for Logic, Methodology, and Philosophy of Science* (Stanford 1962), 442-62; Morton Kaplan, *System and Process in International Politics* (New York 1957); Mancur Olson, Jr., *The Logic of Collective Action* (Cambridge, Mass. 1965); William H. Riker, *The Theory of Political Coalitions* (New Haven, Conn. 1962), etc. See also Robert A. Dahl, *A Preface to Democratic Theory* (Chicago 1956); George C. Homans, *Social Behavior: Its Elementary Forms* (New York 1961); and J. W. Thibaut and H. H. Kelley, *The Social Psychology of Groups* (New York 1959). The last three books make no explicit use of formal rational-choice models, but most of their analysis could be easily restated in these terms.

[10] Modern economic theory (often called neoclassical economic theory in contrast to the classical theory) has considerably relaxed this assumption. Though economic self-interest is still regarded as the dominant motive of economic behavior, it is no longer assumed to be the only important motive.

[11] Anthony Downs, *An Economic Theory of Democracy* (New York 1957).

[12] If the number of adjustable parameters of a given theory is as large as (or is even larger than) the number of independent observations available to us, then the fact that the theory is consistent with these observations does not provide a real confirmation for it, because such a theory can *always* be made consistent with our observations if we choose appropriate numerical values for its parameters. Even if the number of adjustable parameters of the theory is smaller than the number of independent observations, but is only just a little smaller, we cannot ascribe much significance to an agreement between our observations and the theory, because this agreement can easily be a matter of chance. Only if the number of adjustable parameters is *much* smaller than the number of our observations does an agreement between these observations and our theory represent a true confirmation for the latter, and only in this case can we say that our theory provides an explanation for the observed facts.

[13] See John C. Harsanyi, 'Cardinal Utility in Welfare Economics and in the Theory of Risk-Taking', *Journal of Political Economy*, LXI (October 1953), 434-35; 'Cardinal Welfare, Individualistic Ethics, and Interpersonal Comparisons of Utility', *Journal of Political Economy*, LXIII (August 1955), 309-21; 'Ethics in Terms of Hypothetical Imperatives', *Mind*, XLVII (July 1958), 305-16.

[14] See Harsanyi, 'A Bargaining Model for Social Status'.

[15] Harsanyi, 'Explanation and Comparative Dynamics', 136-37.

[16] I owe this point to Nelson Polsby.

[17] By explaining the 'existence' of an institution I mean explaining its emergence at some point of time and its survival ever since.

[18] See Section VIII; cf. also Harsanyi, 'Explanation and Comparative Dynamics'.

CHAPTER VIII

GAME THEORY AND THE ANALYSIS OF INTERNATIONAL CONFLICTS*

I

Game theory is a theory of rational behaviour in the face of opponents expected to behave likewise rationally. Here by 'rational behaviour' we mean the assumption that each participant (or 'player') has a set of well-defined and mutually consistent basic objectives, and will choose his actual policies in accordance with these objectives without any mistake. In technical terms this means that each player has a well-defined 'utility function' expressing the value or 'utility' he attaches to various policy objectives, and that his actual behaviour will be fully consistent with this utility function.

This assumption of rational behaviour of course, if taken quite literally, is certainly unrealistic in many social situations. Policy makers are human and therefore occasionally do make mistakes. Moreover, their policy objectives are seldom quite consistent. For one thing, when people have to choose between two or more very unpleasant policy alternatives, they often find it very hard to make up their minds and follow any of these policies in a consistent manner. For another thing, every policy maker is subject to conflicting pressures from his own constituents, and these may make it very difficult for him to adopt any unambiguous policy line.

For instance, both in international and in internal politics, one often has to choose between trying to reach a mutually acceptable *agreement* with one's opponents, and trying to keep them in check by mere superior *strength*. But usually the worst possible policy is to antagonize and provoke one's enemies even further without the will and the ability to face a showdown with them. Yet this is precisely the irrational policy that many countries have often been following against countries unfriendly to them.

However, in spite of such occasional inconsistencies and mistakes, if we observe a given country's foreign policy over long periods, we can usually discern some fairly stable and consistent basic policy goals pursued by that country, subject only to minor deviations. These basic policy goals seem to undergo only very slow and gradual changes, except possibly at times of major transformations or revolutions in the country's own internal political system. Thus in many cases the assumption of rational behaviour in the game-theoretical analysis of international politics can be regarded as a legitimate simplifying assumption, at least for the purposes of first approximation.

Indeed, apart from economic life, there are probably few areas of social behaviour where rational calculation plays a more important part than it does in international politics. According to common observation, most foreign policy decisions are strongly influenced by weighing the advantages and the disadvantages likely to result from alternative policies; and this fact makes these decisions eminently susceptible to game-theoretical analysis. (In effect, game-theoretical analysis can be quite useful even in situations where some countries tend to follow rather inconsistent foreign policies as a result of conflicting internal political pressures. But of course in such cases we cannot regard each country as being *one* 'player' but rather have to regard it as consisting of that many different 'players' as the number of major political groups with radically different attitudes on foreign policy.)

II

Yet even as far as each country does follow a set of reasonably consistent policy objectives, some further problems still remain. It is not enough to know that each country follows consistent policy goals, we must also know *what* these policy goals actually are if we want to make use of game-theoretical analysis. Let us consider an analogy from ordinary parlor games. The game of checkers can be played in two different ways. Normally each player's aim is to 'win' the game in the usual sense. But sometimes the game is played with the understanding that the player who 'loses' the game (as judged by the usual rules) will win, and the one who 'wins' will lose, so that each player's aim becomes to 'lose' the game as fast as he can. Now suppose a game theorist wants to analyse the situation, either in order to *predict* what a given player's next move *will* be, or in order to *advise* him what his next move *should* be. Then clearly the predictions or advices of our game theorist will make sense only if he knows what the player's actual *objectives* are—whether each player's aim is to 'win' (as under the usual rules) or whether his aim is to 'lose', since these two goals naturally will lead to quite contrary strategies on the part of the players.

Likewise, in international politics we can make predictions about various countries' likely policies, or can give sensible advice to foreign policy-makers, only if we can ascertain what each country's policy objectives actually are. Fortunately, in most cases it is not very hard to find out a given country's policy goals, at least in very general terms. Probably most countries pursue more or less the same general aims, such as national power and military security, as well as certain ideological goals depending on the country's own political creed. The trouble is only that it is not enough if we can simply enumerate all these policy objectives. We also have to know how much *weight* or *priority* a given country will give to its various objectives when it has to *choose* between them: and this is much harder to tell in advance.

For instance, if we want to predict the future behaviour of the Soviet Union then the real problem is how much relative importance the Soviet government will actually give to the goal of increasing the standard of living of its own population, how much importance to various military objectives, and how much importance to helping communist parties abroad or to promoting nationalistic or socialistic revolutions in underdeveloped countries, etc. It is reasonable to assume that the Russian government is in fact interested in *all* these policy goals at the same time. But what we do not know is how far it is willing to go in sacrificing any one of these objectives for the sake of another.

Game theory as such can give us little help in predicting how much weight a given country will assign to its different policy objectives because game theory starts with the assumption that the various players' policy goals (utility functions) are *given,* and bases its own analysis on these given policy goals of the different players. Fundamentally, the only way we can infer a particular country's policy objectives is on the basis of its own past behaviour (including of course verbal behaviour on the part of its leading policy-makers—even though in general naturally we cannot take their policy statements simply at face value). But such inferences are always subject to a certain margin of doubt. On the one hand, a given pattern of past behaviour may admit of interpretation in terms of several alternative hypotheses about a certain country's real policy goals. On the other hand, every country's policy goals are subject to continual change, and it may be very hard to judge how far this change has actually progressed at any given moment. For instance, we know that Soviet foreign policy has undergone certain important changes after Stalin's death. But Western experts find it very hard to decide how far these changes have actually gone with respect to the Soviet Union's basic policy objectives, and in particular with respect to the relative importance attached to any particular objective.

III

Let me now, however, leave all these difficulties on one side, and discuss some of the positive contributions game theory can make to our understanding of international politics.

A fundamental distinction in game theory is the classification of games into three main classes: games with *identical interests*, games with *opposite interests*, and games with *mixed interests*.

As an example for a game with identical interests, consider the two-person game having the following payoff matrix:

	B_1	B_2
A_1	(20,20)	(10,10)
A_2	(0, 0)	(5, 5)

Example 1.

In this game player 1's strategies are A_1 and A_2 while player 2's strategies are B_1 and B_2. As can be seen from the above payoff matrix, the two players here always obtain equal payoffs: thus the more one player wins the more will the other player win also. Hence the two players' interests are exactly identical. If the two players are rational then player 1 will use strategy A_1 while player 2 will use strategy B_1, so that both players will obtain payoffs of 20 units each. Any other combination of strategies would make both of them worse off. Thus in this situation there is no real problem. If the two players are rational enough to recognize the identity of their interests then they will surely cooperate in obtaining the highest possible payoffs for both of them.

In real life of course situations where two or more people's interests are *exactly* the same are not very common though there are many situations where they are at least *approximately* the same. But in any case the concept of games with identical interests is theoretically important because it represents one of the two extreme possibilities.

On the other extreme are games where the players' interests are exactly *opposite*. The most important example is that of *two-person zero-sum* games. In such games one player always wins exactly the amount the other player loses and vice versa. If one player's payoff is X then the other player's payoff will be $-X$, and so the two players' payoffs always add up to $X + (-X) = 0$. Hence the name 'zero-sum game'. Since each player's payoff is always the same as the other player's except for having the opposite sign, it is sufficient to indicate (say) player 1's payoffs in the payoff matrix. (Of course in Example 1 above it would also have been sufficient to indicate only one player's payoffs in the payoff matrix since the other player's payoff was always the same— indeed in that case there was not even a difference in sign.) Consider, for instance, the two-person zero-sum game having the following payoff matrix:

	B_1	B_2	B_3	Row Minima
A_1	15	10	18	10
A_2	9	3	11	3
A_3	20	6	7	6
Column Maxima	20	10	18	

Example 2.

Now each player has three alternative strategies, those of player 1 being A_1, A_2 and A_3, while those of player 2 being B_1, B_2, and B_3. The payoff 10 resulting from the strategy combination (A_1, B_2) represents both the *minimum* of row A_1 and the *maximum* of column B_2. Such a payoff is called a *saddle point*.

If *both* players act rationally then player 1's actual payoff will be exactly the payoff corresponding to this saddle point, viz. 10 units. For if player 1 acts rationally then his payoff cannot be *less* than that, since by using strategy A_1 he can always assure himself at least that much (as no number in row A_1 is less than 10). On the other hand, if player 2 acts rationally then player 1's payoff cannot be *more* than 10, either. This is so because player 2 by using strategy B_2 can always prevent player 1 from obtaining more than that (since no number in column B_2 is more than 10). But if player 2 *can* prevent this then he *will* (if he is rational), because the lower he can depress player 1's payoff the smaller will be his own loss. Thus player 1's payoff cannot be either less or more than 10: hence it will be *exactly* 10.

This means, however, that – if the two players expect each other to act rationally – then player 1's *best* strategy is A_1. For, as we have seen, he cannot expect to obtain *more* than 10. Hence he must concentrate on assuring at least *that much* for himself. But A_1 is the only strategy assuring him this amount (because rows A_2 and A_3 do contain numbers smaller than 10). For similar reasons, players 2's best strategy is B_2: no strategy can reduce his loss *below* 10 if his opponent acts rationally; but strategy B_2 at least ensures that his loss will not rise *above* this figure.

Two-person zero-sum games, as they represent the extreme case of games with opposite interests, are again a concept of great theoretical importance. But in real life few social situations represent two-person zero-sum games because in almost every case the participants will have *some* common interests. Many parlor games are two-person zero-sum games in that one player can win only if the other loses, and if the game is played for money then one player's money gain is the other player's money loss. (Yet even here the two players do have common interests e.g. in making the game mutually enjoyable.) But, neglecting parlor games, the only important social situation having the nature of a two-person zero-sum game is total war, i.e. a war where both sides are interested only in victory – at all costs whatever. But in practice even so-called total wars are not true two-person zero-sum games because the two sides do have a common interest in limiting the intensity of warfare (so long as this does not shift the balance of power in favor of the other side). For instance, in the second world war, which was called a 'total war' and which certainly came closest to a total war among all armed conflicts in modern times, many international agreements were violated by one side or even by both sides. Yet *some* interna-

tional conventions did enjoy general observance: for instance the use of
poison gas was ruled out by mutual consent. Thus even in 'total' war, so
called, there may be *some* limited cooperation between the two sides. (This
of course means that even so-called 'total wars' have not been really total
wars in a literal sense.) Hence even in this case the model of a two-person
zero-sum game can be applied only with important qualifications.

   In any case, most social situations are neither games with identical interests nor games with opposite interests but clearly fall between these two ex-
tremes. That is, they are games with *mixed* interests, where the players' interests are similar in some respects and dissimilar in others. Therefore for
the purposes of the analysis of real-life social situations the theory of mixed-
interest games is the most important part of game theory. But it is also the
most difficult part because games with mixed interests raise much harder
theoretical problems than does either of the two extreme cases. For this
reason the theory of games with mixed interests has been the last part of
game theory to achieve a satisfactory analytical framework.

IV

In the case of two-person games we can represent the differences among the
three main types of games geometrically as follows. Let us measure player
1's payoff u_1 along the horizontal axis and player 2's payoff u_2 along the
vertical axis. Then any point u with coordinates u_1 and u_2 will represent one
particular payoff combination, i.e. one particular conceivable outcome of

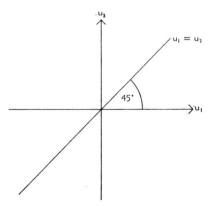

Figure 1.

the game. Any such point u in the u_1 u_2 plane is called a *payoff vector* and we can write $u = (u_1, u_2)$ where u_1 and u_2 are the coordinates of point u.

In the case of a game with identical interests, where both players always obtain equal payoffs, all possible payoff vectors will lie on the $u_1 = u_2$ line, which is the 45° line going through the origin (see Figure 1).

In the case of a two-person zero-sum game, where the two players' interests are completely opposed, all possible payoff vectors lie on the $u_1 + u_2 = 0$ line, which is the —45° line drawn through the origin (see Figure 2).

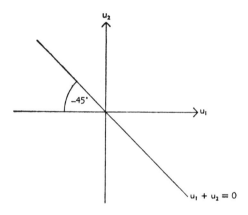

Figure 2.

Finally, in case of a game with *mixed* interests, the possible payoff vectors do not lie on the same straight line but are in general dispersed over a certain two-dimensional area. For instance, Figure 3 represents a game where the possible payoff vectors are the points of the enclosed area *ABCD*, which we call the payoff space. In this game both players will have a *common* interest in moving out to the upper-right boundary *ABC*. For instance, *both* of them will increase their payoffs if they move from point *E* to a point like *B* which lies to the right from *E* and also lies higher than *E*. But the two players will have *opposite* interests in choosing among the various points of this upper-right boundary tiself. For example player 1 will prefer *C* to *B* and will prefer both *C* and *B* to *A* while player 2's preferences will be exactly the other way round. This bears out our statement that the game is one of *mixed* interests: clearly the players' interests are partly similar and partly dissimilar.

In a game with *identical* interests, rational players will always fully cooperate because each of them can only lose by non-cooperation or by less than full cooperation.

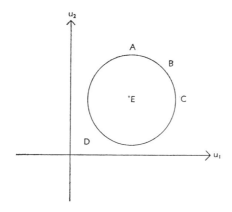

Figure 3.

In a game with *opposite* interests, such as a two-person zero-sum game, the players cannot usefully cooperate at all because they have no common interests they could promote by cooperation.

In contrast, a game with mixed interests usually can be played both as a *cooperative* game and as a *non-cooperative* game. One of the important tasks of game theory is to specify the conditions under which rational players will play a cooperative rather than a non-cooperative game or vice versa. It is at this point, also, where the conclusions of game theory have the most important implications for the analysis of international political situations.

V

Consider the following two-person (non-zero-sum) game:

	B_1	B_2
A_1	(10,10)	(—20,11)
A_2	(11,—20)	(1, 1)

Example 3.

Players 1's strategy A_1 and player 2's strategy B_1 will be called *cooperative strategies,* whereas player 1's strategy A_2 and player 2's strategy B_2 will be called *non-cooperative strategies.* This terminology is justified by the fact that each player will *help* the other player's interests by using what we call his cooperative strategy, and will *harm* the other player's interests by using what we call his non-cooperative strategy. (For instance, if player 1 himself uses strategy A_1, he will obtain the payoff $+10$ if player 2 uses the cooperative strategy B_1 but will obtain the payoff $—20$ if player 2 uses the non-cooperative strategy B_2. Again, if player 1 himself uses strategy A_2, he will obtain the payoff $+11$ if player 2 uses B_1 but will obtain only $+1$ if player 2 uses B_2. Thus, whichever strategy player 1 himself uses, he will be better off if player 2 uses the 'cooperative' strategy B_1 than if player 2 uses the 'non-cooperative' strategy B_2. Likewise, irrespective of the strategy player 2 himself uses, he will be better off if player 1 uses the 'cooperative' strategy A_1.)

The strategy combination (A_1, B_1) under which both players would use their cooperative strategies we call the *cooperative solution* of the game; while the strategy combination (A_2, B_2) under which both players would use their non-cooperative strategies we call the *non-cooperative solution.* Clearly the cooperative solution would be better for both players since it would yield both of them the payoff $+10$ while the non-cooperative solution would yield both of them only the payoff $+1$. In spite of this we shall now argue that the two players will actually use their non-cooperative strategies, so that the outcome will correspond to the non-cooperative solution, less preferred by both of them. We shall argue that this will happen *in spite* of the fact, and indeed precisely *because* of the fact, that both players are assumed to be very rational individuals. This conclusion which we shall now try to establish is called the *Prisoner's Dilemma Paradox.* This name is used in the game-theoretical literature because the first example (proposed by Professor Tucker of Princeton University) for this paradoxical situation involved two prisoners, who had to choose between a cooperative strategy (not 'squealing' on the other prisoner) and a non-cooperative strategy ('squealing'). The argument was that both prisoners will choose to 'squeal', even though this will be disastrous for both of them.

The argument runs as follows. First let us consider the situation from player 1's point of view. If he expects player 2 to use the non-cooperative strategy B_2 then he himself will also use the non-cooperative strategy A_2, because by doing so he will obtain the payoff $+1$ instead of -20. But he will use his non-cooperative strategy A_2 even if he expects player 2 to use the cooperative strategy B_1!!! For by doing so he will obtain $+11$ while if he used his cooperative strategy A_1 he would obtain only $+10$. Thus, whatever player 1's expectations about player 2's behaviour, he himself will always use his non-cooperative strategy A_2. By similar reasoning, player 2 will always use his non-cooperative strategy B_2. But the strategy pair (A_2, B_2) is the non-cooperative solution. This completes the proof.

Clearly a very crucial point in this argument is the fact that the payoff structure of the game rewards the player who himself uses a *non-cooperative* strategy when the other player uses a *cooperative* strategy. (Numerically in our example this 'reward for double-crossing the other player' in this way is $11 - 10 = 1$ unit.) But this payoff structure in itself is insufficient to establish the conclusion. Our argument was crucially dependent on the tacit assumption that the rules of the game do not allow the players to conclude *binding* and *enforceable agreements*. For if the players could make such agreements then both of them could agree to use cooperative strategies, subject to heavy penalties for violating such an agreement. If these penalties were large enough to offset the 'reward for double-crossing' inherent in the payoff matrix of the game (which in our case would mean penalties greater than one unit) then double-crossing would become unattractive to the players. Hence in this case each player could feel quite safe in using a cooperative strategy without the danger of being confronted by a non-cooperative strategy on the part of the other player.

Of course, the players' incentives to keeping agreements need not arise from *externally* imposed penalties for violations. The same effect will be achieved if the players' own *internal* moral attitudes are such as to make violations of agreements unrewarding. In this case we may say that violations of agreements are discouraged by the *interiorized penalties* (disutilities) associated with such violations. From a game-theoretical standpoint external and internal penalties represent the same basic mechanism: they reduce the net payoffs (net utilities) connected with strategies involving violations of agreements. (Here we define the 'net payoff' as the 'gross payoff' *less* the external and/or internal penalty.)

Thus we reach the following important conclusion. In games with mixed interests full cooperation between the players is possible only if they can trust each other's willingness to keep agreements; and this requires that agreements between the players should be fully binding and enforceable by means of external or internal penalties for violations. If agreements are enforceable in this sense then rational players will always play a *cooperative game,* i.e. will try to reach a cooperative solution. But if agreements are not enforceable, i.e. if the players have good reasons to distrust each other's willingness to keep agreements, then they will play a *non-cooperative game* and will reach a non-cooperative solution – in spite of the fact that the cooperative solution would make all of them better off. (Even in what we call a non-cooperative game there may be *some* degree of cooperation between the players, but their cooperation will be restricted to those fields where such cooperation does not require mutual trust.) Accordingly, if the players reach a non-cooperative solution *this may not mean that their behaviour is irrational*: it may only mean that they mutually distrust each other, for which they may have very good rational reasons based on past experience. No doubt, acceptance of a non-cooperative solution is in a way always 'irrational' when a mutually preferable cooperative solution would be available. But this 'irrationality' may not involve any irrationality on the part of the players themselves, but rather may be the result of their very rational behaviour in what may be called an 'irrational' social *situation.*

VI

For instance, we can interpret Example 3 as representing an international political situation, say, one involving a cold war between two countries. The cooperative strategies A_1 and B_1 might involve e.g. a substantial reduction in military preparations and other cold-war activities on the part of country 1 and country 2 respectively. The non-cooperative strategies A_2 and B_2 might correspond to maintaining a high level of military preparations and of other unfriendly activities. Both countries would be better off if the levels of their military and other unfriendly activities could be reduced by mutual agreement, tacit or explicit. But this may not be a practicable policy. In particular, it may happen that both countries would be very keen to double-cross each other if they thought they could get away with it, and both countries may know by bitter experience that this is the case. Then it will be perfectly rational for each side to distrust the other so long as the situation described persists.

Of course, it is quite possible that sometimes two countries *think* they must distrust each other though in actual fact this is not true or is true only to a much lesser extent. For instance, the two countries' political leaders may show much more intrinsic reluctance to double-dealing than they would credit each other with. Or alternatively each side's objective political disincentives against double-dealing may be much stronger than the other side might think, etc. In such cases their mutual distrust may possibly yield to increased information about each other's true attitudes and about each other's true political incentives, etc.

But in general we cannot expect that mutual distrust is merely a matter of mutual misunderstanding. Each side may very well find that it could achieve very *real* political advantages in terms of its own political objectives if it could successfully double-cross the other side; and the political leaders of each side may very well follow moral philosophies that make double-dealing quite permissible in international politics – possibly in all cases, or maybe only in the case of double-dealing against one's ideological opponents. (That is, they may take the view that 'Promises given to Infidels or to Heretics or to Communists or to Capitalists, etc., do not count'.) In such cases the situation cannot be remedied by more information (or by more goodwill) alone. A real improvement can come only from fundamental structural changes in the situation, such as by providing much stronger institutional incentives to keeping international agreements, i.e. by reducing the temptation to violating them; and by changing the basic attitudes of the chief policy makers, as well as those of the general public, toward violations of international agreements and of international law. Of course, such basic attitudinal and institutional changes cannot be achieved from one day to another. The political atmosphere must be prepared for them by first attempting mutual cooperation in minor matters such that do not presuppose a good deal of mutual trust, because they can be reversed without major damage if the other side turns out to be less cooperative or less reliable than one has hoped for.

Clearly, cooperation cannot be achieved merely by one side's willingness to cooperate; and so one must always be prepared for the possibility that the other side may not wish to go further than up to a certain point, at least for the time being. But of course one can never find out how far one can get on the road to mutual cooperation without ever trying a serious start.

To sum up, one of the important contributions of game theory to the analysis of international political situations is realization of the fact that virtually all mixed-interest games, without some mechanism to enforce agreements between the players, lead to a Prisoner's Dilemma Paradox. That is, they are situations where the players *may* have very good reasons to mistrust each other's intentions, so that even very rational players may be driven to the non-cooperative solution, even though the cooperative solution would yield higher payoffs to all of them. The non-cooperative solution will be reached, not because the players act irrationally, but precisely because they act in a rational manner.

This interpretation of international politics sharply contrasts with the view that wars, arms races, and other forms of international conflicts, are merely the results of the policy makers' irrationality, and therefore can be cured by a more rational approach and by better information about the underlying facts. For instance, a famous student of international conflicts, Lewis F. Richardson, who can be regarded as the very Founding Father of the modern analytical approach to the subject, argued that his own theory of international conflicts was:

> ...a mere description of what people would do if they did not stop to think. Why are so many nations reluctantly but steadily increasing their armaments as if they were mechanically compelled to do so? Because... they follow their traditions... and their instincts... and because they have not yet made a sufficiently strenuous intellectual and moral effort to control the situation.[1]

If our own interpretation of international conflicts is right then this is an oversimplified and potentially very dangerous view. For it leads to serious underestimation of the political forces actually generating and maintaining international conflicts; and in particular it precludes understanding of the fact that, with the existing subjective attitudes towards violations of international agreements, and with the existing objective payoffs to countries and individuals violating such agreements, non-cooperative behaviour

may often be the only rational and realistic response to a given international situation. By this means it leads to underestimation of the need for
fundamentally *changing* people's *attitudes* towards double-dealing in international politics and for fundamentally changing the *payoff* that people
and countries can hope to achieve by such behaviour.

VII

In Example 3, strategy pair (A_2, B_2), which we have called the non-cooperative solution, has the following important property. Strategies A_2 and B_2 are
mutually the *best replies* to each other; so long as player 2 uses strategy B_2,
player 1 will maximize his own payoff by using strategy A_2, and conversely,
so long as player 1 uses strategy A_2, player 2 will maximize his own payoff
by using strategy B_2. Accordingly, strategy pair (A_2, B_2) represents a *stable*
situation: once the two players come to adopt this pair of strategies, neither
of them will have any incentive to shift to some other strategy. For this reason we call this strategy pair an *equilibrium point*. More generally, we
speak of an equilibrium point whenever each player's strategy is the best reply to the strategies used by all the other players, so that none of the players
can gain by changing over to some other strategy so long as the other players do not do so. It is easy to check that in Example 3 the strategy pair $(A_2,
B_2)$ is the *only* equilibrium point in this sense. If the players adopted
any other strategy pair then at least one (or both) of them could gain
by shifting to another strategy, even if the other player did stick to
his own strategy without any change. For instance, strategy pair $(A_1,
B_1)$, which we have called the cooperative solution, is unstable because e.g.
player 1 could gain by shifting from A_1 to A_2 if player 2 used strategy B_2,
etc. It is easy to verify that the remaining two strategy pairs (A_1, B_2) and
(A_2, B_1) are likewise unstable and do not have the nature of equilibrium
points.

We can now state our previous conclusion in the following form. In a
non-cooperative game, where the players cannot conclude enforceable
agreements, only an *equilibrium point* can represent a stable situation.
That is, a stable situation can obtain only if each player's strategy is a *best
reply* to the other players' strategies, so that no player will have any incentive to revise his strategy choice. This means that the players cannot adopt a
cooperative joint strategy not having the nature of an equilibrium point,

even if adoption of this joint strategy would be very advantageous to all of them (such as would be adoption of strategy pair (A_1, B_1) in our example).

As we have already argued, if we want to enable the players to adopt such a more desirable cooperative joint strategy then we must transform the non-cooperative game into a cooperative one by making all agreements fully binding and enforceable – ot at least we must change the payoff matrix of the game so as to make the desired cooperative joint strategy an equilibrium point.

This theoretical conclusion may sometimes lead to paradoxical policy proposals. For instance, Professor Morgenstern[2] has made out a strong case for the view that, once the United States has a strong nuclear retaliatory force, it is in her own interest that the Soviet Union should *also* possess one. Otherwise the Soviet Union would feel so insecure as to be tempted to *start* a nuclear war whenever she had the slightest suspicion that the United States might have offensive intentions. In game-theoretical terminology, if *both* nuclear powers had the capability of striking *first* but only *one* side had the capability of striking back *after* a nuclear attack, this would result in a dangerously *unstable* situation, which both sides have an interest to avoid.

Another implication is that in a non-cooperative game any disturbance may easily destabilize an existing equilibrium situation[3], and eventually may lead to a new equilibrium situation less favourable to a given player than the old one was. Hence the players will always be wary of changes in the existing situation. For example, if one player demands concessions – even quite minor ones – from another these usually will be bitterly resisted because the other player will fear that any concession he may now grant will be used only to extract still further concessions from him in the future. Therefore a very important aspect of bargaining skill will be always to reassure the other party that one has only *limited objectives,* and that if one's present demands are now granted this will not be used as a leverage for demanding further and further consessions on later occasions.

For instance, in many cases the employers' resistance to recognizing their employees' trade unions was largely due to the fact that the employers did not know how far the unions would try to encroach upon managerial prerogatives and managerial decision making; and recognition was much more readily forthcoming as soon as a union succeeded in convincing the employer that its interests were in fact limited to improving wages and working conditions within the capitalistic institutional framework.

Likewise in international life one of the main purposes of diplomacy must be in many cases to convince the opponent that one's aims are limited to obtaining certain specific concessions, and do not involve any more fundamental changes in the relative power positions – at least when in fact this is the case. This is of course only another aspect of the general conclusion that in non-cooperative game the most important policy objective is to overcome the justified mutual distrust existing between the players.

VIII

In a sense all these and other conclusions of game-theoretical analysis are based on one general principle, which can be stated as follows. Rationality requires that each player *himself* should have a set of consistent policy objectives, and should not try to run in two different directions at the same time. Rationality also requires that each player should choose his strategies consistent with the *expectations* he can rationally entertain about *other* players' behaviour. For instance, in a two-person non-cooperative game each player must expect that a rational opponent will try to select a strategy that is a *best reply* to his own strategy. Again, in a bargaining game a given player cannot expect that a rational opponent will grant him a certain concession, if in the same situation he himself would refuse a similar concession because, under given conditions, he would not regard it as a rational policy to grant such a concession, etc.

In effect, the main advantage of the game-theoretical point of view is precisely to make us systematically aware of such considerations. It enables us to formulate in more precise terms what it means to act intelligently, and what it means to base our policies on intelligent expectations concerning other intelligent people's reactions to our own policies.

NOTES

* *Australian Journal of Politics and History,* **11** (1965), 292-304.
[1] Lewis F. Richardson, *Arms and Insecurity,* Chicago and Pittsburgh: The Boxwood Press and Quadrangle Books, 1960. p. 12.
[2] O. Morgenstern, *The Question of National Defense,* New York: Random House, 1959.
[3] To a lesser extent this is true also in cooperative games.

CHAPTER IX

MEASUREMENT OF SOCIAL POWER, OPPORTUNITY COSTS, AND THE THEORY OF TWO-PERSON BARGAINING GAMES*

I. INTRODUCTION

Recent papers by Simon (1957), by March (1955, 1957), and by Dahl (1957) have suggested measuring person A's power over person B in terms of its actual or potential *effects*, that is, in terms of the changes that A causes or can cause in B's behavior.[1] As Dahl puts it, A has power over B to the extent to which 'he can get B to do something that B would not otherwise do' (1957, p. 203).

As Simon and March have obtained very similar results, I shall restrict myself largely to summarizing Dahl's main conclusions. Dahl distinguishes the following constituents of the power relation:

(a) the *base* of power, i.e., the resources (economic assets, constitutional prerogatives, military forces, popular prestige, etc.) that A can use to influence B's behavior;

(b) the *means* of power, i.e., the specific actions (promises, threats, public appeals, etc.) by which A can make actual use of these resources to influence B's behavior;

(c) the *scope* of power, i.e., the set of specific actions that A, by using his means of power, can get B to perform; and finally

(d) the *amount* of power, i.e., the net increase in the probability of B's actually performing some specific action X, due to A's using his means of power against B (1957, pp. 203–205).

If A has power over several individuals, Dahl adds a fifth constituent:

(e) the set of individuals over whom A has power—this we shall call the *extension* of A's power.

Dahl points out that the power of two individuals can be compared in any of these five dimensions. Other things being equal, an individual's power is greater: (a) the greater his power base, (b) the more means of power available to him, and the greater (c) the scope, (d) the amount, and

(e) the extension of his power. But Dahl proposes to use only the last three variables for the formal definition and measurement of social power. He argues that what we primarily mean by great social power is an ability to influence many people (extension) in many respects (scope) and with a high probability (amount of power). In contrast, a large power base or numerous means of power are not direct measures of the extent of the influence or power that one person can exert over other persons; they are only instruments by which great power can be achieved and maintained, and are indicators from which we can normally *infer* the likely possession of great power by an individual.

Among the three variables of scope, amount, and extension, amount of power is the crucial one, in terms of which the other two can be defined. For the scope of A's power over B is simply the set of specific actions X with respect to which A has a non-zero amount of power over B, i.e., the set of those actions X for which A can achieve a nonzero increase in the probability of these actions actually being performed by B. Similarly, the extension of A's power is the set of specific individuals over whom A has power of nonzero scope and amount.

While the amount of power is a difference of two probabilities, and therefore is directly given as a *real number*,[2] all other dimensions of power are directly given as lists of specific objects (e.g., a list of specific resources, a list of specific actions by A or by B, or a list of specific individuals over whom A has power). But Dahl and March suggest that at least in certain situations it will be worthwhile to develop straight numerical measures for them by appropriate aggregating procedures—essentially by counting the number of comparable items in a given list, and possibly by assigning different weights to items of unequal importance (e.g., we may give more 'marks' for power over an important individual than for power over a less important one) (March, 1957, pp. 213–220). In other cases we may divide up a given list into several sublists and may assign a separate numerical measure to each of them, without necessarily aggregating all these numbers into a single figure. That is, we may characterize a given dimension of power not by a single number, but rather by a set of several numbers, i.e., a vector. (For instance, we may describe the extension of President de Gaulle's power by listing the numbers [or percentages] of deputies, of army officers of various ranks, of electors, etc., who support him, without trying to combine all these figures into one index number.)

II. TWO ADDITIONAL DIMENSIONS
OF SOCIAL POWER

A quantitative characterization of a power relation, however, in my view must include two more variables not mentioned in Dahl's list:

(f) the opportunity costs to A of attempting to influence B's behavior, i.e., the opportunity costs of using his power over B (and of acquiring this power over B in the first place if A does not yet possess the required power), which we shall call the *costs* of A's power over B; and

(g) the opportunity costs to B of refusing to do what A wants him to do, i.e., of refusing to yield to A's attempt to influence his behavior. As these opportunity costs measure the strength of B's incentives for yielding to A's influence, we shall call them the *strength* of A's power over B.[3]

More precisely, the *costs* of A's power over B will be defined as the *expected value* (actuarial value) of the costs of his attempt to influence B. It will be a weighted average of the net total costs that A would incur if his attempt were successful (e.g., the costs of rewarding B), and of the net total costs that A would incur if his attempt were unsuccessful (e.g., the costs of punishing B).

Other things being equal, A's power over B is greater the smaller the costs of A's power and the greater the strength of A's power.

Both of these two cost variables may be expressed either in physical units (e.g., it may cost A so many bottles of beer or so many working hours to get B to adopt a given policy X; and again it may cost B so many bottles of beer or so many years' imprisonment if he does not adopt policy X), in monetary units (e.g., A's or B's relevant costs may amount to so many actual dollars, or at least may be equivalent to a loss of so many dollars for him), or in utility units. (In view of the theoretical problems connected with interpersonal comparisons of utility, and of the difficulties associated with utility measurement even for one individual, in practice the costs and the strength of power will usually be expressed in physical or in monetary units.[4] But for the purposes of theoretical analysis the use of utility costs sometimes has important advantages, as we shall see.)

Unlike the power base and the means of power, which need not be included in the definition of the power relation, both the costs of power and the strength of power are essential ingredients of the definition of power. A's power over B should be defined not merely as an ability by A to get B to do X with a certain probability p, but rather as an ability by **A** to achieve this at a certain total cost u to himself, by convincing B that B would have to bear the total cost v if he did not do X.

III. THE COSTS OF POWER

One of the main purposes for which social scientists use the concept of A's power over B is for the description of the policy possibilities open to A. If we want to know the situation (or environment) which A faces as a decision-maker, we must know whether he can or cannot get B to perform a certain action X, and more specifically how sure he can be (in a probability sense) that B will actually perform this action. But a realistic description of A's policy possibilities must include not only A's ability or inability to get B to perform a certain action X, but also the *costs* that A has to bear in order to achieve this result. If two individuals are in a position to exert the same influence over other individuals, but if one can achieve this influence only at the cost of great efforts and/ or financial or other sacrifices, while the other can achieve it free of any such costs, we cannot say in any useful sense that their power is equally great. Any meaningful comparison must be in terms of the influence that two individuals can achieve at comparable costs, or in terms of the costs they have to bear in order to achieve comparable degrees of influence.

For instance, it is misleading to say that two political candidates have the same power over two comparable constituencies if one needs much more electioneering effort and expenditure to achieve a given majority, even if in the end both achieve the same majorities; or that two businessmen have the same power over the city government if one can achieve favorable treatment by city officials only at the price of large donations to party funds, while the other can get the same favorable treatment just for the asking.

Of course, a power concept which disregards the costs of power is most inaccurate when the costs of using a given power become very high or even prohibitive. For instance, suppose that an army commander becomes a prisoner of enemy troops, who try to force him at gun point to give a radio order to his army units to withdraw from a certain area. He may very well have the power to give a contrary order, both in the sense of having the physical ability to do so and in the sense of there being a very good chance of his order being actually obeyed by his army units—but he can use this power only at the cost of his life. Though the scope, the amount, and the extension of his power over his soldiers would still be very great, it would clearly be very misleading in this situation to call him a powerful individual in the same sense as before his capture.

More generally, measurement of power merely in terms of its scope, amount, and extension tends to give counterintuitive results when the possessor of power has little or no real opportunity to actually use his power. For example, take the case of a secretary who has to compile various reports for her employer, according to very specific instructions which leave her little actual choice as to how to prepare them. Suppose that her employer then uses these reports as a basis for very important decisions.[5] Physically she could exert considerable influence on her employer's policies by omitting certain pieces of information from her reports, or including misleading information. In this sense, the scope and the amount of her power over her employer is considerable. But normally she will have little opportunity for using this power, and social scientists would hardly wish to describe her as a powerful individual, as they would have to do if they used Dahl's power concept without modification.

In terms of our own power concept, however, the secretary in question has little real power if all dimensions of her power are taken into account. Though she does have power of great scope and great amount over her employer, this fact is normally more than offset by the very high costs of using her power. If she intentionally submits misleading reports she probably will be found out very soon and will be dismissed and/or punished in other ways. Moreover, if she is a loyal employee such flagrant violation of her instructions would in itself involve very high disutility costs to her.

To conclude, a realistic quantitative description of A's power over B must include, as an essential dimension of this power relation, the costs to A of attempting to influence B's behavior.

IV. THE STRENGTH OF POWER

While costs of power must be included in the definition of our power concept in order to ensure its descriptive validity, the variable of *strength* of power must be included to ensure the usefulness of our power concept for explanatory purposes.

As March (1955, pp. 431–432) has pointed out about the concept of influence, one of the main analytical tasks of such concepts as influence or power (which essentially is an ability to exert influence) is to serve as *intervening variables* in the analysis of individual or social decision-making. Therefore we need a power or influence concept which enables us in the relevant cases to explain a decision by a given private individual or by an official of a social organization, in terms of the power or influence that another individual or some social group has over him. But fundamentally, the analysis of any human decision must be in terms of the variables on the basis of which the decisionmaker concerned actually makes his decision — that is, in terms of the advantages and disadvantages he associates with alternative policies available to him. In order to explain why *B* adopts a certain policy *X* in accordance with *A*'s wishes, we must know what *difference it makes* for *B* whether *A* is his friend or his enemy—or more generally, we must know the *opportunity costs* to *B* of not adopting policy *X*. Hence, if our power concept is to serve us as an explanatory intervening variable in the analysis of *B*'s decision to comply with *A*'s wishes, our power concept must include as one of its essential dimensions the opportunity costs to *B* of non-compliance, which measure the strength of *B*'s incentives to compliance and which we have called the strength of *A*'s power over *B*.

For instance, if we want to explain the decision of Senator Knowland to support a certain bill of the Eisenhower administration we must find out, among other things, which particular individuals or social groups influenced his decision, and to what extent. Now suppose that we have strong reasons to assume that it was President Eisenhower's personal intervention which made Senator Knowland change his mind and decide to support the bill in question. Then we still have to explain *how* the variables governing the Senator's decision were actually affected by the President's intervention. Did the President make a promise to him, i.e., did he attach new *advantages*, from the Senator's point of view, to the policy of supporting the bill? Or did the President make a threat, i.e., did he attach new *disadvantages* to the policy of opposing the bill? Or did the President supply new information, pointing out certain already *existing* advantages and / or disadvantages associated with these two policies, which the senator had been insufficiently aware of before? In any case we must explain how the President's intervention increased the opportunity costs that Senator Knowland came to associate with opposing the bill.

If we cannot supply this information, then the mere existence of an influence or power relationship between President Eisenhower and Senator Knowland will not *explain* the latter's decision to support the bill. It will only pose a *problem* concerning this decision. (Why on earth did he comply with the President's request to support the bill, when it is known that he had many reasons to oppose it, and did actually oppose it for a while?)

There seem to be four main ways by which a given actor A can manipulate the incentives or opportunity costs of another actor B:

(1) A may provide certain *new* advantages or disadvantages for B, subject to *no condition*. For instance, he may provide certain facilities for B which make it easier or less expensive for B to follow certain particular policy objectives desirable to A. (For example, country A may be able to induce country B to attack some third country C, simply by supplying arms to B, even if A supplies these arms 'without any strings attached'—and in particular without marking it a condition of her arms deliveries that B will actually attack C.) Or A may withdraw from B certain facilities that could help B in attaining policy objectives undesirable to A. More generally, A may provide for B goods or services complementary to some particular policy goal X, or competitive to policy goals alternative to X, so as to increase for B the net utility of X, or to decrease the net utility of its alternatives; or A may achieve similar results by depriving B of goods or services either competitive to X or complementary to its alternatives.[6]

(2) A may set up *rewards* and *punishments*, i.e., *new* advantages and disadvantages subject to certain *conditions* as to B's future behavior.

(3) A may supply *information* (or misinformation) on (allegedly) already *existing* advantages and/or disadvantages connected with various alternative policies open to B.

(4) A may rely on his legitimate *authority* over B, or on B's personal *affection* for A, which make B attach *direct disutility* to the very act of disobeying A.

Of course, in a situation where A has certain power over B, either party can be mistaken about the true opportunity costs to him of various alternatives. Therefore both in discussing the costs of A's power over B, and in discussing the strength of his power, we must distinguish between *objective* costs and *perceived* costs—between what these costs actually are and what the individual bearing these costs thinks them to be. For the purpose of a formal definition of the power relation, the *costs* of A's power over B have to be stated as the *objective* costs that an attempt to influence B would actually entail upon A, while the *strength* of A's power over B has to be stated in terms of the costs of noncompliance as *perceived* by B himself. The reason is that the costs of A's power serve to describe the objective policy possibilities open to A, whereas the strength of A's power serves to explain B's subjective motivation for compliant behavior. (Of course, a full description of a given power situation would require listing both objective and perceived costs for both participants.)

V. THE STRENGTH OF POWER, AND

THE AMOUNT OF POWER IN

DAHL'S SENSE

Clearly, in general the greater the *strength* of A's power over B, the greater will be A's *amount* of power over B with respect to action X. The relationship between these two variables will take a particularly simple mathematical form if the strength of A's power is measured in *utility* terms, i.e., in terms of the disutility costs to B of noncompliance.[7]

We shall use the following model. A wants B to perform action X. But B associates disutility x with doing X. Nevertheless B would perform X with probability p_1 (i.e., would adopt the mixed strategy $s[p_1]$ assigning probability p_1 to doing X and probability $[1 - p_1]$ to not doing X), even in the absence of A's intervention.[8] B would adopt this strategy because if he completely refused to do X (i.e., if he adopted the mixed strategy $S[0]$) he would obtain only the utility payoff u_0; while if he did X with probability p_1 (i.e., if he adopted strategy $s[p_1]$), then he would obtain the higher utility payoff u_1, making his total expected utility $u_1 - p_1 x > u_0$.

Now A intervenes and persuades B that B will obtain the still higher utility payoff u_2 if he agrees to do action X with a certain probability $p_2 > p_1$ (i.e., if he adopts strategy $s[p_2]$), making his total expected utility $u_2 - p_2 x$. In view of this, B does adopt strategy $s[p_2]$.

Under these assumptions, obviously the *amount* of A's power over B will be the difference $\Delta p = p_2 - p_1$, while the *strength* of A's power over B will be the difference $u_2 - u_1$. As $p_2 \leqslant 1$, we must have $\Delta p \leqslant 1 - p_1$. Moreover, by assumption (cf. Footnote 7), $\Delta p \geqslant 0$.

If B tries to maximize his expected utility,[9] then he will adopt strategy $s[p_2]$ only if

(1) $u_2 - p_2 x \geqslant u_1 - p_1 x,$

that is, if

(2) $\Delta p = p_2 - p_1 \leqslant \dfrac{u_2 - u_1}{x} = \dfrac{\Delta u}{x}.$

This gives us:

THEOREM I. The maximum *amount* of power that A can achieve over B with respect to action X tends to be equal to the *strength* of A's power over B (as expressed in utility units) divided by the disutility to B of doing action X—except that this maximum amount of power cannot be more than the amount of power corresponding to B's doing action X with probability *one*.

The strength of A's power over B divided by the disutility to B of doing X may be called the *relative strength* of A's power over B. Accordingly, we obtain:

THEOREM I'. The maximum *amount* of power that A can achieve over B with respect to action X tends to be equal to the *relative strength* of A's power over B with respect to action X (except that, again, this maximum amount of power cannot be more than the amount of power corresponding to B's doing action X with probability one).

Of course, in the real world we seldom observe B to use a randomized mixed strategy of form $s[p]$, in a literal sense. What we do find is that, if we watch B's behavior over a series of comparable occasions, he will comply with A's wishes in some proportion p of all occasions and will fail to comply in the remaining proportion $(1 - p)$ of the occasions. Moreover, the disutility to B of compliant behavior will vary from one occasion to another. Hence if B wants to comply with A's wishes in pn cases out of n then, other things being equal, he will tend to select those pn cases where compliance is associated with the smallest disutility to him. For example, suppose that a U.S. senator, with political attitudes rather different from the administration's, decides to vote for the president's legislative program often enough to avoid at least an open break with the administration. Then he is likely to select for his support those administration bills which are least distasteful to him and to his constituents. This means that the total disutility to B of a given strategy $s[p]$ (which now has to be defined as a strategy involving compliance in *proportion p* of all cases) will tend to increase somewhat more than proportionally as *p* increases, because should *B* decide to increase the frequency of his compliant behavior he would have to include a higher fraction of 'difficult' cases.

Accordingly, if we restate our model in terms of empirical *frequencies*, rather than theoretical *probabilities*, we must expect that the maximum *amount* of power that *A* can achieve over *B* will increase somewhat less than in proportion to increments in the *strength* of *A*'s power over *B* (measuring this strength now in terms of the *average* utility value of *B*'s incentives for compliance over all occasions). But our Theorem I is likely to retain at least its approximate validity in most empirical situations.[10]

VI. POWER IN A SCHEDULE SENSE

We have just seen that the greater the strength of a person's power over other persons the greater the amount of his power over them tends to be. But likewise, the greater the strength of a person's power over other people, the greater both the scope and the extension of his power over these people. That is, the stronger incentives he can provide for compliance, the larger the number of specific actions he can get other people to perform for him will be, and the larger the number of individuals he can get to perform these actions.

But while the scope, the amount, and the extension of his power are all functions of the *strength* of his power over all individuals, the strength of his power is itself a function of the *costs* of power he is prepared to bear. The greater efforts and sacrifices he is prepared to make, the stronger incentives for compliance he will be able to provide and the greater will be the strength of his power over them.

Therefore, a given individual's power can be described not only by stating the specific values of the five dimensions of his power (whether as single numbers, or as vectors, or as lists of specific items), but also by specifying the mathematical *functions* or *schedules* that connect the costs of his power with the other four dimensions. When power is defined in terms of the specific values of the five power variables we shall speak of power in a *point* sense, and when power is defined in terms of the functions or schedules connecting the other four power variables with the costs of power we shall speak of power in a *schedule* sense.[11]

Power in a schedule sense can be regarded as a 'production function' describing how a given individual can 'transform' different amounts of his resources (of his working time, his money, his political rights, his popularity, etc.) into social power of various dimensions (of various strengths, scopes, amounts, and extensions). The commonsense notion of social power makes it an *ability* to achieve certain things—an ability that the person concerned is free to use or to leave unused. It seems to me that this notion of power as an ability is better captured by our concept of power in a schedule sense than it is by the concept of power in a point sense. (The latter seems to better correspond to the commonsense notion of actually exerted *influence*, rather than to that of power as such.)

If a person's power is given in a mere schedule sense, then we can state the specific values of his five power dimensions only if we are also told how much of his different resources he is actually prepared to use in order to obtain social power of various dimensions—that is, if besides his power schedules we know also his *utility function*. Whereas his power defined in a schedule sense indicates the conditions under which his environment is ready to 'supply' power to him, it is his utility function which determines his 'demand' for power under various alternative conditions.

VII. BILATERAL POWER AND THE 'BLACKMAILER'S FALLACY'

So far we have tacitly assumed that, in situations where A has power over B, A is always in a position to determine, by his unilateral decision, the incentives he will provide for B's compliance, as well as the degree of compliance he will try to enforce. Situations in which this is actually the case may be called unilateral power situations. But it very often happens that not only can A exert pressure on B in order to get him to adopt certain specific policies, but B can do the same to A. In particular, B may be able to press A for increased rewards and/or decreased penalties, and for relaxing the standards of compliance required from him and used in administering rewards and penalties to him. Situations of this type we shall call bilateral or reciprocal power situations. In such situations, both the extent of B's compliant behavior (i.e., the scope and the amount of A's power over B) and the net incentives that A can provide for B (i.e., the net strength of A's power over B) will become matters of explicit or implicit *bargaining* between the two parties.

Of the four ways in which A can increase his strength of power discussed previously, we tend to obtain unilateral power situations in cases (1), (3), and (4), where A's power over B is based on providing *unconditional* advantages or disadvantages for B, on conveying information or misinformation to him, or on having legitimate authority over B and/or enjoying B's personal affection (though there are also exceptions where these cases give rise to bilateral power). For example, it is usually largely a matter for A's personal discretion whether he provides certain facilities for B, whether he discloses certain pieces of information to him, or whether he gives him an order as his legitimate superior. In case (2), on the other hand, when A's power over B is based on A's ability to set up rewards and/or punishments for B *conditional* upon B's behavior, normally we find bilateral power situations (though again there are important exceptions).[12] Here B can exert pressure on A by withholding his compliance, even though compliance would be much more profitable than noncompliance. He may also be able to exert pressure on A by making the costs of a conflict (including the costs of punishing B for noncompliance) very high to A.

For bilateral power situations Theorem I and Theorem I' do not hold true. For these conclusions have been completely dependent on the assumption that if a certain strategy s_1, involving some given degree of compliance by B, is more profitable to B than any alternative strategy s_2 involving a lesser degree of compliance (or none at all), then B will always choose strategy s_1 and will never choose strategy s_2—not even as a result of dissatisfaction with the terms A offers in return for B's co-operation. While in unilateral power situations this assumption is perfectly legitimate (as it amounts to no more than assuming that B tries to maximize his utility or expected utility), in bilateral power situations this assumption would involve what I propose to call the 'blackmailer's fallacy' (Harsanyi, 1956, p. 156).

A would-be blackmailer A once argued that as he was in a position to cause damage worth $\$ 1,000$ to a certain rich man B, he should be able to extract from B *any* ransom r short of $\$ 1,000$, because after payment of $r < \$ 1,000$, B would still be better off than if he had to suffer the full $\$ 1,000$ damage.

But this argument is clearly fallacious. By similar reasoning, B could also have argued that A would accept *any* ransom r larger than nil, because after accepting a ransom $r > \$ 0$, A would still be better off than if no agreement were reached and he did not receive anything at all. What both of these arguments really show is that in any bargaining between two rational bargainers, the outcome must fall between what may be called the two parties' *concession limits*, which are defined by each party's refusal to accept any agreement that would make him actually worse off than he would be in the conflict situation. But the two arguments in themselves say nothing about where the two parties' agreement point will actually lie *between* these two limits. They certainly do not allow the inference that this agreement point will actually coincide or nearly coincide with one party's concession limit.[13] (Only if we know the two parties' attitudes towards risk-taking, and in particular towards risking a conflict rather than accepting unfavorable terms, can we make any predictions about where their agreement point will lie between the two concession limits.)

Either party's actual behavior will be a resultant of two opposing psychological forces. On the one hand, for example, B will admittedly have some incentive for agreeing to any ransom payment less than \$ 1,000. But B will also know that A will likewise have some incentive for accepting any ransom payment greater than zero, and this fact will make B expect to get away with a ransom payment of much less than \$ 1,000. This expectation in turn will provide B with some incentive to resist any ransom payment too close to \$ 1,000. Any realistic theory of B's behavior must take full account of *both* of these psychological forces—both of B's motives for compliance, and of the reasons which make him expect some concessions on A's part which will render full compliance on his own part unnecessary.

VIII. THE ZEUTHEN-NASH THEORY AND THE STRENGTH OF POWER IN BILATERAL POWER SITUATIONS

For analysis of the two parties' behavior in bilateral power situations, and in particular for quantitative assessment of the two opposite psychological forces governing each party's degree of compliance, we shall use the Zeuthen-Nash theory of the two-person bargaining game.[14] Our analysis will be based on the following model.[15]

Just as in the model discussed earlier, A wants B to perform action X. But B associates disutility x with doing X. Nevertheless B would perform X with probability p_1, i.e., would use the mixed strategy $s(p_1)$, even in the absence of A's intervention. This would happen because if B completely refused to do X (i.e., if he adopted strategy $s[0]$) he would obtain only the utility payoff u_0—while if he did X with probability p_1 (i.e., if he adopted strategy $s[p_1]$) then he would obtain the higher utility payoff u_1, making his total expected utility $u_1 - p_1 x > u_0$.

If B completely refused to do X, then A's utility level would be u_0^*. If B did perform X (with probability 1), then A's utility would increase by the amount x^*. Accordingly, if B did X only with probability p_1 then A's expected utility would be $u_0^* + p_1 x^*$.

Now A intervenes and offers B a reward R if B will increase the probability of his doing action X from p_1 to some mutually agreed figure p_2 (i.e., if B adopts strategy $s[p_2]$). In utility units, this reward R would represent a gain r for B, while providing this reward would cost A the amount r^*. Hence, if the two parties can agree on some probability p_2, then A's total expected utility will be

$$(3) \qquad u_2^* = u_2^*(p_2) = u_0^* - r^* + p_2 x^*,$$

whereas B's total expected utility will be

$$(4) \qquad u_2 = u_2(p_2) = u_1 + r - p_2 x.$$

A also sets up the penalty T for B if B refuses to sufficiently increase the probability of his performing action X. In utility units, this penalty T would cause a loss t to B, while enforcing this penalty would cost A the amount t^*. Hence, if the two parties could not agree on the value of p_2, A's total expected utility would be

$$(5) \qquad u_3^* = u_0^* - t^* + p_1 x^*$$

(assuming that B would still perform X with probability p_1), whereas B's total expected utility would be

$$(6) \qquad u_3 = u_1 - t_1 - p_1 x.$$

More generally, we may assume that in a conflict situation *both* parties would use retaliatory strategies against each other, A using strategy T_A and

B using strategy T_B. In such a case t should be redefined as the *total loss* that *B* would suffer in the conflict situation, including both the damages caused to him by his opponent's retaliatory strategy T_A, and the costs to him of his own retaliatory strategy T_B. Similarly, t^* should be redefined as the *total loss* that *A* would suffer in the conflict situation. But otherwise our conclusions retain their validity.

Now, what will be the equilibrium value of the probability p_2 which tends to be agreed upon in bargaining between two rational bargainers?

We already know that it must lie between the p_2 values corresponding to the two parties' concession limits. *A*'s concession limit is reached when $u_2^* = u_3^*$. By (3) and (5), the corresponding p_2 value is

$$(7) \qquad p_2^A = p_1 + \frac{r^* - t^*}{x^*}.$$

With $p_2 = p_2^A$, *A*'s total expected utility would be

$$(8) \qquad u^*_2(p_2^A) = u_3^* = u_0^* - t^* + p_1 x^*$$

while *B*'s total expected utility would be

$$(9) \qquad u_2(p_2^A) = u_1 + r - \frac{x}{x^*}(r^* - t^*) - p_1 x.$$

On the other hand, *B*'s concession limit is reached when $u_2 = u_3$. By (4) and (6) the corresponding p_2 value is

$$(10) \qquad p_2^B = p_1 + \frac{r + t}{x}.$$

With $p_2 = p_2^B$, *A*'s total expected utility would be

$$(11) \qquad u_2^*(p_2^B) = u_0^* - r^* + \frac{x^*}{x}(r + t) + p_1 x^*$$

while *B*'s total expected utility would be

$$(12) \qquad u_2(p_2^B) = u_3 = u_1 - t - p_1 x.$$

It is easy to see (Fig. 1) that in the utility plane u^*, u for the two parties, all possible agreement points $U(p) = [u_2^*(p_2), u_2(p_2)]$ must lie on the straight-line interval connecting the two parties' concession limit points.

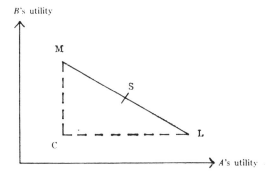

Fig. 1. Zeuthen-Nash utility plane.

$L = U(p_2{}^A) = [u_2{}^*(p_2{}^A), u_2(p_2{}^A)]$ and $M = U(p_2{}^B) = [u_2{}^*(p_2{}^B), u_2(p_2{}^B)]$. (The two parties' payoffs in the conflict situation are indicated by the conflict point $C = [u_3{}^*, u_3]$).

When the locus of all possible agreement points U is a straight line, the Zeuthen-Nash solution takes a particularly simple mathematical form; it is located simply at the midpoint of the distance between the two concession-limit points L and M (i.e., at S).[16] Hence, at the solution point S, A must obtain the expected utility

$$u_4{}^* = \frac{1}{2} \left[u_2{}^*(p_2{}^A) + u_2{}^*(p_2{}^B) \right] =$$

$$(13) \qquad = u_0{}^* - \frac{r^* + t^*}{2} + \frac{x^*}{2x}(r + t) + p_1 x^*$$

where the last equality follows from (8) and (11); while B must obtain the expected utility

$$u_4 = \frac{1}{2} \left[u_2(p_2{}^A) + u_2(p_2{}^B) \right] =$$

$$(14) \qquad = u_1 + \frac{r - t}{2} - \frac{x}{2x^*}(r^* - t^*) - p_1 x.$$

If we set $u_4{}^* = u_2{}^*(p_2)$ and $u_4 = u_2(p_2)$, by (13) and (3) (or by [14] and [4]) we obtain, as the equilibrium value of p_2 corresponding to the solution point S, the expression

(15)
$$p_2 = p_1 + \frac{r + t}{2x} + \frac{r^* - t^*}{2x^*}$$

subject, of course, to the requirement that always

(15a) $p_2 \leqslant 1$.

The Zeuthen-Nash theory also tells us that A will choose the reward R he offers B in such a way as to maximize the expression

$$\Delta r = \frac{r}{x} - \frac{r^*}{x^*}$$

which measures, from A's point of view, the value of R as an incentive, less the cost of providing R for B. Moreover, A will select the penalty T in such a way as to maximize the expression

$$\Delta t = \frac{t}{x} - \frac{t^*}{x^*}$$

which again measures, from A's point of view, the value of T as a deterrent, less the cost of administering T to B. This is so because, according to (13), A will maximize his own final utility payoff u_4^*, by means of maximizing Δr and Δt.

In the more general case where both parties would use retaliatory strategies in the event of a conflict, A (in order to maximize his own final payoff u_4^*) would again try to select his own retaliatory strategy T_A so as to *maximize Δt* when B's strategy T_B is given. On the other hand, B (in order to maximize his own final payoff u_4) would try to select his own retaliatory strategy T_B so as to *minimze Δt* when A's strategy T_A is given. Hence the equilibrium choice of T_A and T_B will be such as to make Δt take its maximin value.

Now clearly, if B adopts strategy $s[p_2]$ corresponding to the p_2 value defined by (15), then the *amount* of A's power over B with respect to action X will become

(16) $$\Delta p = p_2 - p_1 = \frac{1}{2} \left(\frac{r + t}{x} - \frac{t^* - r^*}{x^*} \right).$$

But of course the value of Δp must be consistent with (15a). Hence (16) is subject to the restriction that

(16a) $\Delta p \leqslant 1 - p_1$.

Let X^* denote A's action of *tolerating* B's failure to perform action X on one occasion. (We shall call action X^* the complementary action to action X.) Now suppose that A and B agree that B will perform action X with probability p_2, i.e., that B will *not* perform action X, with probability $(1 - p_2)$. This will mean that A will have to tolerate B's not performing action X, i.e., that A will have to perform action X^*, with probability $(1 - p_2)$. That is, technically, A and B will agree on a *jointly randomized* mixed strategy under which, with probability p_2, B will perform action X while A will *not* perform the complementary action X^*—whereas, with probability $(1 - p_2)$, A will perform action X^* while B will *not* perform action X.

Thus, while A's power over B will primarily consist in A's ability to get B to perform action X with a certain probability p_2; B's power over A will primarily consist in B's ability to get A to perform the complementary action X^* with probability $(1 - p_2)$.

On any given occasion where A performs action X^* (i.e., tolerates B's *not* performing action X), A will lose the utility gain x^* that he would derive from B's performing action X. Therefore A will associate disutility x^* with performing action X^*.

In Equation (16), the sum $(r + t)$ is the sum of the *reward* B would obtain for compliance, and of the *penalty* he would suffer for noncompliance, both expressed in utility terms. This sum measures the *difference it would make* for B to have A as his enemy instead of having him as his friend. It represents the total opportunity costs to B of choosing noncompliance leading to the conflict situation instead of choosing compliance, i.e., some strategy $s[p_2]$ acceptable to A. In brief, it represents the *opportunity costs of a conflict*, from B's point of view. In our terminology, it measures the (gross) *absolute strength* of A's power over B. Accordingly, the quotient $(r + t)/x$ measures the *gross relative strength* of A's power over B with respect to action X.

The difference $(t^* - r^*)$ is the difference between the costs to A of *punishing* B and the costs to A of *rewarding* B, both again expressed in utility terms. This difference measures the difference it would make for A to have B

as an enemy instead of having him as a friend. It represents the net opportunity costs to A of choosing the conflict situation rather than performing action X^* with a probability $(1-p_2)$ acceptable to B, i.e., rather than tolerating B to follow some strategy $s[p_2]$ acceptable to B. (In computing these opportunity costs, r^* has to be deducted from t^*, because in case of a conflict, A of course would save the costs of rewarding B.) In brief, this difference measures the *opportunity costs of a conflict*, this time from A's point of view. In our terminology, it measures the *gross absolute strength* of B's power over A. Moreover, as x^* is the disutility to A of performing action X^*, the quotient $(t^* - r^*)/x^*$ measures the *gross relative strength of B's power over A* with respect to action X^*.

Finally, the difference $[(r + t)/x - (t^* - r^*)/x^*]$ is the difference between the gross relative strength of A's power over B with respect to action X, and the gross relative strength of B's power over A with respect to the complementary action X^*. It may be called the *net strength* of A's power over B with respect to action X. This gives us:

THEOREM II. If both parties follow the rationality postulates of the Zeuthen-Nash theory of the two-person bargaining game, then in bilateral power situations the *amount* of A's power over B with respect to some action X tends to be equal to *half* the *net strength* of A's power over B with respect to the same action X—this net strength being defined as the difference between the gross relative strength of A's power over B with respect to action X and the gross relative strength of B's power over A with respect to the complementary action X^*. (But this theorem is subject to the qualification that the amount of A's power over B cannot be so great as to make the probability of B's performing action X become greater than *unity*.)[17]

Of course, in empirical applications the amount-of-power concept in Theorem II (and in Theorem I) must be reinterpreted in terms of empirical *frequencies*, instead of theoretical *probabilities* (see the preceding discussion of this point).

Simon (1957, pp. 66–68) has pointed out that in bilateral power situations—at least, when none of the participants seriously misjudge the situation—it is impossible to disentangle directly by empirical methods what is due to A's power over B, and what is due to B's power over A, so that we cannot measure separately A's power over B and B's power over A. But of course this does not mean that, given a sufficiently rich theoretical framework, we cannot disentangle, and separately measure, these two power relations by theoretical analysis. In effect, our Theorem II does provide us—at least in principle—with separate measures for the gross strength of each of these two power relations, and with a theory about how these two separate measures have to be combined in order to explain the end result.

IX. RELATIONSHIPS OF OUR STRENGTH-OF-POWER MEASURES TO ALTERNATIVE MEASURES FOR SOCIAL POWER

Theorems I (or I') and II describe how the strength-of-power measures described in this paper are related to Dahl's probabilistic measure for the amount of power, in unilateral and in bilateral power situations. As March's probabilistic measure (1957, p. 224) differs from Dahl's only in taking the absolute value of the difference $(p_2 - p_1)$ rather than the difference itself, these conclusions equally apply to March's measure.

The measure for the net strength of A's power over B in bilateral power situations is also related to the field-psychological measure for social power in small groups, proposed by French (1956), French and Raven (1959), and Cartwright (1959).

It was previously argued that B's (as well as A's) behavior must be explained in terms of two opposing psychological forces, one pressing B for more compliance with A's wishes in view of the rewards and penalties set up by A, and one pressing B for less compliance in view of the concessions B expects A to make in enforcing his demand for compliance. Theorem II now suggests that the strength of these two psychological forces can be measured by the *gross relative strength* of A's power over B, and of B's power over A, respectively. According to Theorem II, the strength of the resultant force, the *net strength* of A's power over B, equals the *difference* between the separate strengths of the two forces.

Similarly, French (1956, p. 183) defines his measure for social power as 'the maximum force which A can induce on B minus the maximum resisting force which B can mobilize in the opposite direction'. However, while the *compliance-inducing* force of French's model is closely related to the one of our own model (as both depend on B's incentives to compliance), the *compliance-resisting* force of French's model does not seem to be connected with B's expectation of obtaining concessions as to the degree of compliance that A requires from him, as is the case in our own model. Moreover, it is not clear whether the two opposing psychological forces of French's model are supposed to follow the same quantitative laws as those of our own model. But in any case the relationship between the two models would be worth further investigation.[18]

Finally, our measure for the net strength of A's power over B in bilateral power situations is also related to the *game-theoretical* measure for power in a committee system proposed by Shapley and Shubik (1954), in that both our and their measures are special cases of the *same* general game-theoretical measure for power in n-person situations.

Our measure for the net strength of power is based on the Zeuthen-Nash theory of the two-person bargaining game. In the following paper I shall discuss how this measure can be generalized for n-person reciprocal power situations, where all n participants mutually possess some power over one another and over the joint policies of their group as a whole. This generalization will be based on my bargaining model for the n-person co-operative game (Harsanyi, 1963; for an earlier version see Harsanyi, 1959), which is itself an n-person generalization of the Zeuthen-Nash theory. This generalized measure for power in n-person situations will be found to contain the Shapley-Shubik measure as a special case.

REFERENCES

Cartwright, D.: 'A Field Theoretical Conception of Power', D. Cartwright (Ed.), *Studies in Social Power,* Ann Harbor: Univ. of Michigan Press, 1959, pp. 183–220.

Dahl, R. A.: 'The Concept of Power', *Behav. Sci.,* 1957, **2**, 201–215.

French, J. R. P., Jr.: 'A Formal Theory of Social Power', *Psychol. Rev.,* 1956, **63**, 181–194.

French, J. R. P. Jr., & Raven, B.: 'The Bases of Social Power', in D. Cartwright (Ed.), *Studies in Social Power*, Ann Arbor: Univ. of Michigan Press, 1959, pp. 150–167.

Harsanyi, J. C.: 'Cardinal Welfare, Individualistic Ethics, and Interpersonal Comparisons of Utility', *J. Polit. Econ.,* 1955, **63**, 309–321.

Harsanyi, J.C.: 'Approaches to the Bargaining Problem Before and After the Theory of Games: a Critical Discussion of Zeuthen's, Hicks', and Nash's Theories', *Econometrica,* 1956, **24**, 144–157.

Harsanyi, J. C.: 'A Bargaining Model for the Cooperative n-Person Game', in A. W. Tucker and R. D. Luce (Eds.), *Contributions to the Theory of Games*, IV. Princeton; Princeton Univ. Press, 1959, pp. 325–355.

Harsanyi, J. C.: 'A Simplified Bargaining Model for the n-Person Cooperative Game', *Intern. Econ. Rev.,* 1963, **4**, 194–220.

Harsanyi, J. C.: 'On the Rationality Postulates Underlying the Theory of Cooperative Games', *J. Conflict Resol.,* 1961, **5**, 179 196.

Luce, R. D., & Raiffa, H.: *Games and Decisions*, New York: Wiley, 1957.

March, J. G.: 'An Introduction to the Theory and Measurement of Influence', *Amer. Polit. Sci. Rev.,* 1955, **49**, 431–451.

March, J. G.: 'Measurement Concepts in the Theory of Influence', *J. Politics*, 1957, **19**, 202–226.

Marschak, J.: 'Rational Behavior, Uncertain Prospects, and Measurable Utility', *Econometrica*, 1950, **18**, 111–141.

Marschak, J.: 'Three Lectures on Probability in the Social Sciences', in P. F. Lazarsfeld (Ed.), *Mathematical Thinking in the Social Sciences*, Glencoe: The Free Press, 1954, pp. 166–215. Reprinted as Cowles Commission Paper, N.S., No. 82.

Nash, J. F., Jr.: 'The Bargaining Problem', *Econometrica*, 1950, **18**, 155–162.

Nash, J. F., Jr.: 'Two-person Cooperative Games', *Econometrica*, 1953, 21, 128–140.

Schelling, T. C.: 'An essay on Bargaining', *Amer. Econ. Rev.*, 1956, **46**, 281–306.

Shapley, L. S., & Shubik, M.: 'A Method for Evaluating the Distribution of Power in a Committee System', *Amer. Polit. Sci. Rev.*, 1954, **48**, 787–792.

Simon, H. A.: *Models of Man: Social and Rational,* New York: Wiley, 1957, pp. 62–78.

Zeuthen, F.: *Problems of Monopoly and Economic Warfare*, London: G. Routledge and Sons, 1930.

NOTES

* *Behavioral Science,* 7 (1962), 67–80.

[1] I am indebted to Professor Jacob Marschak, of U.C.L.A., and to Professors Herbert A. Simon and James G. March, of Carnegie Institute of Technology, for helpful discussions on this and related topics.

[2] But as the probability that B will actually perform a specific action X suggested by A will in general be different for different actions X and for different individuals B, the total amount of A's power (or even the amount of A's power over a given individual B) will also have to be described by a vector rather than by a single number, except if some sort of aggregation procedure is used.

[3] Of course, instead of taking the opportunity costs (i.e. the net disadvantages) associated for B with noncompliance, we could just as well take the net advantages associated for him with compliance—they both amount to the same thing.

[4] A good deal of recent experimental work shows that it is possible, at least under certain conditions, to measure the utilities that a given individual assigns to various alternatives. Interpersonal comparisons of utility can also be given operationally meaningful interpretation (Harsanyi, 1955, pp. 316–320). Note, however, that the main conclusions of this paper, in particular Theorems I and II, do not require interpersonal utility comparisons.

[5] I owe this example to Professor Jacob Marschak.

[6] Case 1 is discussed in somewhat greater detail because power based on providing services or disservices without any conditions attached is often overlooked in the literature. For our purposes, the distinction between unconditional advantages or disadvantages on the one hand, and conditional rewards or punishments on the other hand, is important because the latter lend themselves to *bargaining* much more easily than the former do.

[7] To simplify our analysis, in what follows we shall be concerned only with the case where A is able to influence B in the intended direction, i.e., has a nonnegative amount of power over him. (A can have a negative amount of power over B only if he seriously misjudges the situation, because otherwise he can always make the amount of his power at worst *zero*, by simply refraining from intervention.)

[8] We follow Dahl in considering the more general case where B would do action X with some probability p_1 (which of course may be zero), even in the absence of A's intervention.

[9] On the assumption of expected-utility maximization, see Marschak (1950; 1954, Section 1).

[10] More exactly, in most unilateral power situations. The distinction between unilateral and bilateral power situations will be discussed below.

Note that in empirical applications based on a *frequency* interpretation, a further complication may arise owing to the fact that the utilities to A, and the disutilities to B, of a set of several compliant actions $X_1, \ldots, X_k$ by B may *not* be simply *additive* (as they may have the nature of complementary or of competitive 'goods' from A's point of view, and/or the nature of complementary or of competitive 'evils' from B's point of view).

[11] In analogy to the distinction in economic theory between demand or supply in a point sense and in a schedule sense.

[12] Viz. in cases when A is able to persuade B that he, A, has irrevocably committed himself in advance to not making any concessions to B. See Schelling (1956, pp. 282–287), Harsanyi (1961).

[13] Only in ultimatum games (cf. note 12 above), including all unilateral power situations, is it generally true that one party can extract any degree of concession or compliance from the other party up to the latter's actual concession limit point.

[14] I have set out my reasons for accepting the Zeuthen-Nash theory, and have discussed the theory in some detail, in Harsanyi (1956, 1961). The original references are Zeuthen (1930) and Nash (1950, 1953). For an excellent introduction to game theory in general, see Luce and Raiffa (1957).

[15] See notes 7 and 8 above.

[16] This is obviously true in the special case where the game is perfectly symmetric with respect to the two players. Generally the result follows from the invariance of the Zeuthen-Nash solution with respect to order-preserving linear transformations.

[17] In other words, Theorem II is subject to conditions (15a) and (16a).

[18] Cartwright (1959, p. 193) mentions the fact that while he himself defines social power as a *difference* of two opposing forces, Lewin proposed to measure it as a *quotient* of two opposing forces. According to Theorem II, in bilateral power situations the net force that A can exert on B is proportional to the *difference* of two psychological forces. More generally, if a person has both incentives for and incentives against doing a certain action, then the net strength of his incentives will be the difference between the strength of his positive and negative incentives. (For instance, if B's doing X yields him both rewards and penalties, then his net incentive will be the total value of the rewards less the total value of the penalties.) But note that in the former case Theorem II brings in a coefficient $1/2$, which does not occur in the latter case. On the other hand, both in unilateral and in bilateral power situations the gross strength of the force moving B toward compliance is the *quotient* of the strength of his incentives to compliance, and of the disutility to B of performing the required action X. Here the quotient formula arises because the disutility of doing X enters into the definition of B's expected utility as a *multiplicative* factor (it multiplies the probability of B's actually doing X).

CHAPTER X

MEASUREMENT OF SOCIAL POWER IN
n-PERSON RECIPROCAL POWER SITUATIONS*

I. INTRODUCTION

The preceding paper argued that social power must be defined in terms of five dimensions: the *costs*, the *strength*, the *scope*, the *amount*, and the *extension* of this power. A distinction was made between unilateral and reciprocal (or bilateral) power situations. The former are situations in which a given person A is in a position to determine, by his own unilateral decision, the incentives he will provide for another person B to comply with his wishes, and also the degree of compliance he will try to enforce. The latter are situations in which both parties have the ability to exert pressure on each other, and in which the incentives provided by A and, even more important, the degree of compliance he will try to enforce, therefore become matters of explicit or implicit bargaining between the two parties. Certain simple mathematical relationships between the *strength* and the *amount* of A's power over B were established, both for unilateral and for bilateral power situations.

In *unilateral* power situations, the generalization of these results to the n-person case is quite straightforward. As a matter of fact, the situation where one given individual A has unilateral power over several individuals $B_2, \ldots, B_k$ is already covered in the preceding paper. Thus it is sufficient to consider the case where several individuals $A_1, \ldots, A_k$ simultaneously have some power over the same individual B. Here it is natural to define the *amount* of joint power that $A_1, \ldots, A_k$ have over B with respect to some action X as the *net increase* in the probability of B's actually performing action X because of the intervention of $A_1, \ldots, A_k$. On the other hand, the *strength* of their joint power may be defined as the algebraic sum of the strength of every A_i 's separate power over B (giving a negative sign to the strength of the power of any individual A_i who may try to prevent B from performing action X). It is easy to see that under these definitions Theorem I (and I') retains its validity.

However, the model of bilateral power cannot be directly extended to n-person *reciprocal* power situations, where more than two individuals are able to exert pressures and counterpressures upon one another. To analyze situations of this latter type, the Zeuthen-Nash theory of two-person bargaining must be replaced by a theory of n-person bargaining. The bargaining model for the n-person co-operative game (Harsanyi, 1963; for an earlier version, see Harsanyi 1959) which will be used is an n-person generalization of the Zeuthen-Nash theory. (It is also a generalization of the Shapley [1953] value for the n-person game, in that it extends a certain modified form of the Shapley value from the special case of games with transferable utility, originally considered by Shapley, to the general case.)

To make the model of bilateral power more readily amenable to generalization for the n-person case, the measure for the *amount* of power possessed by each participant must be slightly modified. The amount of A's power over B (that is, A's power over B's *individual policy*) with respect to some action X to be performed by B was defined as the net increase Δp in the probability of B's actually performing action X because of A's intervention. Now a new measure, the amount of A's power over A and B's *joint policy* with respect to some controversial issue $X = (X_A, X_B)$, is defined as the probability p of A's being able to get the joint policy X_A adopted when A favors the policy X_A and B favors a different policy X_B.

Clearly the old model is a special case of the new one, as the controversial issue between A and B may be that B would prefer *not* to perform some action $\overline{X}$ which A wants B to perform. If we denote by $\overline{X}^*$ A's possible action of *tolerating* B's failure to perform action $\overline{X}$, then the joint policy X_A preferred by A will involve B's performing action $\overline{X}$ and A's *not* performing action $\overline{X}^*$, whereas the joint policy X_B preferred by B will involve B's *not* performing action $\overline{X}$ and A's performing action $\overline{X}^*$.

Quantitatively these two measures for the amount of A's power are related as follows. Suppose that, without A's intervention, B would perform action $\overline{X}$ with probability p_1; but because of A's intervention, and as a result of mutual agreement between the two parties, B increases the probability of his performing action X to p_2. Then the amount of A's power *over B* (i.e., A's power over B's *policy* concerning action $\overline{X}$) would be the difference $\Delta p = p_2 - p_1$. On the other hand, the amount of A's power over A and B's *joint policy* would be defined as the *conditional probability* p of B's performing action $\overline{X}$, given that on the present occasion he would not perform action $\overline{X}$ without A's intervention (because a controversial issue between A and B exists only on occasions where B would not perform action $\overline{X}$ without A's intervention). This conditional probability is $p = (p_2 - p_1)/(1 - p_1)$.

It is easy to see that our new measure for the amount of A's power is simply a normalized version of the old measure. For in any particular situation where p_1 is given, the new measure p is proportional to the old measure Δp, as $p = \Delta p/(1 - p_1)$. But while Δp varies[1] between 0 and $1-p_1$, the new measure p varies between 0 and 1. (However, our main concern will be with the n-person analogue of the case where A's and B's preferences are completely opposed with respect to some particular action $\overline{X}$, i.e., where $p_1 = 0$. Then of course $p = \Delta p$ and the two measures coincide.)

II. DEFINITIONS OF THE AMOUNT OF POWER IN THREE TYPES OF n-PERSON SITUATIONS

Case A. Single preferences and no compromise policies

Power relations become relevant in a social group when two or more individuals have conflicting preferences and a decision has to be made as to whose preferences shall prevail. Thus special theoretical interest attaches to the extreme case where n individuals have preferences to dissimilar that no two of them agree in preferring some particular policy X_i to some other policy X_j, and where no 'pure' compromise policies (i.e., policies having the nature of *pure strategies*) exist among the policies preferred by different individuals.

This can be represented by the following model. There are n individuals, called $1, \ldots, n$. Each individual i prefers a different joint policy X_i, but is completely indifferent among all alternative policies X_j, $X_k, \ldots$ preferred by various other individuals j, k, ... (This we shall call the *single preferences* assumption. Its purpose is to rule out the possibility that two or more individuals *jointly* prefer some policy X_i over some alternative policy X_j. For instance, suppose to the contrary that while individual 1's first preference is policy X_1, he is not indifferent between policy X_2 (favored by individual 2) and policy X_3 (favored by individual 3), in that his second preference goes to X_2 and his third preference to X_3. Here 1 and 2 will *jointly* prefer X_2 to X_3, contrary to our assumption.)

Let v_{ij} be the utility that individual i assigns to joint policy X_j. By the single preferences assumption we can write

$$(1) \qquad v_{ij} = \begin{cases} w_i & \text{if } i \neq j \\ w_i + x_i & \text{if } i = j \end{cases}$$

It will also be assumed that between any policy X_i, favored by i, and any policy X_j, favored by j, there is no pure compromise policy X_k that would be preferred by *both* individuals to the policy favored by the *other* individual. (This will be called the *no compromise* assumption). This implies that all possible joint policies other than the policies $X_1, \ldots, X_n$ representing the first preference of one of the n individuals, are inefficient policies and can be disregarded. Therefore we shall identify the controversial issue at stake among the n individuals with the n-tuple $X = (X_1, \ldots, X_n)$.

In this situation it is natural to define the *amount* of individual i's power over the *joint policy* of all n individuals as the probability p_i of his being able to get his favorite joint policy X_i adopted by all individuals. Of course, $\sum p_i = 1$. We shall write $\bar{\bar{p}}$ for the probability vector $\bar{\bar{p}} = (p_1, \ldots, p_n)$.

Case B. Multiple preferences and no compromise policies

There are again n individuals, with each individual i giving his *first* preference to a different[2] joint policy X_i. But now each individual i may also have definite preferences between policies X_j and X_k, even if $j, k = i$ (*multiple preferences assumption*).

We shall still assume, however, that $X_1, \ldots, X_n$ are the only efficient policies (*no compromise* assumption).

We may again try to define individual i's power as the probability p_i of his being able to get policy X_i accepted. But for most purposes this probability will not be an adequate measure of his power. If, e.g., out of three possible policies, individual 1 assigns 10 units of utility to policy X_1, 9 units of utility to policy X_2, and 1 unit of utility to policy X_3, we shall not be able to assess the magnitude of his power if we know only that he has a 10 per cent chance of getting X_1 adopted and do not know how the remaining 90 per cent probability is distributed between policies X_2 and X_3.

Thus we may call p_i, the probability of individual i's favorite policy X_i

being adopted by the whole group, the *amount* of *i*'s *specific power*, because it measures his power to determine exactly the nature of the specific policy to be adopted by the group. (Again, $\sum p_i = 1$.) For most purposes, however, we need a different measure.

A more satisfactory measure will be the whole probability vector $\bar{\bar{p}} = (p_1, \ldots, p_n)$ giving the probabilities for the adoption of each of the alternative policies $X_1, \ldots, X_n$. This may be called the *vector measure* for *i*'s power.

But we can also define a more satisfactory scalar measure as follows. Let v_{ij} again denote the utility that individual *i* assigns to joint policy X_i. Suppose that X_k is the policy alternative least preferred by *i* so that

(2) $v_{ik} = \min_j v_{ij} = w_i.$

We define $x_{ij} = v_{ij} - w_i$. Then for each policy x_j we can write

(3) $v_{ij} = w_i + x_{ij}$

with $x_{ik} = 0$ for the least-preferred policy X_k.

Let $Y(\bar{\bar{p}})$ be the prospect corresponding to the probability vector $\bar{\bar{p}}$, i.e., the prospect that adoption by the group of joint policies $X_1, \ldots, X_n$ has the probabilities $p_1, \ldots, p_n$ respectively. The expected utility value to individual *i* of prospect $Y(\bar{\bar{p}})$ will be

(4) $y_i = w_i + \sum_j p_j\, x_{ij}.$

In order to compare Case B with Case A, we may also consider certain simpler hypothetical prospects $\tilde{Y}_i(\tilde{p}_i)$ which would involve only two possibilities: adoption of policy X_i, most preferred by *i*, and adoption of policy X_k, least preferred by *i*, the former having probability $\tilde{p}_i$ and the latter having probability $1-\tilde{p}_i$. The expected utility value to *i* of any such hypothetical prospect $\tilde{Y}_i(\tilde{p}_i)$ would be

(5) $\tilde{y}_i = w_i + \tilde{p}_i\, x_{ii}.$

There will be a unique prospect $\tilde{Y}_i(\tilde{p}_i)$ which would have the same utility value to individual *i* as prospect $Y(\bar{\bar{p}})$, making $\tilde{y}_i = y_i$. This $\tilde{Y}_i(\tilde{p}_i)$ will correspond to the probability

(6) $\qquad \tilde{p}_i = \sum_j p_j \, x_{ij}/x_{ii}.$

This hypothetical two-way prospect $\tilde{Y}_i$ ($\tilde{p}_i$) may be said to measure the value to i of the n-way prospect $Y(\overline{\overline{p}})$, and the corresponding probability $\tilde{p}_i$ may be used as a scalar measure of individual i's power. What $\tilde{p}_i$ measures is not i's power to get the group to adopt some specific joint policy X_i; this is measured by p_i, the amount of i's *specific* power. Rather, $\tilde{p}_i$ measures i's power to get the group to adopt *some* policy reasonably satisfactory to him, even if this policy is not necessarily the policy *most preferred* by him. This quantity $\tilde{p}_i$ we shall call the amount of i's *generic* power over the group's joint policy. For most purposes it represents the best scalar measure for the amount of i's power.

Of course in Case A previously considered, $\tilde{p}_i = p_i$, and the amount of i's power (without qualification), the amount of i's *specific* power, and the amount of i's *generic* power, are all the same thing.

Case C. Multiple preferences and possible compromise policies

Finally, we shall consider the more general case where the number of efficient alternative policies available is $n + m$, i.e., is greater than n, the number of individuals.[4] Policies $X_1, \ldots, X_n$ will represent the first preferences of individuals $1, \ldots, n$. Policies $X_{n+1}, \ldots, X_{n+m}$ will not represent any individual's first preference, but they still may be adopted as joint policies by the n individuals (or they may be used with positive probability weights in the jointly randomized mixed strategy adopted by them) because they may represent a suitable compromise among the conflicting interests of different individuals.

In Case C, individual i's power can again be measured by the amounts of his specific or generic power, or by the vector measure for the amount of his power. But there are the following differences. The amounts of specific power, p_i, for the n individuals now need not add up to unity (because some probability now may be allocated to policies other than $X_1, \ldots, X_n$). The vector measure $\overline{\overline{p}}$ for the amount of power now is an $(n + m)$-vector, not an n-vector as in Case B.[5] Finally, in Case C the amount of i's *specific* power is an even less satisfactory measure for his power than it was in Case B, and the use of the amount of his *generic* power will become even more necessary. (For instance, if the n individuals agree to adopt some particular compromise policy, say, with probability 1; then every individual will have zero amount of *specific* power, as he had to give up all chances to achieve his own favorite policy. At the same time, the compromise actually adopted may very well be highly satisfactory to all of them, giving all of them a near-unity amount of *generic* power.)

III. DEFINITION OF THE STRENGTH OF POWER

As Cases A and B are special cases under Case C, we shall define the strength of each participant's power for the *general* Case C, and shall later mention some of the simplifications applying in special cases.

The n participants will have more or less conflicting interests concerning a certain controversial issue $X = (X_1, \ldots, X_{n+m})$, i.e., concerning how much probability p_j to allocate to each of the $(n + m)$ policy alternatives X_j. Therefore we shall assume that these probabilities p_j will be determined by explicit or implicit bargaining among the n participants.[6] By definition, the amount of individual i's specific power will be simply p_i. By equation (6), the amount of his generic power, $\tilde{p}_i$, will also be defined in terms of the probabilities p_j. Thus both of these measures for each individual's power can be regarded as results of bargaining among these individuals.

The outcome of this bargaining will depend on two main factors. One is the physical and legal ability of each individual or coalition of individuals to carry through certain policies independently of the consent of other individuals, which we shall call the *independent power* of this individual or coalition. (For instance, in many policy-making bodies a simple or qualified majority coalition of the members will have full independent power to decide on policies.) The other factor is the ability of each individual, or coalition of individuals, to provide incentives (i.e., rewards and penalties) for other individuals to give their consent to policies favored by this individual or coalition, which we shall call the *incentive power* of this individual or coalition. (For instance, a minority which could not decide policies by its own rights may be able to bribe or intimidate the majority into consenting to its policy proposals.)

My bargaining model for the n-person game—on the assumption that each participant's behavior will satisfy certain rationality postulates—predicts the outcome of bargaining among the n participants in terms of all individuals' and all possible coalitions' independent power and incentive power. Thus the *theoretically predicted value* of the amount of a given individual i's *generic power*, $\tilde{p}_i$, can be regarded as a measure of the *strength* of i's *bargaining position*, or of his power to get some policy alternative reasonably acceptable to him adopted by the group. This quantity I propose to call the *strength* of individual i's power.[7] (I propose to use the theoretically predicted value of $\tilde{p}_i$, the amount of i's *generic* power, rather than the predicted value of p_i, the amount of i's *specific* power, because for reasons already indicated I consider $\tilde{p}_i$ as being a much better measure for i's power than p_i.)

We shall consider a bargaining situation of the following kind. The n individuals agree to adopt the jointly randomized mixed strategy $\overline{\overline{p}}$ assigning the probabilitites $p_1, \ldots, p_{n+m}$ to the *policy alternatives* $X_1, \ldots, X_{n+m}$. By Equation (4), strategy $\overline{\overline{p}}$ will yield for individual i the expected utility

$$(7) \qquad y_i = w_i + \sum_{j \in M} p_j \, x_{ij}$$

where $M = (1, \ldots, n + m)$.

At the same time, the n participants also agree on a reward strategy ϱ, under which each individual i will give each other individual j a *reward* R_{ij} in order to get j to agree to a strategy $\overline{\overline{p}}$ favorable to i. (Of course, some or all of these rewards R_{ij} may be nil.) These rewards may take the form of money, commodities, power in *other* fields (i.e., concessions concerning controversial issues other than X—this restriction is necessary to avoid double counting), etc.

Let r_i be the total *net* utility gain that individual i obtains as a result of reward strategy ϱ.[8] The total utility payoff of individual i as a result of strategies $\overline{\overline{p}}$ and ϱ will be

$$(8) \qquad u_i = w_i + r_i + \sum_{j \in M} p_j \, x_{ij}.$$

We also need a set of notations to describe the situation that would arise if the n individuals could not agree on the joint strategies $\overline{\overline{p}}$ and ϱ, in particular to describe the situation that would arise if the n individuals split into two opposing coalitions S and $\overline{S}$, the former having s members and the latter having $\overline{s} = n - s$ members.

We shall assume that, in case of a conflict between coalitions S and $\overline{S}$, coalition S would have the choice among the policy alternatives $X_1, \ldots,$.

X_{n+m} with probability π^S, while coalition $\overline{S}$ would have the choice among these alternatives with probability $\pi^{\overline{S}} = 1 - \pi^S$. If the choice were made by coalition S, alternative X_j would be selected with probability q_j^S ; if the choice were made by coalition $\overline{S}$, alternative X_j would be selected with probability $q_j^{\overline{S}}$. Hence, in case of a conflict between coalitions S and $\overline{S}$, the total probability of X_j being selected would be

(9) $\qquad p_j^S = p_j^{\overline{S}} = \pi^S q_j^S + (1 - \pi^S) q_j^{\overline{S}}.$

If policy alternatives $X_1,..., X_{n+m}$ have probabilities $p_1^S,..., p_{n+m}^S$ associated with them, Equation (4) would give individual i the expected utility

(10) $\qquad y_i^S = w_i + \sum_{j \in M} p_j^S x_{ij}.$

We shall also assume that in the event of a conflict between coalitions S and $\overline{S}$, coalition S would use the retaliatory as well as defensive conflict strategy ϑ^S, while coalition $\overline{S}$ would use the conflict strategy $\vartheta^{\overline{S}}$. To a given member i of coalition S, the conflict strategies ϑ^S (of which he would be a participant) and $\vartheta^{\overline{S}}$ (of which he would be a target of attack) would cause the total *net* utility loss t_i^S . Thus t_i^S would be the total net *cost* to i of a conflict between S and $\overline{S}$ (if, to avoid double counting, we disregard the losses that i would suffer because the conflict might change the probabilities associated with the various policy alternatives X_j).[9]

Thus the total payoff to individual i in case of a conflict between S and $\overline{S}$ would be

(11) $\qquad u_i^S = w_i - t_i^S + \sum_{j \in M} p_j^S x_{ij}.$

Under these assumptions, according to my bargaining model (Harsanyi, 1963, Equation [8.7]) the n individuals will agree on such strategies $\overline{\overline{p}}$ and ϱ which will give each individual i the final utility payoff u_i , defined by the generalized Shapley-value expression:

$$u_i = w_i + z_i \cdot \frac{1}{n}(1 + R) +$$
$$+ z_i \cdot \sum_{\substack{S \ni i \\ S \subset N}} \frac{(s-1)!(n-s)!}{n!} \left[(P^S - P^{\overline{S}}) - (T^S - T^{\overline{S}}) \right]$$
(12)

where N denotes the set $N = (1, \ldots, n)$, and where $z_1, \ldots, z_n$ are certain variables,[10] whereas

$$(13) \qquad R = \sum_{k \in N} \frac{r_k}{z_k}$$

$$(14) \qquad P^s = \sum_{k \in S} \sum_{j \in M} \frac{p_j{}^s x_{kj}}{z_k}$$

and

$$(15) \qquad T^s = \sum_{k \in S} \frac{t_k{}^s}{z_k} \, .$$

The quantities x_{kj} are the constants defined by Equations (2) and (3). On the other hand, the variables of form z_i, r_i, $p_i{}^s$, $t_i{}^s$ are defined implicitly in terms of a set of simultaneous optimizational equations[11] (Equations (10.6) and (10.2a) in Harsanyi, 1963), whose numerical solution in general requires an iterative procedure.

In special cases, however, a more direct approach is possible. In particular, in Case A it is often possible to treat the assumed bargaining game as a game with (locally) *transferable utility*,[12] owing to the participants' ability to redistribute probability, by mutual agreement, between different policy alternatives X_i and X_j. In Case A, Equation (8), in view of Equation (1), takes the simple form

$$(16) \qquad u_i = w_i + r_i + p_i \, x_i.$$

In order to obtain transferable utility, we have to subject all individuals' utility functions to linear transformations, by choosing the quantities x_i as the new units of measurement for each individual i's utility. The transformed value of u_i will be

$$(17) \qquad u_i' = \frac{w_i + r_i}{x_i} + p_i.$$

Summing these quantities, we obtain

$$(18) \qquad \sum_{i \in N} u_i' = \sum_{i \in N} \frac{w_i + r_i}{x_i} + 1$$

which is a constant independent of the probabilities p_i and so satisfies the transferable-utility requirement.

Similarly, Equation (11), in view of (1), now takes the simple form

(19) $\dot{u}_i{}^S = w_i - t_i{}^S + p_i{}^S x_i.$

The transformed value of $u_i{}^S$ will be

(20) $(u_i{}^S)' = \dfrac{w_i - t_i{}^S}{x_i} + p_i{}^S.$

Summing these quantities, in view of (9), we obtain

(21)
$$\sum_{i \in S} (u_i{}^S)' = \sum_{i \in S} \frac{w_i - t_i{}^S}{x_i} + \pi^S \sum_{i \in S} q_i{}^S =$$
$$= \sum_{i \in S} \frac{w_i - t_i{}^S}{x_i} + \pi^S.$$

The last equality applies because in Case A coalition S will obviously distribute all probability among the policies X_i favored by its own members i so that

(22) $\sum_{i \in S} q_i{}^S = 1.$

We see that the summation in Equation (21) also yields a constant independent of the probabilities $q_i{}^S$, and so satisfies the transferable-utility requirement.

However, the possibility of utility transfers satisfying Equations (20) or (21) is restricted by the fact that the probabilities p_i and $q_i{}^S$ can never become negative. For our purposes it is sufficient if the transferable-utility requirement is *locally* satisfied in the neighborhood of the solution payoff vector $\bar{\bar{u}} = (u_1, \ldots, u_n)$ of the game, which will be so if the equilibrium values for all n probabilities $p_1, \ldots, p_n$ are positive (i.e., nonzero).[13] In actual fact, it can be shown that the method to be discussed always furnishes the correct solution in any situation under Case A where it yields positive or zero values for all probabilities $p_i = \bar{p}_i$. But when our method gives negative values for some of the p_i's then the whole solution (including those

p_i's for which we have obtained positive or zero values) must be recomputed by means of the general iterative method not assuming transferable utility.

In cases where the transferable-utility assumption is admissible, equation (12) can be supplemented by the following simple equilibrium conditions:

(23) $z_i = x_i \qquad i = 1, \ldots, n$

(24) $R = \max_\rho R\ (\varrho)$

(25) $T^s - T^{\bar{s}} = \min_{\vartheta^s} \max_{\vartheta^{\bar{s}}} [T^s\ (\vartheta^s,\ \vartheta^{\bar{s}}) - T^{\bar{s}}\ (\vartheta^{\bar{s}},\ \vartheta^s)]$

Moreover, by (22), (1), and (23), we have

(26) $P^s = \pi^s.$

(In the general case without transferable utility, we obtain equilibrium conditions fairly similar to (24) and (25). But the *max* and *min* operators are subject to constraints involving some of the other variables, in such a way that the constraints together form a nonrecursive circular system. This nonrecursiveness generally necessitates the use of an iterative procedure for finding the solution.)[14]

From equations (12), (8), and (6), we obtain the predicted value of $\tilde{p}_i$, the amount of individual i's generic power, as

(27) $$\tilde{p}_i = \frac{z_i}{x_{ii}} \left[\frac{1}{n} + \sum_{\substack{S \ni i \\ S \subset N}} \frac{(s-1)!\,(n-s)!}{n!} (P^s - P^{\bar{s}}) \right] +$$

$$+ \frac{z_i}{x_{ii}} \left[\frac{1}{n} \left(R - \frac{r_i}{z_i} \right) - \sum_{\substack{S \ni i \\ S \subset N}} \frac{(s-1)!\,(n-s)!}{n!} (T^s - T^{\bar{s}}) \right]$$

The expression on the right of this equation is what we propose to call the *strength of* individual i's *power*.

Let us consider the meaning of this mathematical expression more closely. If we interpret Equation (14) in the light of Equation (6), we can see that each variable P^S is essentially a weighted sum of the amounts of *generic power* that the various members of coalition S would possess in case of a conflict between coalitions S and $\overline{S}$. Similarly, by Equation (13), the variable R is a weighted sum of the net *rewards* r_i that the different individuals would receive from one another in case of full agreement. Finally, by Equation (15), each variable T^S is a weighted sum of the *penalties* (or conflict costs) that the members of coalition S would suffer in case of a conflict between coalitions S and $\overline{S}$.

Accordingly, the first term on the right of Equation (27) is a weighted sum (of a constant $\frac{1}{n}$ and) of the amounts of generic power that individual i and his coalition partners would possess in various possible conflict situations, less a weighted sum of the amounts of generic power that members of the opposing coalitions would possess. This term can be regarded as a measure of the *net strength* of individual i's (and of his potential allies') *independent power*, i.e., of his ability to implement his policy preferences without the consent, or even against the resistance, of various individuals who may oppose him (and of his ability to prevent the latter from implementing their policy preferences without his consent).

On the other hand, the second term is a weighted sum of the net rewards that all other individuals would obtain in case of full agreement, and of the net penalties that they would suffer in various possible conflict situations if they opposed individual i, less a weighted sum of the net reward that individual i would obtain if full agreement were reached, and of the net penalties that he and his coalition partners would suffer in conflict situations. This term can be regarded as a measure of the *net strength* of individual i's *incentive power*, i.e., of his ability to provide incentives (or to use incentives provided by nature or by outside agencies) to induce other participants to consent to implementing his own policy preferences.

Finally, the *sum* of these two terms, i.e., the whole expression on the right of Equation (27), which we have called the *strength of i's power*, can be taken as a measure for the full strength of i's *bargaining position*, or of his power to get his policy preferences satisfied within the group, based both on his independent power and on his incentive power. (Under the models in the preceding paper for 2-person situations involving either unilateral power or reciprocal power, A had no independent power with respect to action X to be performed by B, as A was unable to perform an action of B's in place of B. The only way A could get an action of B's performed was to provide incentives for *B* to perform it. Hence the total strength of *A*'s power over *B* was simply equal to the strength of his incentive power. But in *n*-person reciprocal power situations we need a more general definition for the strength of a person's power, admitting the strength of his independent power as a separate term.)

We have derived the mathematical expression defining the strength of an individual's power from a bargaining model for the *n*-person game, based on certain specific rationality postulates. But the above analysis shows that this expression is a suitable measure for the strength of each participant's *bargaining position* or *power* even in situations where the participants do not follow the rationality postulates of this bargaining model. (Of course in such situations the observed *amount* of each participant's generic power will usually *not* be equal to its theoretically predicted value, i.e., to the *strength* of this participant's power.) To put it differently, the rationality postulates of our bargaining model are based on the assumption that all participants will use the strategical possibilities open to them in the best possible and most rational ways. In empirical situations this assumption will not always be fulfilled. But what the outcome would be if all participants did make full rational use of their strategical possibilities will still be a question of great theoretical interest; because the answer to this question will help us to assess quantitatively *what their strategical possibilities actually are*, i.e., what each participant's objective *bargaining position* is, even if the actual outcome does not correspond very closely to the different participant's objective bargaining positions.

To sum up our results, we now state our:

THEOREM III.[15] In *n*-person reciprocal power situations, if the participants follow the rationality postulates of the writer's bargaining model for the *n*-person game, then the *amount* of each participant's *generic power* will tend to be equal to the *strength* of his power, defined as the sum of the strength of his *independent power* and the strength of his *incentive power*.[16]

IV. RELATIONSHIP BETWEEN OUR STRENGTH-OF-POWER CONCEPT AND THE SHAPLEY-SHUBIK MEASURE FOR POWER

Shapley and Shubik (1954) have proposed a quantitative measure for the power of each participant in a committee system, e.g., in a constitutional structure. (For instance, they have found that under the U.S. Constitution the power indices for the President, for an individual senator, and for an individual congressman are in the proportion of 350:9: 2.) In our notations, their power index can be defined as

$$(28) \qquad p_i^* = \frac{1}{n} + \sum_{\substack{S \ni i \\ S \subset N}} \frac{(s-1)!(n-s)!}{n!} \left(\pi^s - \pi^{\bar{s}} \right)$$

which is identical with our measure for the *strength of individual i's independent power* alone in Case A (cf. Equations [23], [26], and [27]).

Shapley and Shubik's power measure is based on the Shapley value for the *n*-person game (Shapley, 1953), while our strength-of-power concept is based on our own bargaining model for the *n*-person game. But in view of the very close mathematical relationship between our bargaining model and the Shapley value, it is not surprising that our strength-of-power concept and their power index are also closely related.

Of course, the intuitive interpretation Shapley and Shubik give to their power index is not the same that we have given to our measure for the strength of independent power, in that their power index is supposed to express (roughly speaking) the *a priori* probability that a given participant *i* will have the *decisive vote* in getting policy proposals finally accepted. But Shapley and Shubik are fully aware of the fact that their power index admits of a number of alternative intuitive interpretations—in effect, they point out that any intuitive interpretation consistent with the axioms defining the Shapley value would necessarily lead to numerically the same power index.

But even at an intuitive level it is possible to translate their definition in terms of our own model. Let us consider the case of *n* individuals each of whom wants to have the decisive vote on some particular policy problem. Let us also make the following two restrictive assumptions:

(1) Each of the *n* participants would be perfectly indifferent as to who should have the decisive vote in case he could not have it himself.

(2) None of the *n* participants can provide any incentives for the other participants.

Assumption (1) brings the situation under our Case A, while assumption

(2) makes the strength of each participant's incentive power equal to zero.

We may consider that the Shapley-Shubik model deals with the special case corresponding to these assumptions. Given these assumptions, both our strength-of-power measure and the Shapley-Shubik power index for a given individual i are defined as being equal to the probability p_i that the decisive vote will be cast by this individual i. Moreover, both our own model and the Shapley-Shubik model yield for this probability the value $p_i = p_i^*$ defined by Equation (28). Thus, under these assumptions their power measure and ours coincide.

In short, the Shapley-Shubik power measure can be regarded as that special case of our own strength-of-power concept where the *single-preferences* and the *no-compromise* assumptions of Case A are satisfied, and where at the same time the *incentive power* of every participant is *nil* (or is disregarded).

That is, compared with the Shapley-Shubik measure, our own strength-of-power measure has the advantage of taking account of the effects that the *incentive power* of various participants has on each participant's power position. For instance, if the participants' utility functions are sufficiently known then our measure makes it possible to compute the increase in the American President's strength of power (and the corresponding decrease in the strength of the power of the Congress), due to a given amount of patronage that he can promise to senators and congressmen, or due to a given amount of influence with the electorate he can promise or threaten to mobilize at the next election for the Congress, etc.

Our strength-of-power measure can also take account of the effects of appliances and party alignments among the participants. Under Case A this can be done only by assuming that the very act of co-operation with the other members of a given possible coalition S would be a source of direct utility or disutility to certain individuals i, with corresponding effects on the values of the quantities t_i^S and T^S.[17] But under Cases B and C, alliances and party alignments can be represented also by similarities among the policy preferences of various participants. In the analysis of most empirical situations one will presumably need both of these methods for representing alliances among the participants. (Shapley and Shubik [1954, pp. 791–792] take account of party alignments by noting the possible discrepancies between their theoretical measure and an analogous empirical measure they introduce, but the existence of a party structure does not enter into their theoretical measure as such.)

Finally, our strength-of-power measure can also take account of improvements in *all* participants' power positions when suitable *compromise policies* are discovered, which may increase the chances, for all participants at the same time, of a reasonably satisfactory outcome (Case C).

REFERENCES

Harsanyi, J. C.: 'A Bargaining Model for the Co-operative *n*-Person Game', in A. W. Tucker and R. D. Luce (Eds.), *Contributions to the Theory of Games*, IV, Princeton: Princeton Univ. Press, 1959, pp. 325–355.
Harsanyi, J. C.: 'A simplified Model for the *n*-Person Cooperative Game', *Intern. Econ. Rev.*, 1963, **4**, 194–220.
Harsanyi, J. C.: 'Measurement of Social Power, Opportunity Costs, and the Theory of Two-Person Bargaining Games', *Behav. Sci.*, 1962, **1**, pp. 67–80.
Shapley, L. S.: 'A Value for *n*-Person Games'; in H. W. Kuhn and A. W. Tucker (Eds.), *Contributions to the Theory of Games*, II. Princeton Univ. Press, 1953, pp. 307–317.
Shapley, L. S., & Shubik, M.: 'A Method for Evaluating the Distribution of Power in a Committee System', *Amer. Polit. Sci. Rev.*, *1954*, **48**, 787–792.

NOTES

* *Behavioral Science*, 7 (1962), 81–91.
[1] To simplify our analysis, we disregard the case of negative power, where $\Delta p < 0$, i.e., where A's intervention actually *decreases* the probability of B's performing action $\overline{X}$ which A wants him to perform. (This can occur only as a result of A's seriously misjudging the situation. For if he knew the effects of his intervention, he always could achieve at least a *zero* amount of power by simply refraining from any intervention.)
[2] As to the case where two individuals i and j prefer the *same* policy $X_i = X_j = X_{ij}$, see note 3 below.
[3] If two individuals i and j prefer the same policy $X_i = X_j = X_{ij}$, we of course have only one probability p_{ij} for the adoption of policy X_{ij}, instead of having two separate probabilities p_i and p_j for the adoption of X_i and X_j. This probability p_{ij} may be regarded as a measure for the amount of *joint* specific power of these two individuals. (We cannot regard p_{ij} as a measure for each individual's separate specific power, because if we counted p_{ij} two times, the specific-power measures of all *n* individuals would not add up to unity.) On the other hand, using equation (6), we can define separate measures for the amounts of *generic power*, $\tilde{p}_i$ and $\tilde{p}_j$, possessed by the two individuals. If, apart from their common first preference for policy X_{ij}, their utility functions for the various policy alternatives are otherwise not identical, then we actually may have $\tilde{p}_i \neq \tilde{p}_j$.
[4] For a situation where the number of policy alternatives is smaller than the number of individuals, see note 3.
[5] But this $(n + m)$-vector will normally have no more than n nonzero components (and in most cases is likely to have much fewer than that). Let $\overline{v}_j = (v_{1j},...,v_{nj})$ be the vector of the utilities that individuals $1,..., n$ associate with each policy alternative X_j. Let us call a set of policies X_j, X_k,... linearly independent if the corresponding utility vectors $\overline{u}_j$, $\overline{u}_k$,... are linearly independent. Then no efficient probability mixture of the policy alternatives $X_1,...,X_{n+m}$ can use more than n linearly independent policies with nonzero probability weights. Moreover, any efficient utility vector that can be attained by a probability mixture of more than n

linearly dependent policies can also be attained by a mixture of *at most n* linearly independent policies. Therefore there is never any advantage in using a probability mixture of more than *n* different policies.

[6] In the real word, of course, the bargaining parties will usually trade in statistical *frequencies*, not in *probabilities* as such. That is, if no direct (i.e., pure) compromise policy is available, they will reach an indirect compromise by letting one party have his way on one occasion and another party on another occasion, with frequencies dependent on each party's bargaining position. But reinterpretation of our model in terms of frequencies rather than probabilities tends to make little difference to our conclusions.

[7] A more exact definition will be given below (see Equation [27]).

[8] When all rewards R_{ij} happen to be *independent goods* for both the giver *i* and the receiver *j*, i.e. when they are neither complementary nor competitive goods, then we can analyze each net utility gain r_i into an algebraic sum of the separate utilities of all rewards received, and the separate utility costs of all rewards given away, by individual *i*. But in general such analysis is not possible because these quantities are not simply additive.

[9] Again, in special cases we may be able to analyze t_i^S into a sum of the *losses that i* would suffer by the opposing coalition's conflict strategy ∂^S, and of the *costs* to him of his own coalitions's conflict strategy ∂^S. The latter in turn may possibly admit of analysis into the costs of retaliatory actions against members of the opposing coalition, the costs of defensive measures, the costs of subsidies (rewards) to be paid to members of his own coalition *less* the value of subsidies he receives from them, etc. But in general such analysis is not possible because these items are not simply additive.

[10] They are reciprocals of the quantities $a_1, ..., a_n$, which I have called the *weights* of the game (Harsanyi, 1963).

[11] By an *optimizational* equation I mean an equation containing the *max* and/or the *min* operator(s).

[12] We speak of a game with *transferable utility* if any player *i* can transfer money or other values (or can transfer power in our case) to any other player *j* in such a way that the *sum* of their utilities (as well as the utilities of all other players) remains *constant* because *j*'s utility gain is exactly equal to *i*'s utility loss.

[13] More exactly, the transferable-utility requirement must be satisfied also for each coalition *S* in the neighborhood of the vector $\bar{\bar{u}}^S$ formed out of the conflict payoffs u_i^S of all members *i* of coalition *S*. This in turn requires that the equilibrium values (as defined by Equations (10.6) and (10.2a) of my 1963 paper) of the probabilities q_j^S for each $j \in M$, and for each $S \subset N$, should be nonnegative.

[14] In cases *B* and *C*, also, the solution of the game takes a simpler form when the solution uses *n* different policy alternatives X_j with nonzero probabilities p_j. (By note 5 the solution never has to use more than *n* different policies, but of course it may use a smaller number of them.) Then the *n* variables z_i become the roots of the following set of *n* simultaneous equations, linear in the reciprocals of the unknowns:

$$\sum_{i \in N} \frac{x_{ij}}{z_i} = 1 \qquad \text{for each } j \in J$$

where *J* is the set of all *j* corresponding to a policy X_j actually used. The equilibrium values of *R* and of the T^Ss are again determined by Equations (24) and (25). But the equilibrium values of the P^Ss are now determined by conditions more complex than Equation (26).

[15] For easier reference I am calling this Theorem III, to follow Theorems I and II of the preceding paper.

[16] Theorem III is a direct generalization of Theorem II. But formally there is no full parallelism, because in Theorem II the strength-of-power measure has to be multiplied by a factor 1/2

while in Theorem III no multiplication is necessary. This is so because we have found it convenient to incorporate the factor $1/n$ (corresponding to factor $1/2$ of Theorem II) into the expression we have chosen to define the strength of a person's power in n-person situations.

We do not have to add a qualification, as we did in the cases of Theorems I and II, concerning the range of variation of the amount of generic power (viz. that $0 \leqslant \vec{p}_i \leqslant 1$), because under the definition given the strength of a person's power always remains within the required range.

[17] The pairs of opposing coalitions S and $\overline{S}$ in my bargaining model are assumed in general to be based merely on *tactical considerations*. But some praticular coalitions of course may also exhibit emotional ties and/or similarities in policy preferences among their members. This fact in our model would find expression in the utility functions of the relevant individuals.

CHAPTER XI

A BARGAINING MODEL FOR SOCIAL STATUS IN INFORMAL GROUPS AND FORMAL ORGANIZATIONS*[1]

Apart from economic payoffs, social status (social rank) seems to be the most important incentive and motivating force of social behavior. This concern for social status is perhaps more conspicuous in those societies, like the American, where the ruling ideology encourages a striving for upward social mobility, for movement to higher social status positions. But it seems to be no less important in those societies, like the traditional Indian caste society, which prevent or strongly discourage upward mobility—for at least downward mobility is possible in every society as punishment for nonfulfillment or certain social obligations. Thus the only difference is that in such less mobile societies, people's concern for social status will take the form of simply trying to *maintain* their existing status and caste positions and of avoiding all types of nonconformist behavior possibly endangering these positions.

If we ever come to the point of developing a general analytical theory of social behavior, then in all probability people's striving for economic gain and for social status will be the two most important direct explanatory variables—even if at deeper levels of analysis these may themselves admit of explanation in terms of some other, still more fundamental, motivating forces.[2] (In particular, I would argue that people's striving for political and social power as such usually admits of explanation as a means to achieving economic objectives and to achieving higher social status.)

Yet, if the striving for social status is to be used as a major explanatory variable for social behavior then it becomes particularly important to reach clearer understanding of the nature of social status itself. We need a theory of social status explaining how the various members' relative rank and status is determined in social groups: a theory explaining what makes social groups grant higher social status to some of their members, and what makes these members themselves seek higher social status within the group. The present paper is meant to be a contribution to such a theory.

I. FUNCTIONALISTIC THEORIES OF SOCIAL STATUS

The theories of social status now prevalent in sociology are based on functionalistic ideas: their purpose is to explain the existence of a social status hierarchy in terms of the functional needs of society as a whole. For instance, in a very influential paper, Davis and Moore (1945) have argued that every society has to grant higher income and higher social status to the occupants of socially important positions requiring scarce natural abilities and/or scarce skills (skills usually acquired by arduous and expensive special training and education). The occupants of such positions must be granted higher income and higher status so as to provide incentives for qualified individuals to fill such positions and to perform the duties associated with them in a satisfactory manner.

In our own view, however, social institutions such as the social status system cannot be adequately explained in purely functionalistic terms. To explain a social institution, we have to explain why the participating individuals actually behave in certain specified ways. But individual behavior cannot be explained in terms of the needs and interests of the society as such; it can be explained only in terms of the personal motivations of the relevant individuals. Social needs can affect individual behavior only as far as they are translated into individual motivations—either by appeal to the various individuals' self-interests in a narrower sense, or by appeal to their personal loyalties—that is, to their personal concern for the interests of some other individuals, or for the interests of some organizations or social groups.

No doubt in some situations, at least when their personal interests and their narrower sectional loyalties are not strongly affected, the behavior of many people will be motivated mainly by their loyalty to the society at large, that is, by what they consider to be the general interests of their national community, or even of mankind as a whole. But such general social considerations are hardly the main motivating forces of people's behavior when they participate in the everyday operation of social institutions. In particular, it would be hardly realistic to assume that people are normally guided by such general social interests when they are shaping social status relationships in their own social environment, for instance when they are seeking higher social status for themselves or when they are accepting or rejecting other people's higher status claims. Our own aim therefore will be to explain social status differences and social behavior related to these differ-. ences in terms of the participants' own individual motivations—in terms of the actual incentives people have to achieve higher status and to grant or not to grant higher status to others.

Apart from this general objection to functionalistic explanations, we also have a more specific objection to the Davis-Moore theory. As far as they explain a person's high social status by the value and importance that his social position and his services have to society, they are committed to the assumption that high social status is in actual fact an indication of true social value and importance. Thus their theory prejudges the empirical is- sue as to how much actual correspondence there is, in any given society and in any given field of social activity, between people's existing social status and the real value of their contributions to general social objectives.

Let me use an analogy from economic theory. Under perfect competition (at least in the absence of external economies and diseconomies) every indi- vidual's income will tend to be equal to the social value of his economic contributions (including the value of the economic services of his land and capital). But economic theory cannot restrict itself to this very special case of perfect competition; it must extend its analysis to situations (monopoly, external economies and diseconomies, consumers' ignorance, and so on) where as a rule this equality breaks down. In the same way, it seems to me, a theory of social status must not limit itself to the very special hypothetical case of perfect correspondence between people's actual social status and the real social importance of their activities, but rather must cover also the case of imperfect or nonexistent correspondence; and indeed it must be able to *explain* why this correspondence will decrease or even disappear in certain empirical situations. A theory of social status must be able to ex- plain not only how great statesmen, scientists, entrepreneurs, and so forth have often achieved high social status by outstanding services to their so- ciety; but must also explain how demagogues, charlatans, confidence men, and even common criminals, have often been able to achieve equally high or higher social status by activities which were much less respectable.

II. SOCIAL STATUS AS INCENTIVE

The primary purpose of this paper will be to analyze social status relation- ships among the members of a given social group, whether an informal group or a formal organization. We shall regard people's social status in the society at large as being determined by their status positions in various smaller groups, that is in the organization for which they work, in their occupational or professional group, in their residential community, in various social organizations, and so on.

The main part of the paper will develop a bargaining model to explain how social status relationships are determined within any given social group. This will be done on the assumption that the various individuals' preferences between social status payoffs and other (such as economic) payoffs are given, without investigating the factors determining the relative importance people attach to status and to nonstatus payoffs.

This bargaining model, of course, has to be supplemented by analysis of the factors actually governing people's preferences between status and nonstatus payoffs, both on the 'demand' side and on the 'supply' side. That is, we have to investigate people's actual incentives to seeking higher social status (possibly at the expense of foregoing some economic and other nonstatus payoffs), as well as their incentives to granting or not granting higher social status to other people (again possibly as an alternative to rewarding them by economic and other nonstatus payoffs). We shall briefly analyze these incentives later. Finally, we shall consider the relationship between the privileges enjoyed by high status members and those enjoyed by rank-and-file members of a social group.

The discussion will start with some provisional definitions, which will later be supplemented as the analysis proceeds. For the time being, we shall say that a person has high social status in a given social group if all or most other members show deferential behavior toward him. In turn, by deferential behavior we shall mean a willingness to defer to (that is, to comply with) a given person's expressed and anticipated wishes—at least when this does not entail significant costs in terms of time, effort, inconvenience, and economic resources in a narrower sense.

Thus, deferential behavior means primarily a general cooperative attitude, a willingness to perform minor personal favors and services for another person. It also involves yielding him a priority of access to various minor privileges, or at least refraining from active competition with him for such privileges—such as offering him a seat, letting him precede in a doorway or in a queue, giving him a first choice among alternatives, and so forth. On the negative side, it involves at least avoiding any action that would needlessly offend, annoy, or inconvenience him, and so on.

This description shows that deference to status superiors consists of much the same type of behavior as does the common courtesy and the general cooperative behavior which all members of the group are expected to show each other, regardless of their relative social positions—equals to equals, and even superiors to inferiors. The main difference is that deference tends to go much further than common courtesy in any given direction; and, more important, deference is an asymmetric relationship: individual B displays deference to individual A if he treats A with much greater courtesy and consideration than he expects to be treated by A in return.

The emphasis is on relative differences in courtesy rather than on the absolute degree of courtesy as such. In some societies and in some social groups, all individuals may receive and may expect to receive very extensive courtesy and cooperation from one another; and in such cases deference will consist in still greater courtesy and still more willing cooperation in relation to some particular individuals. In other groups the members may display and may expect very little mutual courtesy and cooperation; but some members may still receive deference in the sense of being unmistakably by their fellow members with somewhat greater courtesy and cooperation than are the other members of the group.

Thus, under our present definition, to ask why some people in a given social group have higher social status than others is essentially the same thing as to ask why some individuals are being treated with very special courtesy and cooperation, and in particular why some individual B is treating another individual A with greater courtesy and cooperation than conversely.

The most natural answer to this question seems to be that a given individual will be treated with extra courtesy and cooperation, that is, will be shown deference by the other members of the group, if the other members attach particular importance to his presence and to his activities within the group, and if they hope that such deferential treatment will increase his willingness to remain an active member of the group while less respectful treatment might have the opposite effect.

Of course, such considerations can explain B's deferential behavior toward A only if B is in fact personally interested—whether for selfish or unselfish reasons—in the goals served by A's activities, and if he thinks that A really has the ability and the competence to make worthwile contributions toward achieving these goals. Yet, we shall assume that, even if B himself fails to appreciate A's contributions, he may nevertheless treat A with deference as a result of social pressure (anticipated rewards and/or punishments) from the other members of the group, so long as the majority or even a sufficiently powerful minority among the group's members do assign a high value to A's activities.

For instance, suppose a university mathematics department contains a well-known statistican on the faculty. If the other faculty members treat him with deference, this will usually be an indication of the fact that at least *some* of them are very anxious to retain him as a member of the department because they regard statistics as an important activity in a mathematics department, and also regard him personally as a competent statistician who can make valuable contributions to teaching and research in statistics within the department. But other members may not recognize statistics as a worthwhile branch of mathematics at all, or at least may doubt this individual's personal competence as a statistican. Yet they may still treat him respectfully as an important member of the department, simply because they may want to maintain good personal relations with those colleagues who are more appreciative of his professional activities.

Thus our own model agrees with that of Davis and Moore (1945) in assuming that high social status serves primarily as an incentive to people performing important activities. But our approach differs from theirs at the next step, as we have already indicated. They regard social status as an incentive to the performance of activities important from a social point of view, and do not raise the question of what personal motivation the lower status individuals will have to recognize the higher social status of the individuals performing such socially important activities.

In contrast, our own approach is based on the assumption that an individual will be granted high status by the other members of the group fundamentally as an incentive to perform activities personally important to these members themselves (whether for selfish or for unselfish reasons)—quite without regard to the usefulness, unimportance, or even harmfulness of his activities to society at large. Moreover, a social group may grant a person high status as a reward for certain activities having no real value even to the group's own members, so long as these members mistakenly believe that his activities have a real value to them and make real contributions to achieving their own personal objectives. Finally, a person may achieve high social status in a given social group even if most members know perfectly well that his activities are useless or positively harmful to their own interests, so long as at least some powerful individuals in the group assign, rightly or wrongly, high value to his activities from their own personal point of view—or even so long as at least one very powerful individual does so.

In cases where one individual shows deference to another individual, owing to genuine appreciation of his activities, and in order to give him an incentive to continue these activities, we shall speak of *incentive* deference. On the other hand, in cases where an individual shows deference to another individual merely as a result of social pressure, merely in order to obtain rewards and/or to avoid punishments from other individuals, we shall speak of *induced* deference.

Our model easily accounts for various empirical facts which do not admit of explanation in terms of the Davis-Moore model, such as the high social status that criminal gangs may grant to members performing valuable services for the gang, even if these services represent highly undesirable criminal activities from the whole society's point of view; or the high status that some social groups may grant to quacks and frauds in the mistaken belief that the latter perform valuable services for them; or the high status that groups dominated by an autocratic leader may grant to people serving the leader's personal interests to the detriment of all other members' interests, and so forth.

Indeed, under our model, high social status may also be achieved as a reward for what may be called mere negative services, consisting of nothing other than merely refraining from certain obnoxious activities. Thus, in a criminal gang a bully may achieve high social status simply by threatening with violence everybody who does not recognize his status claim—which is equivalent to saying that the members of the gang will grant him high social status as an incentive for him to refrain from violence against them. Of course in a sense, a negative service is a useful 'service': the members of the gang will be better off if the bully does not beat them up than if he does. But it is a 'service' done in the context of an obnoxious disservice: even if the bully refrains from violence in exchange for status (and possibly other) payoffs, he will only remove an agressive threat which he himself has imposed in the first place. He is like a hypothetical doctor who would be asking for a reward to cure an illness which he himself had maliciously inflicted on the patient.

Let me add, however, that human societies rather seldom grant social status as a reward for mere 'negative services' alone. As we shall see, the reason is that human societies tend to resist status claims based on what they regard as 'illegitimate' power; and power based merely on threats of violence or on threats of other disservices is considered to be illegitimate power in most human noncriminal social groups. (But in animal societies, status hierarchies based on a 'pecking order', that is, on threats of violence, are very common.)

Yet, even though high social status is seldom achieved solely by an ability to engage in obnoxious activities, such an ability is very often an important contributing factor to a person's high social status in a given social group. More particularly, if a person performs some useful positive services which in themselves by their own intrinsic value would not qualify him for high social status in the relevant group or organization, he may be able nevertheless to achieve high social status if he is in a position to perform important disservices—for instance, if he can cause great damages to this group or organization by negligence, disloyalty, or malice. In most cases the other members of the group will be prepared to grant him high social status and various other positive incentives, just to keep him in a loyal, careful, and cooperative mood (unless they think he will be sufficiently deterred from all uncooperative behavior merely by the penalties attached to it).

Thus a business executive in charge of a large plant, who could cause great losses to the company, will usually be given high salary and status even if his job requires no great ability, skill, or effort (and even if he needs no more than routine care and average competence to avoid these great losses). Even an ordinary worker operating some expensive machinery which is easy to wreck will have a strong claim to special treatment in terms of wages and status privileges.

In brief, under this theory a person has high social status in a given social group if he is given 'V.I.P. treatment' by the other members; and he, in fact, will be given 'V.I.P. treatment' precisely if he is considered to be a very important person for the other members of the group, owing to his ability to perform very important services and/or disservices for them.

III. SOCIAL STATUS AS A POWER RELATIONSHIP DETERMINED BY EXPLICIT OR IMPLICIT BARGAINING

In recent technical literature on the definition and measurement of political and social power, the concept of power is often defined in a very broad sense—usually simply as an ability to influence other people's behavior in any possible way. In Dahl's words (1957, p. 203), A has power over B to the extent to which 'he can get B to do something that B would not otherwise do.' Though for many purposes such a broad definition has certain advantages, in this paper it will be more convenient to define power in a narrower sense, as an ability to get other people to do things for us by virtue of our ability to deal out rewards and/or punishments to them. (This definition excludes from our power concept, for example, any ability to influence other people by conveying or not conveying information or misinformation to them, or by appealing to their personal friendship, and so on.)

Social status, as has been defined above, is in this sense clearly a *power* relationship. Under our definition, a person has high social status in a given social group if he can get the other members to cooperate with him in certain ways (for example, do minor favors for him) as a result of his ability to reward them (by performing certain services for them) and/or as a result of his ability to punish them (by performing certain disservices). However, social status represents a type of power different from the types of power of primary traditional interest to political scientists: it is not power to influence group policies (political power[3]), or power to implement and to enforce group policies (administrative power). It is rather power to get other members of the group to defer to one's wishes—that is, to get them to cooperate in achieving one's own private ends (for example, by doing minor personal favors). Of course, under our theory, the deferential treatment given to an individual of high social status does very often serve the common ends of the group (as far as it motivates the individual in question to perform activities conducive to these ends, or to refrain from contrary activities); yet intrinsically, deferential behavior consists of a willingness to act in ways conducive to this individual's private ends (in order to motivate him in the desired way).

Accordingly, deferential behavior to people of higher social status differs both from obedience to administrative superiors and from submission to people of superior political power, both of which involve following another person's instructions in matters related to the official policies of the group, and not in matters related to this person's own private wishes as deferential behavior typically does.

To continue our discussion of social status as a power relationship, social status always represents a *reciprocal* power relationship. Usually when a given individual is in a position to perform certain services and/or disservices for the other members of a particular social group, the latter are also in a position to perform certain services and/or disservices for him: that is, both sides are in a position to deal out rewards and/or punishments to each other. Therefore, a given person's social status in a group will depend not only on his own importance to the group, but also on the group's importance to him—though thus far we have discussed only the first side of this relationship. A person will be granted high social status only if in some appropriate sense he is more important to the group than the group is to him. A given individual may perform very important services for the other members, and may still have no claim to higher social status and to deference from the other members of the group, if the latter perform even more important services for him so that he is even more dependent on their good will and cooperation than they are on his.

In two earlier papers (Harsanyi, 1962a, b) we have tried to show that such reciprocal power relationships can be best analyzed by means of game-theoretical bargaining models. More particularly, if we are willing to make the simplifying assumption that a given individual's services (and/or disservices) have the same importance to all the other members of the group then we can base our analysis on a two-person bargaining model. Of course, this simplifying assumption implies that we treat all deferential behavior toward this individual as if it were spontaneous 'incentive deference' (based on a genuine appreciation of this individual's services), and as if no 'induced deference' (induced by social pressure) were involved at all. We obtain a two-person bargaining model by assuming that, in any social group consisting of n members, the social status of any given individual A is determined by mutual bargaining (whether explicit or implicit) between individual A himself and the other $(n-1)$ members of the group, the latter acting as *one* bargaining unit.[4] (For convenience, we shall often speak of bargaining between individual A and the whole 'group', even though we shall actually mean bargaining between individual A and the other $(n-1)$ members.)

In any two-person bargaining situation, the two sides' bargaining positions will depend on the rewards and the punishments they can administer to each other, and on the costs they would themselves incur in administering these rewards and punishments. We can express this fact more concisely by saying that the two sides' bargaining positions will depend on the costs of a possible conflict to each side. Each side will be in a stronger position the smaller its own conflict costs would be and the greater those of the other side. More specifically, the net conflict costs of either side would consist of the following items:

(1) loss of the rewards normally provided by the other side;

(2) damages resulting from the penalties imposed by the other side;

(3) the costs incurred by actively imposing penalties on the other side; less:

(4) the costs of the rewards normally provided for the other side (in case of a conflict these rewards would be withheld and so their costs would be saved).

We can state these relationships in mathematical symbols as follows.[5] The rewards received and the penalties or costs incurred by individual A himself will be denoted by the small letters r, p, and c; whereas the rewards received and the penalties and costs incurred by each of the other $(n\text{-}1)$ members of the group will be denoted by the capital letters R, P, and C. (For brevity we shall often call these variables simply the rewards received and the penalties or costs incurred by the 'group'.) More particularly we shall use the following notations:

r, for the value (utility[6]) to A of the rewards he would normally receive from the group (other than his social status rewards themselves—for example, the value of his economic renumeration, the value he attaches to his participation in group activities, the value he attaches to his influence on group policies, and so on);

$C(r)$, for the cost (disutility) to the group of providing these rewards for A;

R, for the value of A's rewarding activities (his services) to the group;

$c(R)$, for the cost to A himself of performing these rewarding activities (in terms of time and effort, and possibly also in terms of money and other economic resources);

p, for the damages the group could cause to A by punitive (retaliatory) actions;

$C(p)$, for the cost to the group itself of these punitive action;

P, for the damages individual A could cause to the group by punitive (retaliatory) actions;

$c(P)$, for the cost to individual A himself of these punitive actions.

According to our preceding argument, individual A's net conflict costs would be:

(1) $c^* = r + p + c(P) - c(R)$

whereas the group's net conflict costs would be

(2) $C^* = R + P + C(p) - C(r)$.

Of course, in computing these conflict costs for either side, we must take account of the alternative arrangements available to each side in a conflict situation. Thus, in case of a conflict with the group under consideration, individual A might be able to join other groups, and his losses would consist only of those payoffs that these other groups could not provide for him. Likewise, in case of a conflict with individual A, the group might be able to replace him by other individuals, and the group's losses would consist only of those services that these other individuals could not provide for the group.

The strength of individual A's bargaining position vis-à-vis the other members of the group will depend on the quantities c^* and C^* of Equations (1) and (2). The social status he can achieve within the group will be higher the smaller the quantity c^* and the greater the quantity C^*. This means that, other things being equal, individual A will have to be granted *higher* social status by the group:

The *smaller* is r, the value of the rewards other than social status he is receiving from the group (for example, if the group cannot provide him high monetary remuneration then it will be under stronger pressure to grant him at least high social status);

the *smaller* is p, the value of the damages he could suffer as a result of the group's retaliatory actions in case of a conflict;

the *smaller* is $c(P)$, the cost of retaliatory actions to A himself against the group;

the *greater* is $c(R)$, the cost to him of performing the services he provides for the group;

the *greater* is R, the value of these services to the group;

the *greater* is P, the value of the damages he could cause to the group by his retaliatory actions;

the *greater* is $C(p)$, the cost to the group of undertaking retaliatory actions against him; and finally

the *smaller* is $C(r)$, the cost to the group of the rewards provided for him.

The reader can easily verify that these conclusions are in full agreement with our commonsense expectations about these relationships.

More specifically, our bargaining model predicts that d, the amount of deference[7] that individual A will receive within the group, will be given by the mathematical expression:

$$d = \frac{1}{2}\left(\frac{C^*}{C(s)} - \frac{c^*}{s}\right) =$$

(3)
$$= \frac{1}{2}\left(\frac{R + P + C(p) - C(r)}{C(s)} - \right.$$

$$\left. - \frac{r + p + c(P) - c(R)}{s}\right).$$

Here s denotes the value (utility) that individual A himself would assign to a high social status position (more exactly, to the very highest social status position) within the group; whereas $C(s)$ denotes the cost (disutility), the other group members would incur, on the average, by granting him such a high social status position. (Equation (3) corresponds to Equation (16) in Harsanyi, 1962a, p. 77.)

IV. INDUCED DEFERENCE AND INDUCED
SOCIAL STATUS

We have already mentioned that full quantitative analysis of induced deference relationships (established by social pressure), as distinguished from incentive deference (based on genuine appreciation of an individual's services), would have to be based on our n-person bargaining model for social power situations. So we shall here restrict our analysis of induced deference relationships to a few informal qualitative remarks.

Suppose that individual A has the ability to perform important services and/or disservices for individual B, and is therefore treated by B with deference. Normally this deference will involve not only a willingness by B himself to comply with A's wishes but also a willingness by B exert pressure on other individuals, C, that they should likewise comply with A's wishes —since it will be usually A's wish that B should exert such pressure on other individuals. In other words, B's deferential behavior toward A will normally include efforts to get other individuals, C, also to show deferential behavior toward A.

On the other hand, if B in fact tries to induce another individual C to show deference to A, then C will usually comply if B has the ability to perform important service and/or disservices for him. If B has this ability then C will tend to defer to B's wishes and so, if it is B's wish that he should extend his deference also to A, then C will tend to act accordingly, and will in fact show induced deference to A.

In this case, C's willingness to defer to A's wishes and to recognize A's higher social status will not be motivated by rewards (services) or punishments (disservices) expected from A himself, but will rather be motivated by rewards and/or punishments expected from another individual, viz. B. We shall say that in a situation like this B acts as a 'sponsor' of A's higher status vis-à-vis C.

This mechanism tends to make deference a transitive relationship: if C defers to B whereas B defers to A, then C will tend to extend his deference also to A. This will be true even if C's specific reasons for showing deference to B are completely different from, and unconnected with, B's own specific reasons for showing deference to A.

The amount of induced deference that C will show to A will depend both on the strength of B's bargaining position vis-à-vis C, and on the strength of A's bargaining position vis-à-vis B. The stronger the former, the stronger influence will B have over C; and the stronger the latter, the stronger pressure can A exert on B to get him to actually use this influence over C in the desired direction.

We often observe that, when in a given social group G some individual A achieves high social status and is given deference by the other members of the group owing to his ability to perform valuable services for them, then his high social status and his claim to deference will be recognized also by outsiders, who are not members of group G and who do not benefit from his services in any obvious way. Our theory explains this fact by the induced deference mechanism: a high status member A of any given group G will tend to obtain deference also from outsiders, because the latter 'will not want to offend' the members of group G by disrespectful behavior toward an individual enjoying high status in their group. In other words, these outsiders will be motivated by the fact that they will expect the members of group G to act as 'sponsors' of A's social status. That is, they will expect to be rewarded by the members of group G if they treat individual A with deference, and/or will expect to be punished by them if they do not.

Up to now we have assumed that whenever a given individual *B* shows deference to another individual *A*, *B* does this in expectation of specific rewards (services) and/or specific penalties (disservices), either from individual *A* himself (incentive deference) or from some other individual(s) acting as sponsor(s) of *A*'s social status position (induced deference). But no doubt *B*'s deferential behavior toward *A* may also have a less specific moti vation. It may serve simply to demonstrate *B*'s support for the social attitudes (that is, for the 'cause') represented by *A*, as well as to promote public support for these attitudes in society at large. Thus *B* may show great deference to *A* in order to emphasize his own support for the moral attitudes, or the political party, or the scientific activity, or the religious movement, and son on, of which *A* is a leading protagonist—as well as in order to set a 'good example' to other people in supporting these moral attitudes, this political party, this scientific activity, or this religious movement. In such cases we shall call *B*'s deference to *A* *demonstrative* deference.

It may happen that *B*'s deference to *A* is motivated partly by a desire to demonstrate his support for *A*'s 'cause', and partly by a desire to obtain specific rewards and/or avoid specific penalties from *A* himself or from other individuals sponsoring *A*'s social status position. In such cases we shall speak of demonstrative deference only if *B*'s deference to *A* goes beyond what would be necessary to secure these specific rewards and to escape these specific penalties from *A* himself or from his sponsors.

Of course, *B*'s desire to take a public stand on certain moral, political, scientific, religious, and other issues and to set a 'good example' may also make him act in the opposite way: he may wish to demonstrate his opposition to the moral, political, scientific, religious, and other attitudes represented by *A*, and may therefore partly or wholly withhold the deference he would otherwise display toward *A* — even if this means taking the risk of losing *A*'s services and/or incurring his disservices, or of incurring the displeasure of his sponsors. In such cases we shall speak of demonstrative nondeference.

Thus in most societies people will be reluctant to grant deference and high social status in order to reward such services as those of a prostitute, a procurer, a 'fixer', an enemy traitor collaborating with their own country, and so on—even if they are quite willing to make use of such services and to reward them by other means (such as monetary remuneration).

Likewise, people will often show great reluctance to displaying deferential behavior toward a person they consider to possess 'illegitimate' power (for example, the enemy commander in enemy-occupied territory), even if they have to suffer heavy penalties for their uncooperative behavior.

Demonstrative deference and demonstrative nondeference can be incorporated into our bargaining model by assuming that the attitudes underlying these two types of behavior exert their influence by means of decreasing or increasing the quantity $C(s)$, the cost (disutility) which the other members of the group would incur by showing deference to individual A and by recognizing his superior social status.

VI. INCENTIVES TO SEEKING HIGH SOCIAL STATUS

In our preceding discussion we have simply assumed that people usually prefer higher to lower social status. This of course immediately implies that they will be reluctant to grant higher social status to other people (and will do so only if they have special motives, as those suggested, for doing so), because granting higher status to another person means accepting one's own status as inferior to his.

But why should people be so keen on high social status? After all, at least under our definition, high social status means that one is treated with deference by other people, and this involves only minor privileges of little intrinsic value, most of which have mainly ceremonial significance (for example, obtaining small favors from various people, being treated with special courtesy and consideration, being given precedence on various occasions, and so forth).

It is not enough to say that these minor privileges are important because of their symbolic meaning, unless we are also told what their symbolic meaning is supposed to be. On the other hand, we cannot say that their importance lies in the fact that they symbolize possession of high social status as such, because this would lead to a vicious circle. It would amount to saying that people seek high social status because of the privileges attached to it; and they seek these privileges because these are indicators of high social status.

In our own view, high social status carries two main advantages. On the one hand, it indicates that the other members of the group attach real importance to one's services, which gives reasonable assurance that one's services will be in continued demand by the group for some time to come. By this means high social status provides some future security for one's social position within the group. If the members of a given social group want only one once-for-all service from a given individual they will not grant him high social status within the group, but will reward him for his service in some other way (such as paying him a certain amount of money).

On the other hand, high social status usually carries the implication that the other members of the group are willing to extend their association with the individual concerned to activities other than those which originally gave rise to their association. For instance, an individual enjoying high social status in a business organization will usually find ready acceptance not only as a business associate but also as a neighbor, a coreligionist, a fellow club member, a political ally, and so on. More particularly, people of high status tend to be readily accepted as personal associates in private social contact, ranging from formal social activities to informal social intercourse. As a result, people of high social status have relatively free social access to other individuals if they wish, which gives them a much freer choice among desirable potential personal associates (business contacts, personal friends, marriage partners) than people of lower social status can ever have. This is perhaps the most important advantage associated with high social status.[8]

VII. HIGH-STATUS GROUP MEMBERSHIP VS. ORDINARY GROUP MEMBERSHIP

It seems to me that the best way of putting social status relationships in proper perspective is to interpret high social status within a social group simply as a fuller and more complete form of group membership. Apart from full members enjoying all privileges of group membership, many groups also have less-than-full members (associate members, temporary members, candidate members, and so on) enjoying only restricted membership privileges. In contrast, we can say that having high social status means enjoying still fuller membership privileges than even so-called full members of the rank and file. We have argued that the deference shown to high-status members is merely an accentuated form of the common courtesy which all members are expected to show to each other: in the same way,

high-status members also enjoy other membership privileges in an accentuated form.

Indeed, instead of considering high social status as being a superior form
of ordinary group membership, we can take the opposite approach and regard ordinary rank-and-file membership as being an inferior form of the
full membership status enjoyed only by members of higher rank. Thus we
may say that the highest ranking members are the only really full members,
the only ones belonging to the 'inner core' of the group. In comparison with
these high-ranking members, all members of lower rank may be said to
have only restricted membership status. For instance, in describing a feudal
political system, we may say that persons of noble rank had important special privileges over commoners. But instead we may also say that only
members of the nobility were full citizens in the true sense of the word,
while commoners had at best only restricted citizenship within the body
politic.

This interpretation of social status, which makes high social status simply a more complete form of group membership, is fully supported by motivational analysis. The reasons for which people seek high status in a social
group are essentially the same as the reasons for which they seek admission
to ordinary membership of the group; and likewise the reasons for which
people grant or refuse high social status to others are essentially the same as
the reasons for which they grant or refuse them admission to ordinary
membership.

A social group is a set of individuals cooperating in trying to achieve certain common goals and sharing the benefits arising from actual achieve-
ment of these goals. Basically, people seek admission to a social group because they want to gain access to these benefits of group membership; and
they seek high social status in the group because they know that high-status
members tend to have fuller and easier access to these benefits than members of lower status.

Already at a rank-and-file level, a special attraction of group membership is the fact that cooperation and association among the members are
usually not restricted to the primary activities of the group but normally extend to many other fields, including private personal contacts. But here
again, even though mere admission to ordinary membership in itself tends
to assure some degree of social acceptance by the other members, high social status tends to secure a much higher degree of social acceptance and

tends to establish a privileged position in all forms of social intercourse —which, as we have argued in the previous section, is one of the most important attractions of high social status.

A person is admitted to group membership only if the existing members think that his likely contributions to the group will outweigh the costs of his admission (for example, the necessity of sharing the benefits of group membership with him; the necessity of putting up with his possible human weaknesses or unpleasant personality traits, and so on). Likewise, he will be admitted not merely as an ordinary member but as a member with special status privileges, only if his expected contributions are sufficiently important to outweigh not only the costs of his admission to ordinary membership but also the higher costs of granting him these special privileges of high social status. Thus it will depend on the strength of a person's bargaining position vis-à-vis the group whether he will be admitted to high-status membership or merely to ordinary membership—or whether he will be refused admission to the group altogether.

VIII. SOCIAL STATUS AND THE ALLOCATION OF RESOURCES WITHIN THE GROUP

Thus the primary effect of the social status hierarchy in a social group is to establish distinctions between members with various degrees of fuller or less full membership status, and with higher or lower priority of access to the economic and noneconomic resources controlled by the group.

Thus social status can also be regarded as a social mechanism for allocating the use of scarce resources among the individual members of each social group—one supplementing and sometimes even replacing private property as an allocating mechanism. A social group may distribute its resources to individual members for their exclusive use as their private property, or may retain these resources (or some of them) for the common use of its members. In the latter case the actual use of these resources will be typically governed by the members' relative social status within the group, in the sense that, other things being equal, the higher-status members will tend to have a prior claim to their use.

In practice, at least in our own society, social status is an allocative mechanism of much lesser importance than private property. This is so because most social groups and organizations provide rewards for their members mainly in the form of direct transfer of money and other economic resources, rather than in the form of access to resources retained for collective use by their members. In other societies, however, resources retained for collective use may play a much more important role.[9] But however small the importance of these collective resources may be, it is true also in our own society that high-status individuals tend to have preferential access to them—even though in our case this typically only means preferential access to resources having small economic value and having primarily ceremonial significance (such as preferential access to seats in public places).[10]

REFERENCES

Blau, P. M.: *Exchange and Power in Social Life*, New York: John Wiley, 1964.
Dahl, R. A.: 'The Concept of Power', *Behav. Sci.*, 1957, **2**, 201–215.
Davis, K., & Wilbert E. Moore: 'Some Principles of Stratification', *Amer. Soci. Rev.*, 1945, **10**, 242–249.
Harsanyi, J. C.: 'Measurement of Social Power, Opportunity Costs, and the Theory of Two-Person Bargaining Games', *Behav. Sci.*, 1962a 7, 67–80.
Harsanyi, J. C.: 'Measurement of Social Power in *n*-Person Reciprocal Power Situations', *Behav. Sci.*, 1962b, **7**, 81–91.
Homans, G. C.: *'Social Behavior: Its Elementary Forms'*, New York: Harcourt, Brace, & World, 1961.
Maine, Sir H. J. S.: *Ancient Law*, London: J. Murray, 1901.
Wynne-Edwards, V. C.: *Animal Dispersion in Relation to Social Behavior*, Edinburgh: Oliver & Boyd, 1962.

NOTES

* *Behavioral Science,* **11** (1966), 357–369.
[1] The original version of this paper was presented at the Annual Meeting of the American Political Science Association in Chicago, September, 1964. It was distributed as Working Paper No. 94 of the Center for Research in Management Science, University of California, Berkeley.

I have been very gratified to find that—on the basis of very extensive empirical research, and without any reliance on game-theoretical considerations—Peter M. Blau (1964) has arrived at a theory of social status very similar to the theory proposed in this paper, which is based on a game-theoretical bargaining model.

The research reported in this paper was partially supported by a grant from the Ford Foundation to the Graduate School of Business Administration, University of California, Berkeley.

[2] Psychologists at any rate may wish to carry the analysis of human motivation a few steps further, and may wish to explain all human behavior ultimately in terms of people's basic physiological wants, as well as their desire for satisfying perceptual, motoric, intellectual, and emotional experiences, and for human companionship, affection, and emotional security.

[3] We are using the term 'political power' in a broad functional sense. We do not necessarily

mean power related to governmental policies but rather power related to the agreed policies of the social group under consideration. We are not speaking of 'politics' as this term is usually understood, but are rather speaking of the 'internal politics' of the relevant group or organization.

[4] If we want to avoid the unrealistic simplifying assumption that individual A's services are equally important to all other members of the group, and if we want in our formal analysis to maintain the distinction between 'incentive deference' and 'induced deference' as defined in the previous section, then we must analyze social status relationships within any social group of n members explicitly in terms of our n-person bargaining model for reciprocal power situations, as described in Harsanyi (1962b). This latter approach would enable us to take explicit account of the fact that the social status of a given individual A will be determined not only by bargaining between individual A himself and the other $(n-1)$ members of the group, but also by bargaining among the latter $(n-1)$ members themselves, who will in general differ in their evaluation of individual A's services (and/or his potential disservices), and who therefore will differ also in their attitudes toward A's status claim.

However, we can analyze the most important factors determining individual A's social status, already in terms of a two-person bargaining model, and for this reason this is the approach we shall actually use.

[5] The nonmathematical reader may omit the remaining part of this section without loss of continuity.

[6] All variables are assumed to be measured in utility units.

[7] We can measure d by the frequency of deferential acts directed toward A by the other members of the group; or by the probability that A will be shown deferential behavior on any particular randomly selected occasion providing an opportunity for such behavior.

[8] High social status granted to a given individual always shows that the group attaches particular importance to the contributions this individual can make to the activities of primary concern to the group. It therefore shows that this individual is a preferred associate over lower status members, at least for the purposes of these group activities. But other things being equal, he will tend to be a preferred associate also in relation to other activities (such as private personal contacts). Yet other things may not be equal. For instance, there may be special psychological costs attached to closer association with higher-status individuals, and to this extent higher-status individuals may actually become less preferred personal associates. (Cf. Homans, 1961, Chs. 14–15). Thus the high-status members of the group may not enjoy fuller social acceptance for all purposes. This may even go so far that the lower-status members of the group may set up a secondary social status hierarchy competing with the 'official' status hierarchy of the group and excluding those individuals who have high status positions in the former. For example, the labor union movement establishes a secondary status hierarchy which excludes the members of the management group from its own ranks.

[9] Our distinction between private property and social status as allocative mechanisms is closely related to Sir Henry Maine's (1901) celebrated distinction between 'contract' and 'status'.

[10] Already in the animal kingdom we find beginnings of private property and social status in the form of territorial behavior and the pecking order. Just as social status in human societies, this pecking order regulates access to scarce resources (to food, and sexual partners) only in the case of resources not appropriated yet by any particular individual. Each animal is willing to defend the resources of its own territory against all intruders, even against those with a higher rank in the pecking order. The pecking order as such only regulates access to resources located at some 'neutral' territory. It is only outside its own home territory that a lower-ranking animal will meekly submit to a higher-ranking animal and will accept the latter's prior claim to resources coveted by both of them (Wynne-Edwards, 1962).

PART C

SCIENTIFIC EXPLANATION

CHAPTER XII

EXPLANATION AND COMPARATIVE DYNAMICS
IN SOCIAL SCIENCE*

I. INTRODUCTION

Among social scientists there is now an increasing interest in fundamental theory, in *explaining* social facts rather than merely *describing* them. At present the only social sciences possessing a well-developed systematic theory are economics and demography. But there is a clear trend towards greater emphasis on theoretical analysis in social and cultural anthropology, sociology, social psychology, social and cultural history, political science, legal theory, etc. There is also a growing realization of the fact that society is a causal mechanism so closely inter-connected as to require analysis to a large extent in terms of one basic theory common to all social sciences rather than merely in terms of independent theories particular to the various disciplines. The interest of social scientists in recent years has tended to centre upon problems which by their very nature require study by a cooperative effort of specialists in different social sciences, such as the problems of cultural change, economic development, the relation between culture and personality structure, comparative politics, etc.; and experience with interdisciplinary research projects in such fields has made even clearer to what an extent our understanding of social phenomena is restricted by the lack of an integrated explanatory theory of society.

When a social scientist (e.g., a historian) tries to explain the behaviour of a given individual, he will use the social institutions and cultural patterns of the relevant society as explanatory principles without necessarily attempting to explain these institutions and cultural patterns themselves. But at a deeper level of analysis the main task of the social sciences is precisely to explain the institutions and cultural patterns of each society. The purpose of this paper is to propose certain heuristic criteria for explanatory hypotheses and general theory construction at that level of analysis. Of course, heuristic considerations can never save us the trouble of actually setting up specific explanatory hypotheses and testing them against the social facts of the present and the past. But they may help us to devise fruitful hypotheses and to avoid blind alleys if we can make it clearer to ourselves what sort of theory we are after and what kinds of explanations we are looking for.

The most 'natural' explanation for a social fact is in terms of some other social variables belonging to the *same* time period. For instance, the most obvious way of explaining the nature of English literature in the Victorian age is to refer to certain characteristics of English society in that period. But a little reflection will show that this type of explanation cannot be pressed very far. For, English literature of the Victorian age evidently carried forward (or reacted against) the English literary traditions of earlier ages and was also subject to literary influences from abroad. Hence, what contemporaneous English social conditions can explain about Victorian-age English literature are not so much the prevailing *literary patterns* themselves as are rather the *deviations* that occurred from the literary patterns of the previous period (as well as from the foreign models used). That is, what contemporaneous social conditions directly explain are not the relevant social *variables* themselves but are only their *time trends* (time derivatives[1]), i.e. the directions and rates of their change.

Following the terminology used by economists, we shall speak of *static explanation* when a social variable is explained exclusively in terms of variables belonging to the *same time period*; and we shall speak of *dynamic explanation* when at least some of the explanatory variables used belong to an *earlier period* than the variables to be explained. More generally, we shall speak of dynamic explanation also if what we directly try to explain, and/or what we offer as explanation, involve not only the *values* of certain social variables at a given time, but also their *time trends* (time derivatives), i.e. the directions and rates of their change.

Social scientists making use of a static explanation often do not sufficiently realize how restrictive the assumptions are to which they are committed by adopting this type of explanation. A static explanation implies a static model of the social system. That is, it implies the assumption that all social variables relevant to the problem on hand always adjust to one another (and to the variables defining the natural environment) without any considerable time lag. More pratically, if the value of a certain variable Y is to be explaned in terms of the contemporaneous values of some other variables $X_1, \ldots, X_n$, then the following assumptions have to be satisfied:

(1) At any moment the values of $X_1, \ldots, X_n$ must determine an equilibrium value for Y.

(2) Should Y be removed from this equilibrium value by any disturbing force, it must return again without any significant delay[2] to this equilibrium value when the disturbing force ceases to operate.

(3) Should there be any change in the values of $X_1, \ldots, X_n$, then Y must move to its new equilibrium value (determined by the new values of the X's) also without any significant delay[3].

Clearly, these are very strong assumptions, in particular (2) and (3). No doubt, there are within the social system subsystems to which static models are applicable at least as crude first approximations. For instance, the analysis of economic and political institutions in terms of static models and in terms of the concepts of economic or political equilibrium (balance of power) does have its usefulness. But the social system as a whole can hardly be regarded as a static mechanism. If nothing else, at least the evident inertia of cultural traditions and of social institutions must prevent any immediate all-over adjustment to changing conditions as would be required by a static model.

Therefore, in general we have to use dynamic models, which allow for slow, delayed or staggering adjustment, and which include the social conditions of earlier periods (and/or the time trends due to the changes going on in society) among their explanatory variables. This means that normally the explanation of a given cultural pattern or social institution will have to refer to the cultural patterns and social institutions of the previous period; and the conditions of the present will explain no more than the cultural and institutional *differences* between the present period and the previous one.

Very often when empirical observation fails to discover any consistent relationships between two important groups of social variables, we can quite confidently expect to find meaningful relationships between *changes* in these two groups of variables. For instance, the examples of the United States, Great Britain and the Soviet Union show that there is no uniform connection between the productive technology of a society and its economic and political institutional framework, as in each of these societies basically the same productive technology is associated with very different economic and political institutions. In contrast, between *changes* in technology and the consequent changes in economic and political institutions (as well as the other way round) there do appear to exist well-defined recognizable relationships. For example, we already know a good deal about what economic and political changes tend to follow the adoption of Western technology by a non-Western country (and how the nature of these changes depends on the economic, political and cultural conditions of the country prior to Westernization). Similarly, we also have a good idea of the social and cultural changes that regularly tend to follow technological innovations in Western countries.

The point is that dynamic laws represent the general case of causal laws while static laws form a very special case, found only in causal systems of special descriptions[4]. Therefore society must be subject to dynamic laws if it is subject to causal laws[5] at all, but there is no reason to expect that it will be subject to static laws, except for certain special fields.

Greater care in distinguishing between static and dynamic models would no doubt enhance the theoretical value of certain analytical tools now commonly used by social scientists. For example, social institutions and cultural patterns are now often explained in terms of the *functional adjustment* hypothesis. It is argued that every society must display a certain minimum degree of functional efficiency, i.e. correspondence between social needs and social institutions – at least as much as is needed for the very survival of the society. This leads to the inference that all social institutions tend to serve some real social needs and that all important social needs tend to be catered for by some social institutions: the task of empirical research is simply to find out which social institutions are connected with which social needs and vice versa.

Another, closely related, analytical tool is the hypothesis of *cultural consistency* (see Benedict, 1934). It is assumed that the value-attitudes, beliefs and activity patterns of each society form a well-integrated self-consistent system. Once certain basic value-attitudes of the society are given, the other elements of the culture can be explained to a large extent in terms of this consistency requirement.

Both the functional adjustment and the cultural consistency hypotheses certainly contain a good deal of truth: there are strong forces that tend to adjust social institutions to social needs or alternatively to eliminate socie-

ties with extreme institutional maladjustments; and there are also strong
forces that tend to iron out inconsistencies among the cultural patterns of a
given society. But it is sufficiently clear that all these forces are often quite
slow in operation (and often have to work in the face of strong counteracting forces which try to preserve maladjusted institutions or inconsistent cultural patterns) so that the requirements of a static model are not met. Consequently there is no presumption whatever to the effect that the institutions and cultural patterns of any given society will be found to be particularly well adjusted or particularly consistent. Undue insistence on such
hypotheses can only lead to existing functional maladjustments or cultural
inconsistencies being explained away. A satisfactory model of functional
adjustment and cultural integration cannot be static but rather has to include specific assumptions, at least in a rough qualitative sense, about the
speeds at which the relevant adjustment and integration processes operate
in different parts of the social system(as well as about the strength of the
counteracting forces they have to overcome).

III. EXPLANATION AS A PROBLEM OF COMPARATIVE DYNAMCS

If society were a static mechanism the task of social science would be to explain differences and similarities between different societies or different
parts of the same society in terms of certain basic social variables of the
same period. That is, the fundamental problem would be a problem of
comparative statics. As, however, society is a dynamic system the fundamental problem becomes a problem of *comparative dynamics*. The problem is to explain similarities and differences in the development over time
of different societies or of different parts of the same society, in terms of the
initial conditions (i.e. the conditions prevailing at some arbitrary point of
time chosen as the starting point of our investigation) and in terms of the
subsequent *external influences* (boundary conditions) affecting their development. On reflection it turns out that the explanation of *any* social fact is
always a problem of comparative dynamics even if at first it is not stated in
this form. For example, explaining the existence of industrial capitalism is
the same thing as explaining why the Western society of the 18th century did
produce a capitalistic industrial revolution while other societies, even those
at comparable levels of economic and cultural development, did not have
independent capitalistic industrial revolutions of their own. It was one of

Max Weber's greatest contributions to social science to point out the reducibility of every question about explanation to a question in comparative dynamics.

Indeed, if an explanation proposed for a social fact does not explain why this fact appears or appeared in some societies or social groups but not in others – i.e., if it does not supply an explanation in a comparative dynamic sense – then we cannot accept it as full explanation of this social fact at all (though we may very well accept it as an important step towards a future explanation). For instance, even if the scapegoat theory of racial prejudice should be correct as far as it goes it cannot be regarded as full explanation of racial prejudice so long as it cannot explain why racial prejudice emerged in some societies or social groups but not in others, or why it is increasing in some social environments but is decreasing in others.

The fact that the social system is a dynamic system means that all problems in social science have an essential historical dimension and that in effect the main task of social science is to *explain historical development*. So it is most unfortunate that it has become customary for social scientists with a sense for theoretical analysis to neglect history and for social scientists with historical scholarship to keep themselves innocent of theoretical analysis.

Of course, in many cases the reluctance of historians to offer explanations (exept on rather superficial levels) for the course of social development is simply a matter of there being no worthwhile analytical theory they could have drawn upon. For instance, so long as we have no theory to speak of on the dynamics of political institutions, we cannot blame historians if they fail to offer a satisfactory explanation for the fact that democracy works reasonably well in some countries but could never take firm roots in some other countries at comparable levels of cultural development. Even in economic history, progress in explaining the patterns of historical development was up to quite recently greatly hindered by the fact that available economic theory did not provide a satisfactory theory of economic growth. Only in the last few years have both economic theorists and economic historians shown a more active interest in explaining the differences in the rate and direction of economic development among various societies at different periods, and in setting up dynamic models consistent both with sound economic theory and with the established results of historical research.

As the main purpose of a comparative dynamic theory of society would be to explain the course of historical development, our present interest in comparative dynamics to some extent represents a return to problems that used to occupy the evolutionary theorists of the 19th and early 20th centuries – in contrast to the anti-theoretical, or at best static, approach fashionable in the more recent past (roughly in the inter-war period)[6]. But of course there are also fundamental differences. Evolutionists were looking for a law determining a uniform sequence of evolutionary stages for all societies. Comparative dynamics, on the contrary, is based on the idea that different societies often show very different patterns of development, and its main objective is to explain these differences in development in terms of differences in the initial conditions and the external influences.

Instead of assuming a law directly determining the course of social development (as a uniform sequence of evolutionary stages), a dynamic theory of society will have to explain social development in terms of the basic causal laws governing the interaction among the various social and environmental variables. It will have to set up analytical models based on specific – and, if possible, quantitive – assumptions concerning the causal influence that each major social and environmental variable has on the other variables, and concerning the causal mechanisms which transmit this influence. And of course ultimately all these causal laws will have to be explained in terms of interaction among the social groups – and, more fundamentally, among the individuals – who make up the social system.

IV. EXOGENOUS VARIABLES AS EXPLANATORY VARIABLES

Among explanatory variables, special logical status belongs to variables *exogenous* to the social system, i.e., to the variables describing the natural environment of the society, and the biological properties of the population, in their aspects independent of human intervention. For, if a social scientist suggests an explanation for a social fact in terms of other social facts (i.e., in terms of variables endogenous to the social system), his explanation will be incomplete so long as he cannot offer explanation for these latter social facts themselves. But if he puts forward explanation for a social fact in terms of variables genuinely exogenous to the social system his analytical task will be completed, as it will not be his business as a social scientist to find an explanation for these exogenous variables themselves. In this sense the exogenous variables represent the only vehicles of 'ultimate' explanation in social science.

For instance, if the differences between Western European and Indian economic development could be fully explained in terms of differences in the natural resources (as they in fact cannot), no further explanation would be required. But if we try to explain these economic differences, say, in terms of the religious differences (as between Christianity and Hinduism), this explanation wil be incomplete so long as we cannot explain these religious differences themselves. Indeed, any explanation of the economic differences in terms of religion will carry full conviction only if there is some evidence that the religious differences themselves in turn can be explained by factors *independent* of the economic differences we have started from in the first place.

To be sure, experience shows that we very often cannot follow all causal chains back to the basic exogenous variables. In effect, if we want to restrict our analysis to a period shorter than the whole history of the human race, we have to admit as explanatory variables initial conditions which are already social variables; and if we want to limit our attention to a social system smaller than mankind as a whole, we have to admit as explanatory variables influences coming from other societies. But even apart from the natural limitation of the scope of our analysis in time and in space, the failure of all theories of environmental determinism (and the even more complete failure of theories of racial determinism) shows that our explanation of social development can hardly ever be so complete that we could avoid admitting 'historical accidents', i.e., events that we can subsume only under statistical laws. This means that the connection between the known exogenous variables and the detailed course of social development has to be visualized in terms of stochastic (probabilistic) rather than deterministic models.

Of course, the concept of historical accidents must be handled with great care to make sure that its use will satisfy the requirements of probability theory. For instance, suppose that a given society did not make a certain invention in a given period even though there would have been a strong social need for it and even though all basic technological principles required were known. Then, as inventions are no doubt to some extent matters of luck, we may legitimately regard this failure to make the invention in question as a mere historical accident, if the period involved was reasonably short. But if the invention failed to occur over a long period the assumption that this was due to mere chance will have a very low probability, and a specific explanation, e.g., in terms of negative social attitudes towards invention, will be required.

But, even though explanation in terms of exogenous variables is not always possible, whenever it is possible it has a very special theoretical interest; and one of the basic tasks for a causal theory of the social system will be to discover the causal (deterministic or statistical) laws according to which the natural environment and the other exogenous variables influence the social variables, and to identify the causal mechanisms which transmit this influence. Not only the exogenous variables themselves have a privileged position as explanatory variables but so do all endogenous social variables which bear the direct impact of major exogenous variables and play a principal role in transmitting the latter's influence to the rest of the social system.

One of the reasons why explanation of social phenomena in terms of *economic* forces is often so fruitful lies in the fact that the economic system is one of the main channels through which the natural environment (in particular, the presence or absence of natural resources and of natural routes of communication) acts upon the social system. To be sure, the economic system is not the only causal channel through which the environment exerts its influence. For instance, geographical conditions have an important effect on the sizes and boundaries of political units; climate influences patterns of recreation and social intercourse, etc. In trying to explain differences in the development of different societies, of course, all these influences of the natural conditions have to be taken into account.

V. STABLE ENDOGENOUS VARIABLES
(SOCIAL INSTITUTIONS AND CULTURAL TRADITIONS)
AS EXPLANATORY VARIABLES

Social institutions and cultural traditions have an important role as explanatory variables fundamentally because of their *stability*.

Though only the exogenous variables are fully independent of the other variables, any stable endogenous variable also represents a relatively *independent source of causal influence* in that (so long as it maintains its stability) its value is independent of changes in the other variables.

The task of a dynamic theory of society is to explain social development in terms of the initial conditions associated with some arbitrary 'initial' period (and in terms of the subsequent external influences). Hence special theoretical interest attaches to those causal channels which transmit the influence of the initial conditions to later periods. These causal channels are represented primarily by the stable variables of the social system. A given initial condition tends to have a persistent influence on later development either if it itself represents a relatively stable social variable (a stable social institution or cultural tradition) or if it has a lasting effect on another variable with a high degree of stability (e.g., the social conditions, themselves possibly of short duration, which give rise to a lasting institution or cultural tradition). In effect, the influence of *any* initial condition can always be represented in principle by a constant parameter in the equations describing the behaviour of the system over time – though this constant parameter may not always correspond to a directly observable constant variable of the system.

To be sure, the effect of a stable social variable on social development, even if persistent, need not be large. In particular, variables connected with some causally isolated part of the social system may exhibit great stability – maybe precisely as a result of their isolation from influences coming from other parts of the system – and may still have very little influence on the rest of the system. For example, the social structure of an isolated rural community may reamin practically constant for centuries without this fact having any important effect on society at large. But any social or cultural variable that tends *both* to show a high degree of stability *and* to remain in close interaction with other important variables can hardly fail to be a variable with a significant long-run influence. Even if the influence of such a stable variable should remain small in the short run, its long-run influence will tend to be considerable as it will represent the cumulative effect of a force persistently pressing in the same direction over a long period.

In view of the great causal importance of such relatively stable social institutions and cultural traditions, it is of particular interest to explain the behaviour of these institutions and traditions themselves – both their stability over time and the changes, if any, they display.

There are, of course, certain familiar stabilizing mechanisms which help to preserve all institutions and cultural traditions once they exist – such as education by teaching and example, social pressure for conformity, fear of the new and unfamiliar. But social scientists from Marx to the modern functionalists agree that an institution or cultural pattern cannot persist for long unless it satisfies some specific *interests* or psychological *needs* on the part of society as a whole or on the part of particular social groups. This means that the *stability* of all other social variables greatly depends on those *fundamental structural variables* which determine the common interests and psychological needs of the society as well as its division into the major social groups, and the separate interests and psychological needs of these groups themselves. These fundamental structural variables include the natural environment of the society and its way of utilization; the society's position among, and relation to, other societies; the prevailing basic value attitudes and the basic personality structure of the members of the society[7]; the social structure and its major subdivisions according to class, status, occupation, residential area, ethnic origin, religion, etc., as well as the basic economic, political and social relations among these groups. These fundamental structural variables, or rather changes in them, also play an important role in explaining *changes* in other social institutions and cultural patterns (if the relevant time lags are allowed for). Hence the differences between two societies in these fundamental structural variables must go a long way towards explaining the differences in their other social variables.

VI. ACCUMULATIVE VARIABLES

If we apply the method of comparative analysis, not to two different societies, but rather to two different periods of the same society, obviously we cannot explain the observed differences in terms of completely stable social variables, which did not change from one period to the other. Rather, we have to rely on variables which did significantly change from one period to another but which at the same time remained approximately constant within each (short) period under comparison – that is, on variables which tend to change at a very slow rate but so that this adds up to large changes in the long run. Such variables may be called *accumulative* (or decumulative) *variables.* Examples are: population, the stock of capital, the stock of natural resources (the latter is a 'decumulative' variable subject to depletion), the 'stock' of technological knowledge, the sizes of slowly growing social organizations, etc. Obviously accumulative variables of this sort represent very important causal links in explaining the fundamental long-run changes that occur in a society in the course of social development. In the short run they can be regarded as constant, and therefore as independent variables, while in the long run they are themselves subject to the moulding influence of other social variables.

These latter, i.e., the social and cultural conditions that decide the rate and direction of change in each of these accumulative variables, are of course another most important class of explanatory variables. For instance, it would be a major advance in economic theory if we could decide which are the main economic and social variables that determine the rate of increase in capital and in technological knowledge.

We have argued above that one reason for the fruitfulness of an economic analysis of social institutions lies in the fact that the economic system is one of the main causal channels through which the natural environment acts upon the social system. We can now add an additional reason: the economic system (if defined so as to include productive technology as one of its variables) contains at least three of the major accumulative variables, viz., capital, natural resources and productive technology. Therefore a good deal of the differences between the social conditions of two different periods can be explained in terms of economic differences. But of course a full explanation will have to bring in cumulative variables which are not 'economic' in nature, e.g., population, the 'stock' of pure scientific knowledge, military technology, communication and organization methods, etc.

VII. INTERACTION BETWEEN DIFFERENT SUBSYSTEMS OF THE SOCIAL SYSTEM

Perhaps the most interesting methodological problem facing a social scientist is what working hypothesis to adopt about the likely direction of the causal influence between certain major groups of social variables (i.e., between different subsystems of the social system). Should we, with Max Weber, assign causal priority to the religious-ethical variables and explain the emergence of Capitalism in terms of Protestant ethics, or conversely should we, with Karl Marx, assign causal priority to the economic variables and explain Protestantism itself in terms of the economic conditions of late-medieval towns? Should we explain economic development in terms of political factors and regard Capitalism the by-product of the fiscal policies of national governments or should we adopt the opposite explanation and make the national governments themselves the agents of Capitalistic economic interests?

Sometimes attempts have been made to dismiss all problems of this kind with the pronouncement that in society all causal relations are two-way affairs and that no social variable has causal priority over any other. But this is not, in my view, a fruitful approach. Maybe most causal relations run in both directions but no doubt one direction is often much more important than the other, and if so this fact will be very interesting information to us. In particular, so long as we have to work with very rough and often non-quantitative models, the only way of gaining insight into the causal structure of the social system is to find out the principal directions of causal influence among the major social and environmental variables.

In effect, hypotheses as to causal priority can always be translated into comparative dynamic hypotheses concerning the causal importance of the relevant social variables as initial conditions. For instance, Max Weber's theory is essentially a hypothesis on what difference it would have made to later economic development in Western Europe if Protestantism had not figured among the initial conditions of the relevant period. Likewise, the Marxian theory on the causes of the Reformation is a hypothesis about what difference it would have made to Western European religious development if the economic conditions of late-medieval towns had been different. Of course, without the possibility of experimental testing (and we cannot set up a society similar to Western European society of the relevant period, except for the absence of Protestantism, and then observe what will happen), hypotheses of this sort can be supported only by indirect evidence. As in other nonexperimental sciences, the analysis of historical facts may be a partial substitute for experimentation. For example, Max Weber was able to test his thesis up to a point by comparing the economic development of the Western European society with that of other societies with different religions but otherwise more or less similar social institutions. But of course observation is never a full substitute for experimentation. The societies Max Weber used for comparison inevitably differed from Western European society in many other respects besides religion, e.g., in certain economic and political characteristics, and this involved the possibility of alternative interpretations for the historical facts.

However, this type of historical evidence may be supplemented by study of the causal mechanisms operative in social development and by investigation of the dynamic behaviour of the relevant social variables.

What does it mean to ascribe causal priority to one subsystem of the social system over another? It essentially means to assume that, while the main aspects of the first subsystem's development can be explained in terms of internal factors, i.e., in terms of interaction among its own variables, the second sub-system's development has to be explained in essential respects in terms of influences coming from the first subsystem. Obviously all parts of the social system and all parts of culture show some measure of relatively autonomous development and on the other hand none of them can claim full autonomy. But the various subsystems seem to exhibit conspicuous differences as to the degree of autonomy they possess. Philosophy, art, religion, law, etc., may for a while apparently follow their own internal logic in their development, but soon this development takes an unexpected turn, old ideas are abandoned for no apparent good reason and new ideas emerge which in no way represent a further development of the old. If an attempt is made to explain these developments in terms of their internal logic alone they remain profound mysteries. But if we bring in external factors, such as social, political and economic changes, things become at once meaningful and understandable. The economic system (and even more so the larger system including, besides the economic variables, also technology, political organization and the size and composition of the population) shows a much higher degree of autonomy. If someone wants to explain Capitalism as a product of Protestant ethics he has to find an explanation for the emergence of Protestant ethics itself – presumably in terms of the autonomous evolution of Christian theology. But Max Weber himself admits that Protestant ethics is by no means a logically necessary implication of Protestant theology; indeed he thinks that fatalistic ethics would have been logically more consistent with the doctrine of predestination. So the explanation of Protestant ethics in terms of autonomous theological developments fails at the very first step, and extra-theological social factors have to be invoked to explain why the early Puritans adopted the ethical attitudes so highly favourable to the development of Capitalism. On the other hand, if we try to explain Portestantism as a result of the social conditions prevailing in late-medieval towns, we have no fundamental difficulty in explaining how these social conditions themselves emerged as a result of economic, technological and political developments.

Over relatively short periods, of course, practically any subsystem of the social system may show largely autonomous developments, which may then have important effects on other parts of the social system. The point is only that in may subsystems such spells of relatively autonomous developments tend to be soon interrupted by outside influences. Indeed, as Kroeber (1944) has pointed out, many fields of culture simply do not possess the ability to display continual development in one particular direction indefinitely: if no outside influence intervenes they will soon exhaust their internal developmental possibilities and simply stop or exhibit endless repetition of the same patterns.

VIII. CONCLUSION

To sum up, we have tried to show that the fundamental problem of social science is to explain social facts in terms of a *comparative dynamic theory* of social development.

We have argued that among explanatory variables special theoretical importance attaches to those which are relatively independent of the other variables of the social system, and which are therefore in a position to exert relatively *independent causal influence* on the other variables.

On the basis of this criterion we have discussed six groups of important explanatory variables, viz., (1) exogenous variables; (2) endogenous variables that mediate the influence of major exogenous variables; (3) endogenous variables with a high degree of stability (i.e. stable institutions and cultural traditions); (4) basic structural variables, which determine the values, interests and psychological needs of the members of the society and that way largely determine the stability of other social variables; (5) accumulative variables, connected with the basic changes of society in the long run; (6) the variables that determine the rate of growth of the accumulative variables.

We have used the same criterion of relative causal independence also for judging the likely direction of causal influence between different subsystems of the social system. We have argued that a subsystem is more likely to have causal priority over other subsystems the more it is intrinsically capable of persistent autonomous long-run movements of its own, and the more it is able to preserve these movements against distrubing influences coming from other parts of the social system.

REFERENCES

Benedict, Ruth: *Patterns of Culture,* Boston: Houghton Mifflin Co., 1934.
Kardiner, A., Linton, R., DuBois, D., & West, J.: *The Psychological Frontiers of Society,* New York: Columbia Univ. Press, 1945.
Kroeber, A. L.: *Configurations of Culture Growth,* Berkeley: Univ. of Calif. Press, 1944.

NOTES

* *Behavioral Science,* 5 (1960), 136–145.

[1] As we are here concerned only with the basic logic of explanatory models, we shall neglect the distinction between differentials and finite differences, or between differential equations and difference equations.

[2] For, the equilibrium value of Y can be used to explain the actual value of Y only if Y is most of the time actually at or near its equilibrium value.

[3] See the previous note.

[4] Any system subject to static laws is always also subject to dynamic laws but not vice versa. This is so because any static law can always be expressed in the form of a dynamic law, e.g. by adding a vacuous conditional clause involving a variable of the previous period, etc.

[5] This is true irrespective of whether these causal laws are deterministic or merely statistical.

[6] Economic theory in many ways followed a course different from that of most other social sciences in that if felt the influence of extreme evolutionist doctrines much less, and later largely avoided the anti-theoretical current that swept over sociology and anthropology. But it likewise went through a period of purely static theorizing and of neglect for development problems.

[7] The basic value attitudes and basic personality structure themselves may be determined by the prevailing type of family organization and child-rearing practices. See A. Kardiner, Linton, DuBois, and West (1945).

CHAPTER XIII

POPPER'S IMPROBABILITY CRITERION
FOR THE CHOICE OF SCIENTIFIC
HYPOTHESES*¹

I

The publication in English of Karl R. Popper's *The Logic of Scientific Discovery* (London, Hutchinson, 1959) twenty-five years after the appearance of the German original, is an important event. At the time when many philosophers questioned the cognitive value of scientific hypotheses (and even of the most down-to-earth empirical generalizations), Popper has shown how to reconcile the free use of bold explanatory hypotheses with an insistence on empirical testing. Many of Popper's views have now been accepted even by most of his earlier opponents, which is no small tribute to a philosopher who had challenged an important current of opinion. But, though the basic aspects of Popper's theory have attracted considerable attention in recent years, some of his finer points have received insufficient discussion. It is hoped that the publication of this important book in English translation will now help to remedy this situation.

In the present note I propose to discuss a somewhat paradoxical point of Popper's theory, viz. his advocacy of the methodological rule that, out of several alternative hypotheses equally consistent with the empirical data, we should always accept the one possessing the *lowest a priori* probability (he uses the term 'logical probability').

The actual procedure Popper suggests is this. Out of the various hypotheses compatible with the known empirical facts, the *a priori least probable* hypothesis is selected at first merely for the purpose of very careful further empirical *testing*. It will be tentatively *accepted as true* only if it survives all these tests, i.e. if it remains compatible with all known empirical facts even when all these tests have been completed. And of course it will maintain its status as an accepted hypothesis only so long as subsequent research does not happen to produce new empirical facts incompatible with it.

We should give preference, according to Popper, to the *a priori least probable* hypothesis for two reasons. On the one hand, the greater the *informative content* of a hypothesis the lower its *a priori* probability (i.e. the more is required to make it true). Hence science has to choose between great content and high probability – between making greatly informative though uncertain statements and between saying possibly very safe but empty platitudes – and the choice must be in favour of the former. On the other hand, the greater the informative content of a hypothesis (and therefore the lower its *a priori* probability) the more specific predictions it can make about empirical facts and the more easily its predictions will be falsified by empirical testing if the hypothesis is in fact wrong. Hence, a second reason for preferring hypotheses with lower *a priori* probabilities is the fact that they posses higher degrees of empirical *testability* (or falsifiability).

This view of Popper seems intuitively paradoxical as nothing appears to be more obvious than that we should always give preference to the more probable hypothesis; and it is the point where Popper's theory most sharply differs from probabilistic theories of hypothesis confirmation, such as Keynes's, Jeffreys's or Carnap's. (For our purposes the main issue is between Popper and the probabilistic school as a whole, and the difference among the various members of this school are of minor importance. As Jeffreys's theory is the one most specific on the numerical probabilities to be assigned to quantitative scientific hypotheses, I shall contrast Popper's views mainly with Jeffreys's).

The air of paradox is not removed, it seems to me, by the fact that Popper wants us to accept the *a priori least probable* hypothesis only after careful empirical testing. For, even after the most extensive and most rigorous tests there will still be infinitely many alternative hypotheses which are equally consistent with the results of our tests as well as with all other known empirical facts; and so it will still sound paradoxical if we are told always to choose, out of all these hypotheses equally consistent with the empirical facts, precisely the one that has the *lowest a priori* probability.

II

In practice the difference between Popper's theory and such probabilistic theories as Jeffreys's is smaller than might appear at first sight. For, both parties agree that, out of several alternative hypotheses equally compatible with the observations, we always have to accept the *simplest* one. There is also considerable agreement on the actual criteria for judging the simplicity of alternative hypotheses. Both Jeffreys and Popper consider a quantitative hypothesis (quantitative law) simpler the smaller the number of adjustable *parameters* its equation contains. For instance, a linear equation is simpler than a general quadratic equation because it involves a smaller number of coefficients; similarly a quadratic equation is simpler than a general cubic equation; or a plain sine law is simpler than a law involving the sum of several sine expressions, etc.[2]

The difference is only in the philosophical interpretation of this common simplicity requirement. Of two hypotheses, Jeffreys always assigns a *higher a priori* probability while Popper always assigns a *lower a priori* probability to the simpler of the two. Thus Jeffreys says, Other things being equal, always choose the simplest hypothesis because it has the highest *a priori* probability. In contrast, Popper says, Choose the simplest hypothesis *in spite of* the fact that it always has the lowest *a priori* probability.

More specifically, for a more precise statement of the difference between the two theories we have to distinguish between various interpretations of each scientific hypothesis. Consider, for instance, the two alternative hypotheses that

(1) A certain planet has a *circular* orbit; and that
(2) The same planet has an *elliptic* orbit.

Of course, under both Popper's and Jeffreys's theories (1) is a simpler hypothesis than (2) because for fully determining a circle fewer parameters have to be specified than for fully determining an ellipse.

Now ellipses can be defined either so as to include circles as a special case or so as to exclude circles. Accordingly, hypothesis (2) can be taken either in a *neutral* sense, which leaves open the possibility of a circular orbit – or in an *exclusive* sense, which rules out this possibility.

On the other hand, each hypothesis may be given either a *generic* or a *specific* form according as the parameters of the circle or ellipse are left unspecified or are assigned specific numerical values.

In terms of these distinctions, under Jeffreys's theory the *exclusive* generic form of hypothesis (2) (i.e. the assumption that the planet's orbit is some unspecified ellipse other than a circle has a *lower a priori* probability than the generic form of hypothesis (1) (i.e. the assumption that the orbit is some unspecified circle) – while under Popper's theory the opposite is true. But, of course, under Jeffreys's theory just as much as under Popper's the *neutral* generic form of hypothesis (2) (i.e. the assumption that the orbit is some unspecified ellipse, not excluding the possibility of its being a circle) has a *higher a priori* probability than the generic form of hypothesis (1) (i.e. the assumption that the orbit is some circle) because the former is always true when the latter is true and is true in other cases as well (viz. when the orbit is an ellipse other than a circle). Indeed, according to the additivity axiom of the probability calculus we must have:

(A)   Prob (*neutral* gen. form of hyp. 2) =
           = Prob (gen. form of hyp. (1)) + Prob (*exclusive* gen. form of
hyp. (2))
which implies

(B)   Prob (*neutral* gen. form of hyp. (2)) $\geq$ Prob (gen. form of hyp.
(1))

In fact, if we assign a non-zero probability to the exclusive form of hypothesis (2), we can replace the sign $\geq$ by a straightforward $>$ sign in (B). As inequality (B) directly follows from the basic axioms of the probability calculus, it has to be accepted by everybody who assigns probabilities to scientific hypotheses at all, and it is clear from Jeffreys's argument that he fully accepts this inequality.

At the same time, if both hypotheses are taken in their *specific* (rather than their generic) forms, Jeffreys *a fortiori* will assign a lower *a priori* probability to hypothesis (2) than he assigns to hypothesis (1). He will now have two independent reasons for doing so. On the one hand, he has already assigned a smaller *a priori* probability to the exclusive generic form of (2) than he has assigned to the generic form of (1). On the other hand, going over from the generic forms to the specific forms of the two hypotheses, the total probability assigned to each generic form has to be distributed among the various specific possibilities subsumed under it. Now, there are infinitely 'more' different ellipses than there are circles in that the set of all possible ellipses has higher dimensionality than the set of all possible circles has (the dimensionality being equal to the number of adjustable parameters). Therefore in the case of hypothesis (2) an already smaller total probability has to be distributed among a larger number of claimants than in the case of hypothesis (1). Thus the *a priori* probability assigned by Jeffreys to each specific form of hypothesis (2) will be smaller than that assigned to each specific form of hypothesis (1), for two reasons at once.

In contrast, Popper would assign the *same a priori* probability to a particular *specific* form of hypothesis (1) and to a particular *specific* form of hypothesis (2), because once definite numerical values are given to all parameters neither hypothesis will contain unspecified parameters and both will equally become fully specific statements. (But of course Popper would argue that the relevant comparison is not between the specific forms of the two hypotheses but is rather between their generic forms, because in scientific practice only the generic forms of quantitative laws are assumed *as theoretical hypotheses* – whereas the numerical values of the parameters are chosen not on theoretical grounds but rather by directly estimating them from the empirical data.)

To sum up, Popper assigns equal *a priori* probabilities to all fully *specific* quantitative hypotheses, irrespective of their complexity. But he is mainly concerned with the *generic* forms of these hypotheses, and assigns *lower a priori* probabilities to simple generic hypotheses than he assigns to more complex ones because a simple generic hypothesis always covers a smaller number of alternative specific possibilities than does a more complex generic hypothesis. On the contrary, Jeffreys starts with assigning *higher a priori* probabilities to simple hypotheses already in the case of *generic* hypotheses (provided that each generic hypothesis is given an exclusive, rather than a neutral, interpretation). Consequently, in the case of fully *specific* hypotheses, he *a fortiori* assigns *higher a priori* probabilities to simple hypotheses. For, not only is the total probability *higher* that he assigns to a simple generic hypothesis; but with a simple hypothesis this total probability assigned to its generic form also has to be distributed among a *smaller* number of possible specific cases corresponding to different possible values of the parameters.

III

Though Popper's and Jeffreys's theories assign different numerical *a priori* probabilities to scientific hypotheses, it does not follow that one of the two theories must be inconsistent. For, as Carnap has shown, there are infinitely many alternative ways of assigning *a priori* probabilities to scientific statements – i.e. there are infinitely many different probability metrics – equally consistent with the principles of logic and the axioms of the probability calculus.

To be sure, Popper does try to show that Jeffreys's definition of numerical probabilities is inconsistent (pp. 378–86). But his main argument (based on his theorem (1) on p. 381) actually shows only that Jeffreys's definition of probabilities is inconsistent with the probability metric that Popper himself uses (i.e. with the Wittgenstein probability metric,[3] see below). That is, it only shows that Jeffreys uses a different probability metric from Popper's.

Apart from this, Popper correctly points (p. 384) to certain vacillations in Jeffreys's definitions of numerical probabilities. These vacillations are due to the fact that Jeffreys's basic postulates do not quite uniquely determine how to assign numerical probabilities to various scientific hypotheses but allow several alternative ways of doing this (though the differences between these alternatives are of little theoretical or practical importance); and it is true that Jeffreys is not always quite consistent in choosing between these alternatives (e.g. in connection with different laws containing the same number of parameters, as indicated by Popper, *loc. cit.*). But this does not affect the validity of Jeffreys's argument (in his *Scientific Inference,* Chapter IV) to the effect that his method makes it *possible* to assign numerical probabilities in a consistent manner[4] – or rather in several alternative manners, each equally consistent in itself.

But even if we admit both Popper's probability metric and Jeffreys's probability metric (or rather the various slightly different alternative probability metrics allowed by Jeffreys's theory) are equally consistent in a formal sense, the choice between them may not be a matter of indifference, because one metric may be more appropriate for one purpose, and the other for some other purpose; and in philosophical contexts in particular, one probability metric may do more justice to the philosophical problems involved than the other does. In actual fact, I shall argue that for the purpose of choosing between alternative hypotheses Jeffreys's probability metric is more appropriate than Popper's.

Popper uses what has become known as Wittgenstein's probability metric (cf. Tractatus Logico-Philosophicus, 5. 152), which is based on the assumption that any two possible combinations of (a given number of) 'atomic facts' are *a priori* equally likely, so that different events are always independent in probability. (That is, the occurrence of one event never makes the occurrence of another event *a priori* either more likely or less likely.) In other words, his probability metric envisages a world devoid of any lawlike regularities and exhibiting only purely accidental regularities due to chance. Hence, his probability metric essentially answers questions of this kind: In a world without general laws what would be the probability that our observations should still accidentally conform to some particular regular pattern? (For example, what would be the probability of finding our astronomical observations to conform by mere chance to, say, Kepler's laws?).

This metric is no doubt the proper one to use when we want to measure how much restriction a given hypothesis imposes on empirical observations (in comparison to an imaginary world where possible observations would not be restricted by any general law). Hence this metric is the proper one to use in mathematical expressions constructed for measuring the *empirical content* of a hypothesis, such as the measures discussed by Popper on pp. 402–3 of his book.

But this metric seems to be less appropriate to use for measuring the *a priori* probabilities of various hypotheses from the standpoint of a scientist who wants to choose among alternative hypotheses on the basis of all empirical and conceptual evidence available. For, his primary interest will not be in the question, what are the chances that his observations will purely accidentally follow a given regular pattern in case there are *no* systematic lawlike connections in nature between different events; his main interest will be rather in the question, what are the chances that a given particular hypothesis expresses a true law of nature in case *there are* laws of nature establishing connections between different events (or, more specifically, in case there are laws of nature at least in the particular field he is concerned with).

Jeffreys's probability metric, contrary to Wittgenstein's, is based explicitly on the assumption that there are general laws in nature (and that there are laws of nature in the particular field under consideration), though it is *a priori* unknown to us what mathematical form each particular law takes. Hence his main problem is to find a probability metric which does not *a priori* exclude any possible hypothesis arbitrarily by assigning zero initial probability to it. He has shown that the axioms of the probability calculus taken in conjunction with this non-zero requirement largely (though not completely) determine the probability metric to be used for judging the *a priori* probabilities of alternative scientific hypotheses.

Jeffreys's probability metric also has the advantage of avoiding Popper's paradoxical conclusion that preference should be given to the *least probable* hypothesis. Instead, Jeffreys's theory leads to the intuitively more satisfactory methodological rule of always choosing the hypothesis *most probable* in the light of all available evidence (i.e. the hypothesis with the highest *a posteriori* probability); and, in the special case where several alternative hypotheses are equally confirmed by the empirical data, by Bayes's theorem this means choosing the hypothesis with the highest *a priori* probability as well.

IV

Scientists always tend to prefer more specific theories to less specific ones. For instance, a doctor will not be satisfied with the unspecific hypothesis that a certain patient has lung trouble of some sort. Rather, if possible, he will try to set up a more specific hypothesis, e.g. that the patient has lung tuberculosis.[5] Now, a more specific hypothesis in general has a smaller *a priori* probability than a less specific one because it involves additional assumptions. (This is true irrespective of the probability metric we use because it follows from the basic axioms of the probability calculus, which any probability metric has to satisfy.) Thus, in certain cases at least, scientists seem to prefer less probable hypotheses to more probable ones, and this seems to contradict probabilistic theories of hypothesis confirmation, such as Jeffreys's.

But in actual fact the probabilistic theories require that more probable theories should be preferred *only* in the case of choosing between mutually exclusive and incompatible theories. But a less specific and a more specific theory on the same subject may not be incompatible. Rather, the more specific theory may include and entail the less specific one. Having lung tuberculosis entails having some sort of lung trouble. The fact that the presence of lung trouble in general, will possess a higher probability than the presence of lung tuberculosis, only means that our doctor will be able to hold the former hypothesis with more confidence than the latter. He may attach 90 per cent probability to the presence of lung trouble of some sort but may attach only 70 per cent probability to the presence of lung tuberculosis (assigning the remaining $90 - 70 = 20$ per cent probability to the possibility of a lung disease of non-tuberculotic origin).

V

The rule that simpler hypotheses should be assigned higher *a priori* probabilities can be justified in various ways. Jeffreys has shown that this rule directly follows from the axioms of the probability calculus if we add the requirement that no possible hypothesis should be allotted zero probability. For, the sum of all probabilities cannot exceed unity; and this is possible only if, listing all the infinitely many admissible hypotheses in order of increasing complexity, the probabilities assigned to them form a diminishing number series (possibly with a finite number of exceptions).

There is, however, I believe a more fundamental philosophical reason why simpler hypotheses should be assigned higher *a priori* probabilities. This reason is that they involve a *smaller number of independent assumptions*. Thus the rule that preference should be given and higher *a priori* probability should be assigned to a simpler hypothesis is just another way of stating the *principle of parsimony*[6] in selecting one's independent basic assumptions.

The fact that the simplicity of a hypothesis depends on the number of independent assumptions it involves comes out most clearly in the case of existential hypotheses. When we try to explain empirical facts in terms of certain underlying forces, factors, elements, microphysical particles, etc., we always regard an explanatory hypothesis as being simpler the smaller the number of essentially different forces, factors, elements, particles, etc., it has to assume.

For example, it is a simpler hypothesis that people's performance on intelligence tests can be explained in terms of, say, *ten* different independent factors (ten different basic abilities) than is the hypothesis that it has to be explained in terms of *eleven* different independent factors – because each new factor represents an additional independent assumption. Accordingly, psychologists will always stick to a hypothesis involving a smaller number of factors so long as the empirical facts do not make it clearly necessary to shift to a hypothesis involving a larger number of factors.

Likewise, it is a simpler hypothesis that matter consists of *simple* atoms (perhaps envisaged as more or less homogeneous spherical particles) than is the hypothesis that the atoms themselves are *composed* of smaller particles. Again, we find that scientists stuck to the simple atomic hypothesis so long as the empirical facts did not make it necessary to recognize the existence of subatomic particles.

By the same token, a unified field theory would be fundamentally a simpler hypothesis than is the assumption that gravitation, electromagnetism and nuclear forces represent independent aspects of physical reality.

The same principle applies in other cases. Even plain induction can be interpreted as the choice of the simpler hypothesis, i.e. the hypothesis involving a smaller number of basic assumptions. For instance, if we find that all ravens so far examined have been black, it is a simpler hypothesis that the inventory of the world contains only black ravens than is the hypothesis that it contains both black ravens and ravens of some other colour, because the latter hypothesis would involve an additional existential assumption.

In the case of quantitative hypotheses (quantitative laws), we have seen that a hypothesis is simpler the smaller the number of adjustable parameters its equation contains. But this rule is again a special case of the same principle. In effect, in order to derive the observed facts from a given quantitative hypothesis, we always have to assign specific numerical values to all parameters. But this means that to the main hypothesis in its generic form (with unspecified parameters) we have to add as many independent assumptions as there are different parameters. (Even if the parameters are estimated from the observations, the estimated numerical values represent assumptions independent of the basic hypothesis itself taken in its generic form.) Hence a simpler hypothesis always involves a smaller number of independent assumptions.

To sum up, we regard a hypothesis as being simpler the smaller number of independent assumptions (in particular the smaller number of independent existential assumptions) it involves. This explains why most of us tend to feel that a simpler hypothesis is *a priori* more likely than is a more complex hypothesis, and why we are reluctant to accept a complex hypothesis instead of a more simple one so long as the empirical evidence does not very definitely favour the more complex hypothesis.

The same principle also accounts for the common view that, other things being equal, a simpler hypothesis gives a more satisfactory explanation (or is able to 'explain more') than a more complex hypothesis. This is so because every explanatory hypothesis must leave its own basic assumptions unexplained. Hence a simpler hypothesis, which involves a smaller number of independent basic assumptions, leaves a smaller number of facts without explanation. For instance, the simpler hypothesis that the orbit of a certain planet is a circle will leave unexplained:

(1) Why the orbit is a circle;
(2) Why it is located on the plane where it is;
(3) Why its centre is where it is on this plane; and
(4) Why the length of its radius is what it is.

In contrast, the more complex hypothesis that the planet's orbit is an ellipse will leave unexplained:

(1) Why the orbit is an ellipse;
(2) Why it is located on the plane where it is;
(3) Why its centre is where it is on this plane;
(4) Why the length of its major axis is what it is;
(5) Why the length of its minor axis is what it is; and
(6) Why it has the orientation it has in its plane.

(Presumably all these facts left unexplained by either hypothesis can be explained by some additional hypotheses, such as a general theory of gravitation and a special theory on the origin of the solar system.[7] The point is only that the first hypothesis leaves fewer facts for these other hypotheses to explain than does the second.)

VI

To conclude, Popper's theory and such probabilistic theories of hypothesis confirmation as, e.g., Jeffreys's agree in accepting the methodological rule that, given several alternative hypotheses equally consistent with the known empirical facts, one should always choose the *simplest* hypothesis. But, whereas the probabilistic theories base this rule on the assumption that the simpler a hypothesis the higher its *a priori* probability, Popper on the contrary holds that the simpler a hypothesis the *lower* its *a priori* probability. Accordingly, he takes the somewhat paradoxical view that if the empirical facts available are equally consistent with several alternative hypotheses we always have to choose the *a priori least probable* one.

I have tried to show that Popper's views are based on the use of Wittgenstein's probability metric, which is less appropriate for judging the *a priori* probabilities of different scientific hypotheses than are alternative probability metrics, e.g. Jeffreys's. I have argued that the basic philosophical reason for giving preference, and for assigning a higher *a priori* probability, to a simpler hypothesis is the fact that a hypothesis is called *simpler* the *smaller the number of independent assumptions* it contains. Thus the rule of preferring a simpler hypothesis is equivalent to the principle of parsimony in selecting one's independent basic assumptions.

NOTES

* *Philosophy,* **25** (1960), 332–340.

[1] I am greatly indebted to Professor John A. Passmore for his critical comments. But of course he bears no responsibility for the views expressed in this note.

[2] Recently John Kemeny has developed a more general theory on the criteria for judging the simplicity of a quantitative hypothesis (see his 'The Use of Simplicity in Induction', *Philosophical Review* **57**, 1953, pp. 391–408).

[3] This is so because the proof on pp. 380–1 of theorem (1) essentially depends on the assumption that any possible combination of n atomic facts is equally likely – which is true only under Wittgenstein's probability metric.

[4] Jeffreys's proof is based on the fact that the set of all possible, essentially different, quantitative hypotheses is a denumerable set; therefore it can be arranged in a linear order; and we can assign the probabilities $\frac{1}{2}, \frac{1}{4}, \frac{1}{8}, \ldots$ to the successive members of the set. Under this arrangement each hypothesis will have a non-zero *a priori* probability and the sum of all probabilities will be unity as required.

[5] I am indebted for this example to Professor John Passmore.

[6] Popper uses this principle only to discourage the introduction of unjustified auxiliary hypotheses (see p.145). But it seems to me it has a much wider application and indeed is one of the most fundamental principles of scientific method.

[7] But of course these hypotheses in turn will leave their own basic assumptions without explanation.

INDEX

Agent normal form 108
Arrow, Kenneth J. 19, 22, 60–61
Average (or mean) utility level for society 19–20, 45, 67, 97

Bargaining models, cooperative,
 for power, 169–181, 191–198
 for social status 204, 207, 211–216, 217, 222, 224n
Bargaining models, noncooperative 109–111
Bayesian theory of rational behavior 38, 47, 65, 67, 78, 82, 84, 90, 96, 114
 and maximin principle 39
 rationality postulates of 47, 65–71, 74, 77, 78
 and social welfare functions 77, 80, 83
 and a solution concept for noncooperative games 112–115
 and subjective probabilities 20, 46, 73, 95, 113
 See also Decision theory, Bayesian
Bayes's theorem 250
Behavior,
 explanation of 227
 humanistic codes of 35
 idealistic codes of 35
Behavior, deferential, and social status 207–211, 212
Bergson, Abram 6
Best-reply strategy, in a noncooperative game 114, 159
'Blackmailer's fallacy' 172–174

Cardinal utility functions, in theory of risk-taking 3
 in welfare economics 3, 6–15, 48–49, 64–68
Cartwright, D., and social power 184
Causal influence, in social development 235, 241
Causal mechanisms, in comparative dynamics, 233
 in social systems 138, 239, 240

Changes, in accumulative variables 237–238
 in social behavior 132
 in social institutions 136, 138, 237
 in social values 131, 133, 135
 in social variables 229
 in technology, and comparative dynamics 230
Cognitive-utilitarian model, of social values 131, 134, 135
Collectivistic interpretation, of social function 136–138
Common interests, in ethics 98
Comparative dynamics. *See* Dynamics, comparative
Competition, perfect, and social status 206
Conceptual (philosophical) problems 64
Concession limits 174, 176
Conflict, and social power 191–192
 and social status 214
Conformist theories, vs. rational-choice models 118
 of social values 133–135
Conversion ratios, for utility units 77–78
Cooperation, in achieving social status 208
Cooperative games 109, 153
 limitations of solutions for 110
 Nash's concept of 110–111
 noncooperative bargaining models for 109–111
Cooperative solution, in prisoner's dilemma problem 102, 104, 154–155
Courtesy, and social status 208
Criterion-satisfaction model, of rational behavior 94
Cultural consistency hypothesis, in social institutions 230–231
Cultural integration, in comparative dynamics 231
Cultural variables, stability of 236

Dahl, R. A., and amount of social power 169–170
 and measure for social power 181
 and social power 162, 163

and social status 212
and strength of social power 169–171
Davis, K., and Moore, Wilbert E., theory
    of social status 205–206, 209–210
Decision rule, Bayesian 38
Decision rule, maximin principle as 38,
    46–47
Decision theory, Bayesian 20, 38, 45,
    46–48, 65, 69, 74, 77, 78, 80–83,
    94–96
    as a branch of the general theory of
    rational behavior 97
Decreasing marginal utility. See Marginal
    utility, decreasing
Deference, demonstrative, in social status
    218–219
Deference, incentive, in social status 210
Deference, induced 216
Deference, and social status 210
Demonstrative deference. See Deference,
    demonstrative
Demonstrative nondeference. See Non-
    deference, demonstrative
Diamond, Peter, and the sure-thing prin-
    ciple 67, 69, 71
Difference principle, Rawls's 4, 41, 42,
    53
    and saving 54
    unacceptable implications of 41
Downs, Anthony, theory of political
    behavior of 56–57, 122
Dynamic models, in social science 129–
    131, 228–229, 231–233, 241
Dynamics, comparative, analytical models
    in 231–233, 241
    causal mechanisms in 233
    and changes in technology 230
    and cultural integration 231
    and economic theory 232, 238
    endogenous variables in 233
    exogenous variables in 233
    and functionalist models 231
    and initial conditions 231
    and political institutions 232
    and probability theory 234
    Weber's contributions to 231–232
Dynamic theory, of social development
    233, 235–236, 241
    of social institutions 139–140

Economic analysis, of social institutions
    238
Economic forces, in social development
    235

Economic motivation, assumed in theories
    of social behavior 125, 127–128
    vs noneconomic motivation 123
Economic system, and other social sub-
    systems 240
Economic theory, and analysis of behavior
    under risk and uncertainty 94
    and comparative dynamics 232, 238
    and motivational assumptions 122
    rational-behavior model of 92–94, 120
    and social status 206
Egalitarian preferences, and social welfare
    functions 80–81
Egalitatian theory. See Super-egalitarian
    theory
Empirical testing, in Popper's theory 243
Equilibrium points 100–105
    imperfect 105–109
    and noncooperative games 100–105,
    159–160
    multiplicity of 112
    perfect 105–109
Equilibrium strategies, in prisoner's di-
    lemma games 107
Equi-probability model, of moral value
    judgments 4, 14, 45–46, 66–67
Errors, in interpersonal utility comparisons
    17, 51, 80
'Ethical' preferences 14. See also, Moral
    preferences, and Social preferences
Ethics, as a branch of the general theory
    of rational behavior 97
Expected-utility maximization, Bayesian
    principle of 38, 45

Fleming, M., ethical postulates of 6, 7, 10
Foreign policy, and game theory 148
Formal groups, and social status   204,
    206–207
French, J. R. P., Jr., and theory of social
    power 181
Friedman, Milton 3
Functionalist theories   118, 136–139,
    230–231

Games, classification of 148
    cooperative. See Cooperative games
    with indentical interests 148–149
    with imperfect information 98, 99
    with incomplete information 98–100
    with mixed interests 148, 151, 152
    noncooperative. See Noncooperative
    games

with opposite interests 148, 149–151
Game-theoretical analysis, of international
politics 145–161
and policy objectives 147–148
of power 174–181, 191–198
and rational expectations 161
of social institutions 138–139
of social status 213–216
Game theory, as a branch of the general
theory of rational behavior 97
Goal-directed behavior 91
Goals, in social groups 221
Group membership, and social status 212,
220–222

Hare R. M. 24
discussion of hypothetical imperatives
34
Harrod, R. F. (Sir Roy), theory of moral
obligations 32–34
Hedonism, and utilitarianism 30–31
Homans, George C. 118–119
Human values, and rational-choice models
140–142
Humanism, in ethics 35
Hypotheses, scientific, choice of 244–254
generic 245–247
the number of independent basic assumptions in 251–253
simplest 253–254
specific 245–247
Hypothetical imperatives, as analytical
truths 34
causal 24
as consequences of an analytical and an
empirical premise 34
formal 25
vs Kantian categorical imperatives 29
non-causal 25
Hypothetico-deductive theory, and rational-choice models 119

Identical interests games. See Games with
identical interests
Impartiality, postulate of 'low-cost' 125
Imperfect equilibtrium points. See Equilib-
rium points, imperfect
Imperfect information, in games 98–99
Improbability criterion, in Popper's 243
Incentives, in seeking social status 207,
218–219
Incomplete information, in games 98–99
Individualism, in ethics 6, 10, 19, 20, 66,
68

Individualistc interpretation, of social
functions 136, 138–139
Individual preferences 10 See also Personal
preferences
Individual rationality, postulate for social
welfare functions 66
Individual utilities, pre-Pareto 13
in social welfare functions 83
Individual utility function. See Utility
function, individual
Induction, and scientific hypotheses 252
Informal groups, and social status 204
Interest-aggregation postulate 125–126
Interests of social groups 237
International conflicts, and game theory
145–161
Interpersonal utility comparisons 15–20,
50–52, 77–80
cannot be avoided 79
vs intrapersonal utility comparisons 50
Inventions, and social development 234,
235
Irrational behavior 128–129
noncooperative behavior need not be
irrational 156

Jeffreys, Harold 244
Jeffreys's theory, and adjustable parameters in scientific hypotheses 245,
247
and most probable hypothesis 250
probability metric used by 245–246,
248–250, 251

Kant, Immanuel 42, 43
Kant's principle, of treating persons as
ends and not as means 42–43

Laplace, principle of indifference 46
Least probable hypothesis, and Popper's
criterion 243, 244
Limited rationality, Simon's theory of 120
Linear social welfare functions 12, 65, 82
Little, I. M. D. 19, 22

March, James G., and social power 162,
163
and measure for social power 181
Marginal utility, decreasing 73–75, 77
Marschak, Jacob, axioms (rationality postulates) of 7, 10, 14, 21
Marx, Karl, on class interests 121
on economic determinism 238–240

Maximin principle 38
  in the original position 40–43
  paradoxes of 39–40, 48
  and social welfare functions 71
  valuable uses of 61
  violates continuity requirement 40
Means-ends model, of rational behavior
  90–94
Metaphysical problem, in interpersonal
  utility comparisons 15
Mixed interests games. *See* Games with
  mixed interests
Mobility, and social status 204
Moral consensus, problem of 82–83
Moral criteria, and interest-aggregation
  concepts 126
Moral obligations, and rule utilitarianism
  32–34
Moral preferences 46, 66. *See also* Ethical
  preferences, *and* Social preferences
Moral rules 24, 30
  as advices 28
  content of 30
  as hypothetical imperatives 26
  as interpreted by intuitionist theories
  27
  as interpreted by subjectivist theories
  27
  logical form of 30
  as non-causal imperatives 28
  objective validity of 34
  See also Value judgments
Moral theory, Adam Smith's, of an impartially sumpathetic observer 28–
  29, 31, 35
Morgenstern, Oskar, On international
  politics 160
  See also von Neumann-Morgenstern
  utility functions
Motivational theory, postulates of 121–
  128
Mutually consistent expectations in games
  100

Nash, John F. 110–112
  See also Zeuthen-Nash theory
Negative service, and social status 210–
  211
Noncooperative bargaining models, for
  cooperative games 109–111
Noncooperative behavior, in international
  conflicts 158
Noncooperative games 100–105, 109–
  111

Bayesian solution concept for 112–
  115
best-reply strategies in 114, 159, 161
binding commitments impossible in
  100
equilibrium points in 100–105, 110–
  111, 159–160
objectives pursued in 103–104, 160–
  161
prior probability distributions in 113
and the prisoner's dilemma problem
  100–105, 154–155, 158
and solution process 114
and tracing procedure 114
Noncooperative solution, in prisoner's
  dilemma problem 154–155
Nondeference, demonstrative, and social
  status 218–219
Nonlinear social welfare functions 64–85
n-person power situations. *See* Power, in
  n-person power situations

Objectives, in international politics 146,
  160–161
Opportunity costs, of a conflict 179–180
  of power 164–169
  and rational behavior 93–94
Opposite interests games. *See* Games with
  opposite interests
Optimal savings, utilitarian theory of 55
Original position, in Rawls's theory 38,
  40–41, 44–48

Parameters, adjustable,
  of a given theory 144n, 245, 247, 252
  of utility functions 124
Pareto, V. 6
Parsimony, in scientific hypotheses 251
Parsons, Talcott, and functionalist models
  118–119
Payoffs, specifying the payoffs in a
  prisoner's dilemma game 103–104,
  154–155
Perfect equilibrium points. *See* Equilibrium
  points, perfect
Perfect information, in games 98
Personal preferences (subjective preferences, or individual preferences) of
  an individual 10, 14, 46, 65
Political behavior, Downs's theory of 122
  rational-choice models of 118
Political institutions, and comparative
  dynamics 232

Popper, K. R. (Sir Karl) 243–254
  hypothesis, the least probable, to be chosen 243–244, 250
  vs Jeffreys 244–250
  and Wittgenstein's probability metric 248–249, 254
  hypothesis, the simplest, to be chosen 245, 253
Positive Correlation Fallacy, and rational-choice models 142
Power, bilateral 172–181
  and the 'blackmailer's fallacy' 172–174
  in n-person power situations 185–187
Power, concept of 162–165
Power, in n-person power situations
  amount of power 185–191, 192
    generic 190–192, 197–198
    specific 190–191
    vector measure 189
  bargaining model for 191–198
  with multiple preferences and no compromise policies 188–190
  with multiple preferences and possible compromise policies 190–191
  with single preferences and possible compromise policies 187–188
  strength of power 191–198
    for incentive power 191, 198
    for independent power 191, 198
    and the Shapley-Shubik measure 182, 199–201
Power, reciprocal 172–181, 186–191, 191–201
Power, and social status 211–216
Power, in two-person power situations,
  amount of power 162–163, 169–171
    frequency interpretation of 170–171
    probability interpretation of 170–171
  bargaining model for 169–181
  base of power 162–163
  constituents of power 162–165
  costs of power 164–169
  Dahl's theory of power 162–163, 181
  dimensions of power 162–165
  French's theory of power 181–182
  March's theory of power 162–163, 181
  means of power 162–165
  opportunity costs of power 164–169

power, as an explanatory (intervening) variable 167–169
power, in a schedule sense 171–172
scope of power 162–163
Simon's theory of power 162, 180
strength of power 166–169, 169–171, 174–182
Power, unilateral 162–172, 185
Preferences, 'irrational' 32
  preferences – opportunities model of rational behavior 93–94
  'true' 32
Prima-facie obligations, in terms of ordinary utilitarianism 32
Principle of average utility 45, 67, 97
Prior probability distribution, in Bayesian solution concept 113
Prisoner's dilemma problem 100–105, 154–155, 158
  specifying the payoffs in 103–104, 154–155
Privileges, of social status 219–220
Probabilities, assigned to scientific hypotheses,
  under the author's theory 251–253
  under Jeffreys's theory 245–246
  under Popper's theory 243–244, 245–250, 253–254
  under Wittgenstein's probability metric 248–249, 254
Protestant ethics, and Weber's theory 238–240
Psychological problem, in interpersonal utility comparisons 16–18

Ramsey, Frank P. 54
Rational behavior, Bayesian concept of 38, 46–48, 65–66, 74, 94–96, 120
  concept of 89, 119–120
  criterion-satisfaction model of 92
  game-theoretical concept of 96, 120, 145–150
  general theory of 96–98
  economic model of 92–93
  means-ends model of 90–93
  preferences-opportunities model of 92-93
  problem of defining 65
  theory of, and motivational assumptions 122, 125–128
  and utility maximization 94, 95
Rational-choice models vs conformist theories 118

in economic theory 141
vs functionalist theories 118
and human values 140–142
motivational postulates for 125–128
of noneconomic social behavior 121
as normative models 141
of political behavior 118, 121–123
and Positive Correlation Fallacy 142
and scientific methodology 124–125
Rationality. *See* Rational behavior
Rawls, John 37–63
   and the difference principle 41–42, 53
   and interpersonal utility comparisons 50–51
   and the maximin principle 38, 40–43, 59–62
   and the *original position* 38, 40–41, 44–48
   and probabilities as used in the original position 46–48
   and saving, as a moral duty 54–56
   and social stability 56–58
   and social welfare functions 71–72, 73, 75, 76
   and the *veil of ignorance* 37
   and von Neumann-Morgenstern utility functions, as used in ethics 48–49
Reciprocal power. *See* Power, Reciprocal
Ralative utility weights. *See* Utility weights
Reward, and social power 192
   and social status 209–210, 211, 214
Richardson, Lewis F., and international conflicts 158
Risk, in decision making 94–95
Robbins, L. 18

Samuelson, Paul A. XI
Satisfaction, susceptibility to 18
   and utility functions 15
Saving, as a moral duty 54–56
Scientific explanation, in social science 227
Scientific hypotheses, additivity axiom in 246
   and induction 252
   and Jeffreys's theory 247–248, 251, 253–254
   and Popper's improbability criterion 243
   and Popper's theory 247–248, 253, 254
Second-order rules, and difference principle 53
Selten, Reinhard 108–109, 112–113

Sen Amartya K. 71–77
   and Rawls's theory 71–73
   and utility dispersion argument 74, 76–77
Shapley, L S., and Shubik, M., and measure for power 182, 198–201
Shapley value, in *n*-person situations 186, 193, 199
Simon, Herbert A., and social power 162, 180
   theory of limited rationality 120–121
Smith, Adam, moral theory of 28–29, 35
Social-acceptance motivation, postulate of, in motivational theory 127
Social behavior, dynamic explanations of 129–131
   relation to social status 204
   theory of 118
Social change 139–140
Social development, and exogenous variables 234
   invention and 234, 235
   stochastic models for 234
Social functions, collectivistic interpretation of 136–138
Social groups, benefits of 221
   and comparative dynamics 232
   goals of 221
   interests of 237
   needs of 237
   resource allocation in 222–233
Social institutions 118
   causal influences on 235
   change in 136, 138, 237
   and cultural consistency hypothesis 230–231
   dynamic theory of 139–140, 235–236
   economic analysis of 235, 238
   and functionalist theory of 230
Social power. *See* Power
Social preferences 7, 8, 10, 66. *See also* Ethical preferences, *and* Moral preferences
Social rationality, postulate for social welfare functions 66
Social science, and comparative dynamic theory 241
   explanation in 227
   endogenous variables in 241
   exogenous variables in 241
   and independent causal influence 241
Social stability, factors contributing to 57

in just society 58
Social status, advantages of 219–220
    and allocation of group resources
        222–223
    bargaining model for 204, 207, 213–
        216, 217
    as behavioral goal-object 128
    and contributions to the group 224n
    and cooperation 208
    costs of 214–216
    and courtesy 208
    Davis-Moore theory of 205–206,
        209–210
    deferential behavior in 207–211
    differences in 206.
    functionalistic theories of 205–206
    and game-theoretical bargaining models
        for 213
    and group membership 220–222
    incentives to seeking 206–211, 219–
        220
    induced, and bargaining position 217
    induced, and induced deference 216
    negative service in 210–211
    penalties imposed in 214–216
    as power relationship 211–216
    and privileges in 219–220
    and reciprocal power 213
    rewards and 209–210, 214
    reward for negative service in 211
    and social behavior 206
    and two-person bargaining model
        213–216
Social subsystems, ascription of causal
        priority in 240
    autonomous developments in 240
    causal relations in 239
    and economic system 240
    interactions among 238–241
    and Marx's theory 238–239
    Protestant ethics in 238–239, 240
    and Weber's theory 238–239, 240
Social system, maintenance of 137
Social values, and ignorance 132
    and cognitive-utilitarian model 131
    and conformist approach to rational
        theory 118
    conformist model of 133–135
Social variables, and dynamic explanation
        228–229
    stability of 236, 237
    and static explanation 228
Social welfare functions, axioms for 7–8,
        10, 66

based on Bayesian rationality postulates
    77
based on maximin principle 77
individualism in 6, 10, 19, 20, 66, 68
as linear functions of individual utilities
    6, 12, 65, 82
as mean of individual utilities 19–20,
    45, 67, 97
moral disagreements on 83
as nonlinear functions of incomes 64,
    74
as nonlinear functions of utilities 74,
    77
Rawls's theory and 71–72
Special obligations, and rule utilitarianism
    33
Stability, of social institutions 56–58,
    235–238
    of social variables 235–238
    See also Social stability
Static explanation, of social behavior 130
    and social variables 228
Statics, comparative, problems of 231
Status, social. See Social status
Stochastic models, in social development
    234
Strategy, in game theory 102, 150, 176,
    179, 198
Structural-functional approach. See Func-
    tionalist approach
Subjective preferences. See Personal prefer-
    ences
Subjective probabilities 46, 47, 113
Substitution principle. See Sure-thing
    principle
Super-egalitarian theory, of social welfare
    functions 80–81
Supererogatory actions, and utilitarianism
    52
Sure-thing principle 68–71, 95, 96
Symbolic behavior. See Irrational behavior

Testability, in Popper's theory 244
Theil, Henri, XI 67
Tracing procedure, in non-cooperative
    games 114
Transferable utility, in n-person bargaining
    games 194–195
Two-person bargaining model, for power
    166–181
    for social status 213–216
Two-person situations. See Power, in two-
    person power situations

Two-person zero-sum game 109, 149, 150, 152–153

Uncertainty, in decision making 38, 94–95
Universalistic attitudes, in society 134
Universalizability, Kant's axiom of 29
Unwarranted differentiation, principle of 29
Utilitarianism, and Rawls's theory 37
  common-sense objections to 30
  consequences of general practice 33
  consequences of single act 33
Utilitarian model, of social values 134, 135
Utility, transferable. *See* Transferable utility
Utility comparisons, interpersonal *See* Interpersonal utility comparisons
Utility-dispersion argument, about lotteries 73
  about social welfare, of Sen 74, 76-77
Utility functions, used in explaining human behavior 123–128
  changes in 131
  in noneconomic behavior 122
  parameters of 124–125
  von Neumann-Morgenstern. *See* von Neumann-Morgenstern utility functions
Utility-maximization, and rational bahavior 94–95
  See also Rational behavior
Utility theory 97
Utility weights, problem of 123–125

Value-attitudes, in society 134
Value judgements, concerning social welfare 3–4

on distribution of income 4
  as hypothetical imperatives 24
  moral 3–4, 44–46
Variables, accumulative, in comparative dynamics 237–238
Variables, changeable personal variables 17
Variables, endogenous, in comparative dynamics 233–235, 238
  in social science 241
Variables, exogenous, in comparative dynamics 233–235
  in social science 241
Variables, explanatory 238
  in social phenomena 235
Variables, social, changes in 229
  and dynamic models 229
Variables, structural, fundamental 237
Variables, unchangeable personal variables 17–18
von Neumann-Morgenstern 7, 10, 109, 143n
von Neumann-Morgenstern utility functions, in definition of justice and moral values 7, 10, 49, 61
  as measures of subjective importance 49

Weber, Max 231–232, 238–240
Wittgenstein, probability metric of 248–249, 254

Zero-savings, between generations 54
Zero-sum games, two-person. *See* Two-person, zero-sum game
Zeuthen-Nash theory,
  generalized to *n*-person bargaining games 186
  of two-person bargaining games 174, 182

THEORY AND DECISION LIBRARY

An International Series in the Philosophy and Methodology

of the Social and Behavioral Sciences

Editors:

Gerald Eberlein, *University of Saarland*

Werner Leinfellner, *University of Nebraska*

1. Günther Menges (ed.), *Information, Inference, and Decision.* 1974, viii + 195 pp.

2. Anatol Rapoport (ed.), *Game Theory as a Theory of Conflict Resolution.* 1974, v + 283 pp.

3. Maria Bunge (ed.), *The Methodological Unity of Science.* 1973, viii + 264 pp.

4. Colin Cherry (ed.), *Pragmatic Aspects of Human Communication.* 1974, ix + 178 pp.

5. Friedrich Rapp (ed.), *Contributions to a Philosophy of Technology. Studies in the Structure of Thinking in the Technological Sciences.* 1974, xv + 228 pp.

6. Werner Leinfellner and Eckehart Köhler (eds.), *Developments in the Methodology of Social Science.* 1974, x + 430 pp.

7. Jacob Marschak, *Economic Information, Decision and Prediction. Selected Essays.* 1974, three volumes, xviii + 389 pp.; xii + 362 pp.; x + 399 pp.

8. Carl-Axel S. Staël von Holstein (ed.), *The Concept of Probability in Psychological Experiments.* 1974, xi + 153 pp.

9. Heinz J. Skala, *Non-Archimedean Utility Theory.* 1975, xii + 138 pp.

10. Karin D. Knorr, Hermann Strasser, and Hans Georg Zilian (eds.), *Determinants and Controls of Scientific Developments.* 1975, ix + 460 pp.

11. Dirk Wendt, and Charles Vlek (eds.), *Utility, Probability, and Human Decision Making. Selected Proceedings of an Interdisciplinary Research Conference,. Rome, 3-6 September, 1973,* 1975, viii + 418 pp.